STONEFACE

DISCARDED

Caitlin Press Inc.
3375 Ponderosa Way
Qualicum Beach, BC V9K 2J8
www.caitlinpress.com

Text design and cover design by Vici Johnstone
Cover photo by Dick Gordon
Photos, unless otherwise identified, are from the Kakfwi family collection.
Edited by Dick Gordon and Holly Vestad
Printed in Canada

Caitlin Press Inc. acknowledges financial support from the Government of Canada and the Canada Council for the Arts, and the Province of British Columbia through the British Columbia Arts Council and the Book Publisher's Tax Credit.

Library and Archives Canada Cataloguing in Publication
Stoneface : memoir of a defiant Dene / Stephen Kakfwi.
Names: Kakfwi, Steve, author.
Identifiers: Canadiana 20220440654 | ISBN 9781773861074 (softcover)
Subjects: LCSH: Kakfwi, Steve. | LCSH: Premiers (Canada)—Northwest Territories—Biography. | LCSH: Legislators—Northwest Territories—Biography. | CSH: First Nations legislators—Northwest Territories—Biography. | CSH: First Nations—Northwest Territories—Biography. | LCGFT: Autobiographies.
Classification: LCC FC4174.1.K35 A3 2023 | DDC 971.9/304092—dc23

STONEFACE

A DEFIANT DENE

STEPHEN KAKFWI

CAITLIN PRESS 2023

Dedicated to the Miracles in my life; Kyla (Willowtips), Daylyn (River Rapids), Keenan (Man Without Arrows); our granddaughters Maslyn Talawetsin (Feather Maker), Sadeya (Little Sunshine); our grandsons Tydzeh (Three Hearts), Ry'den (Born Again Medicine Man). And to Marie, who, through her love, made us all possible.

CONTENTS

MAP OF FORT GOOD HOPE – 8

TIMELINE – 9

FOREWORD – 11

PREFACE – 12

INTRODUCTION – 14

SUGHA THE STORYTELLER – 17

DEFIANT LITTLE DENE – 22

THE HORROR OF GROLLIER HALL – 31

SWEET SUMMER OF SIXTY – 40

MY NAME IS GHA FEE – 46

MY FATHER, NOGHA – 54

FATHER POCHAT – 62

MY COUSIN TEACHES ME – 69

MY PSYCHEDELIC SHIRT – 72

LEARNING FROM MY ELDERS – 75

A YOUNG DENE IN RESIDENTIAL SCHOOL – 83

THE ROAD TO ACTIVISM – 89

THE BERGER INQUIRY – 98

SWEET MARIE – 104

ANOTHER PIPELINE – 108

TALKING FISH CREEK – 110

MARIE ON THE MACKENZIE – 115

FORT GOOD HOPE LEADS THE WAY – 121

Koh Yeh Ley Gho Dene – 128

A Promise Is a Promise – 130

Lynda Sorenson – 134

John Paul II – 141

Dance with the Devil – 152

The Creation of Nunavut – 159

Stoneface – 162

The Three Children of Stoneface – 167

The Dene and the Diamonds – 175

The Devil in Me – 180

Trouble at the Top – 188

Walking Out on the Prime Minister – 191

I'd Better Leave before I Decide to Stay – 194

In the Walls of His Mind – 201

Sacred Work – 211

Three Brothers – 216

Saying Goodbye to Georgina – 223

Born in the Bowl of a Pipe – 228

Acknowledgements – 239

About the Author – 240

MAP OF FORT GOOD HOPE

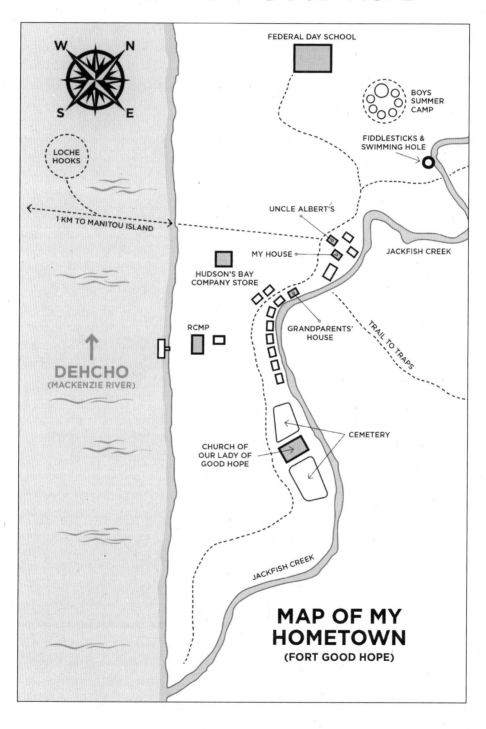

TIMELINE

1950: November 7: Born in a bush camp at Rahdeghotue (Yeltea Lake), NWT.

1960: Taken to Grollier Hall residential school.

1963: Recruited by Bishop Piché to attend Grandin Home residential school in Fort Smith.

1968: Aunt Bella passes away under suspicious circumstances in Norman Wells.

1970: Studies at Akaitcho Hall in Yellowknife.

1970–72: Intermittently attends teacher education program in Fort Smith.

1971: Sister Jean passes away in Fort Good Hope.

1971: Takes summer courses at the University of Alberta; teaches as an intern in Fort Simpson.

1972: Drops out of the University of Alberta.

1972–73: Teaches adult education in Fort Good Hope.

1973: Diagnosed with tuberculosis; goes to Charles Camsell Hospital in Edmonton.

1974: Teaches adult education in Hay River and elementary school in Fort Providence; hired by Georges Erasmus as a fieldworker with the National Indian Brotherhood.

1974–76: Berger Commission hearings.

1975: Father Noel passes away.

1976: Grandfather Gabriel passes away.

1976: Meets Marie Wilson in London, Ontario, while travelling for the Berger Commission.

1977: Berger Commission report released.

1980: Leaves the Dene Nation; runs against Georges Erasmus for Dene Nation presidency and loses.

1981: Marries Marie in Quebec City and they move to Fort Good Hope; joins the NWT Housing Corporation; Dene support the call for the division of the NWT.

1981: Daughter Kyla is born.

1983: Elected president of the Dene Nation.

1984: Travels to Rome to meet Pope John Paul II and organize the papal visit to the NWT.

1986: Daughter Daylyn is born.

1987: Gets Treaty status back.

1987: Pope John Paul II visits Fort Simpson; Stephen is the national host.

1987: First elected to NWT legislature as MLA for the Sahtu and immediately joins the cabinet. His list of portfolios over the next sixteen years include:

— minister of justice

— minister of national constitutional affairs

— minister for the status of women

— minister of Aboriginal Rights and constitutional development

— minister of intergovernmental and Aboriginal Affairs

— minister of resources, wildlife and economic development

— minister of renewable resources

— minister of economic development and tourism

— minister of energy, mines and petroleum resources

— minister of education

— minister responsible for Worker's Compensation Board

— minister in charge of personnel

— minister of the NWT Housing Corporation

1988: Son Keenan is born.

1991: Elected as MLA for the Sahtu for the second time; diamonds discovered in the NWT.

1992: Part of the negotiations for the Charlottetown Accord; signs Gwich'in Comprehensive Land Claim; division of NWT and creation of Nunavut is approved.

1993: Signs Sahtu Dene and Métis Comprehensive Land Claim Agreement.

1995: Elected as MLA for the Sahtu for the third time.

1999, April 1: Formal creation of Nunavut; elected as MLA for the Sahtu for the fourth time.

2000: Elected premier of the NWT.

2003: Walks out on Jean Chrétien at first ministers' meeting.

2003: Leaves politics.

2010: Father Jean Pochat passes away.

2011: Brother Everett passes away.

2016: Mother Georgina passes away.

2020: Begins writing memoir.

FOREWORD

In all my years in business and in government, I learned that as soon as you think you know someone, you're bound to be surprised. I often had the pleasure of working with Stephen Kakfwi when we were both in politics; one day a technical matter regarding the financial relations between the NWT and Ottawa, the next a constitutional question, or a matter of education or health care. He was always well-prepared and serious, and always careful to make sure that he put the interests of Indigenous People and residents of the North first. We worked closely together on "Canadians For a New Partnership" after the Truth and Reconciliation Report was released.

I knew that Stephen came from Fort Good Hope and I knew that he, along with so many others, had suffered the direct and inherited abuses of the residential school system, but it was only in the pages of this book that I learned the depth of the difficulties that he and his family faced. Reading *Stoneface* is like listening to Stephen speak. He holds you with that penetrating stare of his, his words are direct and arresting, and yet he also shows us the humour that is so much a part of him and his Dene heritage. In these stories I learned just how Stephen overcame his own demons and addictions, not just to survive, but to become one of our nation's Indigenous leaders. As he tells of his own spiritual awakening and personal search for reconciliation, he becomes more than a storyteller; he is an Elder, a teacher, and this book is essential reading for those who want to share that knowledge.

— The Right Honourable Paul Martin

PREFACE

At the time of writing this preface, the book is done, the summer is over and I'm waiting for a publishing contract to arrive. It's six o'clock in the morning and I am sitting with my coffee among the spruce and birch trees in my backyard in Yellowknife. I hear a plane starting up and I can tell it's a Beaver. It's coughing and sputtering, slowly revving up its motor, and then I hear it roar through the water, taking off. I think of 1955, when a Beaver took my mother away. She left us six times over the course of twelve years, and she was gone for a total of six years. She spent all that time in hospitals getting treated for TB. And as I listen again to the sound of that float plane, sixty-seven years later, I have tears in my eyes, thinking of how she must have felt leaving us behind, wondering if she would live or ever see us again. Her brothers, sisters and parents had already died from TB.

A few days before she passed away, my mother said, "I'm praying to Jesus to come and take me. I'm ready to go." Then she paused and said, "Why is he taking so long?"

As I relive moments of my life, I agonize over the dark times, some full of fear and horror, and I wonder, Why do the demons and the pain take so long to leave?

I no longer believe in the institution of the Catholic Church, but I do believe in Jesus, that he healed people, performed miracles, cast out demons and rose from the dead. All our people know about these things and they think he was one great Medicine Man—a Healer, a spiritual person. Sometimes when I look back, I think I should have maybe stuck with Jesus. But then it was his priests and his nuns who turned on me.

"Jesus wept."

It is the shortest verse in the Bible. I never knew why he cried. Did he cry because he feared death—or did he see the centuries to come, where the church founded in his name would go on crusades and instigate wars and subjugate, colonize and brutalize people all over the world? Maybe that's why he cried.

I realize that I have been driven in large part by rage, a desire for revenge against the government that took our land and against the church that tried to take our identity. I wanted to make things right and to seek justice and truth. I guess that's why I talk about revenge. I want them to admit that what they did was wrong.

Looking back, I think I should have listened more to the Elders, to the old Chiefs and to the leaders around me. Maybe I could have learned more, learned it better and a lot sooner, but instead I took a path of defiance. I thought that I knew what needed to be done and I had very little patience with outside advice. I know this. Growing up as a child away from my family changed me; I should have realized it then. I wish I had. It would have taken me less time to recognize that the trauma I had suffered made me the way I am and that maybe I wasn't born like this.

But I have been an outsider all my life and I seem to enjoy that.

People think they understand me, but I don't think I ever really understood myself. Writing these stories and researching the events in my life have forced me to look at myself. Maybe it was a good thing that I never took stock of myself until I started this book, because maybe the truth and reality would have stopped me in my tracks.

I spent a lot of time reconstructing my life, year to year, month to month, talking to my family and friends, reviewing notes, letters, journals and daily planners as far back as 1969. I wanted it to be accurate, so I asked other people to verify the renditions and stories. The pandemic and the restrictions that came with it gave me the time. The initial notes and pages contained an enormous amount of anger. I wrote it the way I saw the world in my younger years.

But as the drafts were written and rewritten, and as I relived my life by working on these pages, I realized that I have changed. I am seventy-one. I now have much more compassion, even a fledgling sense of humour and some self-deprecation. In the last five years, I started to sleep up to six hours each night and there've been almost no nightmares. I now accept darkness as a natural part of Creation. It's no longer a place of evil and ugly creatures. Now I work to enjoy everything I do, and I try to be happy because I believe I deserve to be happy. It's not a natural state for me but I'm getting the hang of it. I even have my own dog again and he has the same name as the dog I had as a boy: Skip.

I know I have touched the lives of some people; I know I've hurt some people, too, and broken at least one heart. I have deep regrets about many things and I will probably carry these to my grave. The stories in this book have taken a turn toward compassion and a greater appreciation of the gift each one of us carries. I can see that together we have made our own world a little better for our children, our people and everyone who lives in Canada.

I offer these stories to you as my act of reconciliation so there can be more forgiveness around us, and a little more love and compassion.

INTRODUCTION

When I was in my mid-twenties, I had a recurring dream where I'd hear the voice of a child crying. I always wondered, Who is that child? Why is he crying? Why does he sound so forlorn, so lonely? It took me years to consider that maybe it was me; maybe it was my voice from sometime during my childhood when I used to cry in my sleep.

I don't know what that voice is, but it's slowly disappearing.

In a way, I've spent the last ten years of my life getting ready to die, trying to find some peace and the ability to be collected and compassionate about what I do and what I see around me. How long does that take, to become centred, at peace with everything around you? Does it take days or months or years? I don't know, but I do know that when it's my time to go, I don't want to go kicking and screaming. I would like to be calm and ready to meet my Maker, meet my ancestors.

I was going crazy with the trauma that I suffered in residential school. Counselling wasn't doing it for me, so I needed to do something myself, and writing down the things in my life, keeping notes about everything, was my therapy. I wrote stories, and I wrote the dates and the years when those things happened. I'm always thinking, Maybe I just dreamt this up. Maybe it didn't happen. Sometimes, the doubt I feel when trying to remember is like the doubt that follows being sexually abused in a dark room. You think afterward, It couldn't have happened.

But I talked to people, people like my brothers, my parents, my uncles and my cousin, and said, "Here's a story that I'd like to tell. Have I got it right or am I making a mistake someplace?" So, all the stories are as accurate as they can be. And what I've learned is that every time you tell your story, you feel that much better. It's almost like every time you tell it, there is a little less pain, anger and hate.

Back in the nineties, when students from residential schools started telling their stories, I said to them, "That's great, I admire you guys for doing it and you should go out and tell everybody." And they came back to me and said, "You do it, too, you tell your story. You're one of our leaders. Why don't you tell your story?"

I didn't want to because I was a public person and I had so little privacy left already. I didn't want to tell people, "Oh yeah, me too. I got sexually abused when I was nine and when I was a teenager, and this is what they did to me."

But people kept saying, "You've got to tell your story because you *are* a leader. If you feel that our stories must be told, you must go out and tell your story too." So, I started doing that, and at first, usually two days before the speaking event, I couldn't sleep. I'd be getting all cramped up and stressed out and by the time it came for me to have a session or talk about my time in residential school, I was physically sick. It does something to you. There's incredible shame in it; there's incredible pain in it. Sometimes the pain is so much that people, my friends and colleagues, have killed themselves. They couldn't live with the pain that comes from being sexually abused as children and then hiding it. Sometimes I'd break down and be angry, and the whole day after telling my story, I'd be violently sick. But then I got defiant about it. I said, "I'm not going to let those bastards get me, whoever they are. I'm going to get better at it." And so I kept doing it, and I would tell my audience, "I get sick every time I do this and I'm sick of it, so I'm going to keep doing it until I stop getting sick."

When you start telling it, you hate those people who abused you and you want to kill them. But as you tell it, over and over, you start to become more compassionate. You realize that they were children once; once, they were held by a mother or loved by a father, and something happened to them. Whatever it is, you don't want to hate them anymore. It's too much to carry. So, if you can find a way to make a little less hate, anger, pain and suffering in the world, you must do it. You must tell your story.

There are moments in my life that have led me to certain places and sometimes these moments feel like dots, one-time events that have no seeming relevance to anything else in my life. But I know that these dots are connected and I have realized that you cannot see unless you look back. At the same time, you must go forward and follow your instincts, intuition and vision.

I've had the extraordinary privilege of serving the Dene Chiefs and the Dene people for so many years of my life. I have also had the honour of serving all the people of the Northwest Territories as premier and as a cabinet minister before that. I travelled the entire North and across Canada time and time again. I have seen the beauty and tried not to blink or flinch at the ugliness. I sometimes found it hard to hear the voices of my people—the youth, the mothers, the fathers, the Elders and the workers—especially in the din of politics with government leaders and officials telling you what they want you to hear, or what they think you want to hear. It's easy to get lost.

These are sketches, moments of my life. These are stories about the great events that I was part of. They are stories about incredible people who deserve to be known, named and given recognition. The stories are examples of what we can do when we persevere. As you'll see, I have not always been right or compassionate. I cannot change the past, but I can help show our youth, all young Canadians and Indigenous Peoples of this land, how they should strive to be. In the end I believe that we all shine, although only at certain times.

CHAPTER ONE

SUGHA THE STORYTELLER

One summer, when I was in my twenties and still single, my older cousin Michel said, "We've got to go hunting. We've got to get some ducks for my family."

This was the beginning of September and the ducks were starting to fly south for the winter. Even though it was still summer weather in Fort Good Hope, we loaded a snowmobile and a winter toboggan into a twenty-foot flat-bottom plywood boat. It was hard work, but we got it all in and we headed down the Mackenzie River. We had guns and enough food for two or three nights.

On the way downriver we passed four fish camps on the shore; families were living there in canvas tents with their dog teams, setting nets. They were making dry-fish for the winter, for their dogs and themselves and to sell to the Hudson's Bay Company.

It was good to be outside that day: there was a clear sky and a light wind making small waves on the river. We passed a place on the west side of the Mackenzie River called *Ohn khy feh tlah*, Bird Rock Creek. There were about seven tents. That shoreline is mostly sand sprinkled with gravel and pebbles, and right behind them was a one-hundred-foot-high sloping bank of silt and small rocks. We could see that the camp was busy: there were many dogs and boats, and as we went by that afternoon people were working away and waving at us. We landed a couple of miles below that camp on the shore. We unloaded the snowmobile and the toboggan, and then we took the motor off the boat and pulled it high up on the bank so it would be safe in case the river level went up while we were gone.

We loaded the toboggan with our gear and hooked it up to the snowmobile. Michel started it up and pulled me and everything else up that hundred-foot bank through the dirt and gravel. I had to cover my eyes to protect them from the dust and little rocks flying everywhere. Once we got to the top, we saw an abandoned airstrip and we went along the trail next to it, still driving the snow machine on the dirt, about a mile inland. We had to keep stopping to make sure the snowmobile didn't overheat.

When we got to the lake, we took out our hunting canoe. We jumped in, paddled out and started shooting ducks. We shot ducks until it got too dark to see, then we headed to a place where there was a little open piece of shoreline, just enough room for a fire and two people to sleep. It was no more than two or three inches above the water level. It was a perfect little place, and that's where we camped.

When we lay down to sleep, with our eyes almost at water level, this beautiful yellow crescent moon started to rise slowly from behind the trees on the other side of the lake. It was the most beautiful thing. As it appeared, with its reflection mirrored on the surface of the lake, I remember thinking that I had to be the luckiest guy in the world.

The next day, we hunted. As we always did on duck hunting trips, we cut off the birds' wings and plucked them as well as we could, but we had to gut every one of them so they wouldn't spoil.

Late that afternoon, Michel said, "I've got to get back to town, it's getting late." So, we loaded up and went back the same way. We threw the canoe on top of the toboggan, started up the snowmobile and dragged everything back down the trail. I walked behind the toboggan as we made our way down the riverbank, holding the toboggan with a rope so it didn't slide too quickly, and then we loaded everything into the boat and pushed off from shore.

By the time we were on the river it was getting dark, and this time we were going against the current, which was fairly strong. We also had many ducks, so it was slower going than we expected. When we got close to that busy fish camp that we'd passed the day before, we noticed that nobody was there and all the tents were closed, with sticks across the front—except for one little tent where smoke was coming out of the stovepipe. My cousin was in a hurry but said we should check in and see what was going on.

When we got close, we saw a tall older woman, in her sixties or seventies, step out of the tent. It was Elizabeth Grandjambe, a woman everyone called Sugha—that's Dene for *sugar*. She came down to the shore and started talking as soon as we landed.

"Oh, it's so good to see you, my little brothers. I know you went duck hunting. I hope you did okay. Everybody left. I'm the only one here, but it's okay because the dogs are here with me. Everybody ran out of tea and sugar and lard and had to go to town to get supplies, but they left me behind. It's okay, you know, I'm all right by myself."

She goes on and on. "Oh, I'm all alone, I don't have anything, but I'm okay, you know. The weather's not good. They're supposed to have been back this afternoon but the wind was blowing and… Oh, maybe they'll come tomorrow; we'll see about the weather. I think the weather's gonna be bad tomorrow, but it'll be okay. I don't have any tea, I have no sugar, I have no flour, but I've got some fish. Come, have some fish."

It was getting dark and we had to be on our way, but we couldn't say no: it would have been rude to refuse her offer. So, we beached our boat and went up to her tent. She showed us a little bowl and said, "This is leftover flour from the last bannock I made two days ago. I kept it for you guys; it's all I have. I've got no oil, no lard, but I've got fish oil, so I'm going to mix fish oil with the leftover flour and make pancakes for you guys. You can have it with your fish."

"Well, I've got some tea," Michel said. "I got some stuff in the boat, so…"

"Well, it's up to you," she answered—then added, "Go ahead, you know."

Michel and I went back to the boat and put a bag of ducks together for her. Michel took his grub bag (inside was tea, sugar, leftover lard and treats, like the bannock that his wife had made, that were meant for us), and he gave everything to her. She had quite a haul. She made us some tea and then those fish oil pancakes.

Oh my God, that was hard eating, I tell you. Fish oil is ripe, but we had to be respectful so we ate the darn things and then took off. As we cut east across the river, we could clearly see her on the shoreline waving to us. Soon she disappeared into the grey of the evening, and I remember thinking then and for years after that what she did for us was the perfect example of Dene sharing. She had absolutely nothing, and what little she did have—leftover flour and fish oil—she was too eager, too generous to offer. That was as Dene as you can get. I love that memory. For years I would tell that story as an example of what it means to share in the bush.

But one day, when I was older and more aware of her skill as a storyteller, I thought about it again. Did everyone in the camp really pack up and tell Sugha, "We have to go to town to get our supplies, and we'll get your stuff for you, but can you stay"? Would they really leave an older woman on her own with no supplies?

Sugha knew that we were down the river and that we had to come back at some point. The afternoon that we were coming home, she was probably lying in her tent, thinking, When they come, I wonder what kind of story I could tell them…

Did she have any tea, sugar, lard or flour? I don't know. If she did, did she tuck it all away to make up a story? That's a storyteller. Here's Sugha, twenty miles down the Mackenzie River from the closest town. She's all by herself, with nobody around except thirty dogs. She doesn't feel sorry for herself at all, but she still points it out to us: "I'm all alone. There's nobody here. They're supposed to come back, but it's okay, I'm all right, I got the dogs here with me. I have nothing, no tea or sugar, but it's okay. I got some fish and some leftover stuff, and I can prepare that for you…" We couldn't possibly say no to that.

Here's what I think about this story now: Sugha prepared the story of having nothing and sharing the last of her food with these two young guys. As she watched us head home into the greyness of the river, she would have been thinking, Well, they're happy. I gave them a good story.

That is the essence of a storyteller, and as I was to learn later, Sugha was one of the best. Dorothy Cotchilly, an older woman from Good Hope, once told my mother, "Sugha was born in the mountains and long before she came out of them, word had arrived about her big imagination. People knew that Sugha was a storyteller."

I can illustrate this with another story about Sugha. In March 2005, I was hanging out at the Gold Range bar writing lyrics and trying out the songs I liked on the guitar. It was Yellowknife's Caribou Carnival, so people from many communities were in town. Around three o'clock in the afternoon, before the bar got busy, who should come in but Sugha. She was with her daughter, who helped Sugha travel from Good Hope so she could have something done with her legs at Yellowknife's hospital. She was moving slowly with the help of a walker. She could barely walk—that's an important detail to remember. For some reason, the staff at the Gold Range decided, "Now this is a special lady. We're going to give her the royal treatment." They gave her the best table: two back from the stage, dead centre. The staff made sure she had all the beer she wanted and she sat there for the whole afternoon.

Now by four o'clock, the jam session had started and the Gold Range was packed. There were incredible musicians there, like Charlie Furlong from Aklavik and Angus Beaulieu, the famous fiddler from Fort Resolution. It was awesome music.

I was approached by Therese Pierrot, a lady in her seventies who was not even five feet tall, from Good Hope. In Dene, she said, "*Say shillay dalay whee-tlay.*" My little brother, let's go dance with everybody else.

So off we went, and we danced maybe two or three songs until the dance floor got so packed that it was too hard to see her. We sat down, and while she smiled and caught her breath Therese told me how much she enjoyed it, how it made her feel young. And of course, I caught Sugha sitting there smiling from ear to ear. She saw how much we enjoyed ourselves.

That summer I went back to Good Hope for the Wood Block Music Festival. It was called that because chairs were scarce and people would sit on their chopping blocks. The whole community was gathered out in the field having a big cookout. I was greeting and shaking hands with people I hadn't seen for a while. I walked by a table of grandmothers and Therese was there. She yelled out to me, "Hey, Little Brother, remember when we were dancing at the Gold Range? It's such a happy memory for me!"

Then I hear Sugha, sitting at the next table, say, "Yeah, me too, I remember the good time we had, me and my little brother dancing at the Gold Range."

That was Sugha's way of creating a story. It wasn't true, but she threw it in there anyway. She'd look you straight in the eye and dare you to call bullshit, you know? You see, Dene storytelling has always been an important part of our culture. During the long, dark nights of winter, when it's cold and people are hungry or grieving, storytelling was given high regard because that's all there was to do. Storytelling is an essential part of our lives, as necessary as sleeping or eating.

I think that when Christianity came to our people, the priests started saying, "Thou shall not tell lies. If it is not true, then it is a lie and you are a liar." That really changed things for storytellers. *Liar* in Dene is *Goh-tsi*, one who lies. The best storytellers would hear somebody say something and then build on it and change the story. They'd catch it in mid-air and say, "Ah, yes, that reminds me of the time when..."

Rene Fumoleau was the Catholic priest in Good Hope when I was growing up. He took many photos of the Dene and wrote a book called *As Long as This Land Shall Last*. I think he understood the Dene because he once said to me, with a smile, "If I tell a story, then it must be true." I think he did something to redeem what the Catholic Church did, at least in Good Hope, which was to label storytellers as liars.

After Sugha passed on to the Spirit World, one of her sons told me he was not happy with the way some people had treated his mother. I was surprised to hear him say that, so I told him, "I liked your mother. People liked your mother, you know. She told stories, and there was never a time when you heard that Sugha is down or Sugha needs to be cheered up. She was the one who was always positive and cheering other people up. That's what I remember about her. I respect your mum. She's a part of the circle of Elders that we have."

I have thought a lot about what Sugha's son said to me, and it's one of the reasons why I decided to tell stories and write songs about the Dene people I have met. I want to write about the people that I grew up with. When I'm done, a lot of people are going to know who Sugha is, and others as well.

CHAPTER TWO

DEFIANT LITTLE DENE

I was born in the Dene camp of Rahdeghotue (Yeltea Lake) in November 1950. One of my earliest memories is of a spring bush camp with four or five other families. The snow was gone and the sun was warm, but the leaves weren't out yet. The sounds of spring were everywhere: small birds were singing and ducks were flying overhead. The men were out hunting. My mother, Georgina, and the other women were in camp. They talked and laughed as they cleaned and stretched beaver and muskrat skins. Suddenly a squirrel entered the camp, and the chase was on. All the women ran after it, calling out and chasing it, until it escaped back into the trees. I still remember the sound of my mother laughing.

I suppose I remember that moment of joy so well because in the years that followed I never got to know my mother well. She was in the hospital being treated for tuberculosis six years out of the first twelve of my life. She was often sent to the TB hospital in Aklavik, hundreds of miles away from us. In 1961, she had one of her lungs removed to stop the TB from spreading. I don't know how she survived. During these times, my father couldn't cope with all of us kids on his own, so my oldest sister Cathy and my younger brother Tommy stayed with our grandparents. My other siblings Jean and Everett and I spent a lot of time at our grandparents' too, although we mostly stayed with Dad. By the time Mum came home from the hospital, I was heading off to residential school.

My mother never spoke of her own childhood or family. It was only when she turned eighty that she told us that she, too, had been taken to residential school; she left home when she was five and didn't return for ten years. Soon after she got home, her family passed away in an epidemic. All of them. She didn't speak of her family or childhood because she had no stories to tell.

But I have a story.

I was run over by a truck when I was three and a half years old. That was quite an unusual thing because there was only one road in Fort Good Hope. And there was only one truck.

I understand this story now as one of my earliest acts of defiance. Defiance is going to run through a lot of these stories, stories of my mother, father and grandfather. This defiance runs through all of us.

It was September and it was raining. I saw the truck, my uncle Jonas's truck, at the top of the hill. Deciding to be a little daredevil, I started running back and forth across the muddy road at the bottom of the hill—until my rubber boots got stuck in the mud. I was too small to pull them out. I was going to die with my boots on and I was only three years old!

I found out later that the truck's brakes failed as it was coming down the hill. I remember facing the truck, watching it come toward me and, at the very last moment, throwing myself backwards. The truck cut my face from my chin to my forehead, leaving a scar that began on the left side of my chin and ran up beside my nose, past the inside of my left eye and onto my forehead. All throughout my childhood, I had that scar. My mother told me many years later that I jumped right back up afterward, but I soon fell back down and was unconscious until later that night.

When I woke up, I saw that there were a lot of people around me. It was dark. My mother was crying and Father Robin, an old priest with a beard, was praying. We called Father Robin *Eh-way-chee-lay*, or Ragged Voice, because he had such a hoarse way of speaking. My mother said he prayed over me, but the church doesn't give last rites to kids because it's assumed that the little one will go straight to heaven anyway. I guess they didn't know if I

was going to live or die. I woke up and I was terrified. I was in a long christening gown, so they must have been planning to bury me in that gown.

An old man, Hyacinthe Ritias, with the Dene name of *Eh-Koo-Leh*, heard about the commotion, so he came from the other side of town where he lived to see what the fuss was all about. *Eh-Koo-Leh* walked across the room and spoke to my mother using her Dene name. "*Neh Chi Lay*," he asked, "why are you crying?"

"My son just got run over by a truck."

Eh-Koo-Leh came over to me, touched my face and then looked at my mother. He was annoyed and said, "You quit crying

Stephen posing with the truck that ran him over in 1954, when he was three years old.

for him; he's going to be okay. He's going to live to be quite an old man, so quit your crying." Then he turned and walked off like he was irritated by the triviality of the whole thing. My mother said she was reassured by his words.

Mum told me that for a year after my accident, I wouldn't talk—not a word—and I would never let her go. I was so traumatized that I was scared to be alone. And for years afterward, I had this recurring nightmare: I would hurtle through the universe, past stars, planets, clouds and coloured lights. I've always wondered if I came close to death that day and if I went somewhere when I was unconscious. That dream was both exhilarating and terrifying.

That scar is not so clear anymore; you have to be pretty close to see it, but I remember how I used to feel about it, particularly in high school. At Grandin College residential school, every fall there'd be new kids and there were always a few that had to come up to me and say, "Hey, where'd you get that big scar from?"

I never had an answer for it because no one had ever told me that my scar was a result of the accident with the truck, and I never thought to ask. I didn't like the scar and it made me feel self-conscious around girls.

The funny thing is that after I joined the Indian Brotherhood and started doing fieldwork, I began to like my scar. I still didn't know where I had got it, but I was proud of it. I was an Indigenous man with a scar. I felt like a warrior. Even though I didn't know where it came from, I romanticized it.

In 2014, two years before my mother passed away, she told me the story of the accident. I was sixty-three. It says something about our life—that I never thought to ask her and she never thought to tell me. There was so much trauma and distance between everybody that I never once thought that I should find out where my scar came from. A few years after Mum passed on, I looked in the mirror and I remarked to my wife, Marie, "You know what? I used to have a scar down the side of my face and I think it's disappearing."

And she just said, "Yeah, I know."

Not long after my accident, my mother was once again sent away to a TB hospital, and that was when a woman named Victoria Douglas came into town as a teacher from the south. I was too young to go to school but I was often there because my father was the janitor. I was still very afraid to be on my own, so when Victoria finished class, she'd take me home with her. She's the one who later told me what I was like back then. I couldn't be left in a room by myself, and when she had to change out of her teaching clothes, there was no way to leave me alone so, as she tells it, I'd crawl under the bed so that she could change her clothes. I didn't know it then, but Victoria Douglas would come back into my life many years later.

Some of the happiest memories of my youth were the times when my whole family was living out on the land. My father hunted and trapped and in the wintertime we lived in a camp until one day in the spring, we'd hear our parents say, "We're moving today." We didn't know where, but we were always excited to live in a new place.

I remember waking up one morning to a bright and sunny day. Spring was coming and it was "moving day." We washed up, got dressed and ate a great meal of oats and bannock. Mum and Dad sent us kids outside so they could start packing up the tent. I was four years old, my sister Jean was eight and my brother Everett was six.

We went to play in the snow houses we had built among the trees and willows. After, we went to the river and slid down the bank on our caribou-skin toboggans. Our parents had made the toboggans for us, splitting and freezing the smooth hide from caribou legs. It was a fun time for us.

When Mum and Dad called for us, we went back to the campsite. They had not taken the tent down and the spruce-bough floor was still there. There was fresh bannock and the small stove had a frying pan full of caribou meat. We had lunch, but everything started to feel strange for me. After we ate, Mum emptied the hot coals and ashes from the stove onto the snow. The large dog toboggan was outside the tent and almost full of everything Mum and Dad had packed from inside the tent. The little toboggan that was meant for us was empty, but once the stove was cool, Mum packed the pipes inside it and tied it on top of our little toboggan, tying a pillow on top of the stove for us to sit on. We were almost ready to leave. I looked around our beautiful camp, and my excitement for a new place was replaced by a sadness to be leaving our snow houses, sliding hill and everywhere we had learned to play hide-and-seek.

Mum and Dad took down the tent, untied it from the poles and rolled everything up. Once everything was packed, the dogs started barking, excited to get going. Dad hitched up five dogs and their leather harnesses to the big toboggan and one dog to our little toboggan. Mum walked us down the hill to the lake, picked me up and set me down on the pillow. I didn't want to leave; by this time I was very sad. Everett and Jean told me not to cry, that we were going to travel together to our new camp. Mum said not to worry: our dog would follow her and Dad's sled.

Dad came down the bank with the dog team and a very full toboggan. Mum ran alongside it and jumped on, and the dogs raced down the ice on the lakeshore until they disappeared around the bend. Our toboggan began to follow. Everett stood at the back and Jean sat on the stove, holding me. I was really crying now.

"Look, Steve," Jean said suddenly. "Look at the moon and the trees—they're moving with us!" When I looked up, I saw the yellow crescent moon in the morning sky behind the trees. And it was true, it was moving with us. As we raced along the shore, the moon and the distant trees all seemed to be moving with us. I watched in utter amazement.

"See," she said, "the moon and trees, they're moving with us." Suddenly it was all right. Jean, Everett and I were heading down the trail toward a whole new adventure. As our dog pulled us toward a new camp, I knew there would be new hills to slide down and snow houses to build.

—

I want to talk more about my mother, Georgina. I remember marvelling at how hard she worked. One of my strongest memories of her came during the winter of 1968–69, when I was eighteen and home from residential school. I went out woodcutting with her. We needed to collect wood for a big barrel stove that heated the house and for the smaller kitchen stove. We'd leave town early in the morning, when it was still dark, carrying our packs, two axes, snowshoes and a Swede saw. We would put on our snowshoes, leave the trail and find a place where we knew there was a good stand of dry wood. We would spend the whole day cutting and piling up wood. We always had a fire going to stay warm, and we'd have our lunch and our tea in front of it too. We worked hard with that Swede saw. Everett usually came out with his dog team, but if he didn't, I went back and hauled the wood into town. Woodcutting with my mother that winter was the most time I ever spent with her.

My mother had eleven children; two passed on to the Spirit World in infancy. My parents also adopted three of their grandchildren to raise as their own. My father passed away young, in his early fifties, but my mother continued raising all the children that were still with her. Confident and determined, she took them out on the land by herself, even in the harshest of the winter months. She would set her tent, cut wood, gather the spruce boughs, cook, and feed and care for the children on her own. She had a reputation for making wonderful bread. She tanned moose and caribou hides and she excelled at sewing, beadwork and embroidery. She made mukluks, mitts, gloves and moccasins for all her children, and for others as well.

In the summer months, Mum would take the children to a fish camp where she had her own canoe and tended to the nets by herself. In the spring, her camp was closer to town, where she and the other women would work on the moosehides and caribou hides. One spring, a black bear started coming into that camp and her friends were worried, so they took their tents down and headed back into town. That left Georgina on her own. She

Stephen's mother, Georgina, and father, Noel, at the baptism of Stephen's little sister Irene with Father Rene Fumoleau (1957). ©NWT Archives/Rene Fumoleau fonds/N-1995-002: 0086

was angry that the bear had scared off her companions, so one morning when the bear came back into camp, she picked up her rifle and shot it. The news spread quickly in the community, and she was jokingly referred to as Georgina the Bear Slayer.

Of all the people in my family, I was closest to Everett. He was two years older than me. We went to residential school at the same time and we played together as young boys in Good Hope. He taught me a lot—especially when he was dying, and even after he passed away. I'll talk about that later, but I want to tell a different story about Everett first.

Shortly after Everett was born, my mother went back to the hospital for the umpteenth time. My father couldn't take care of Everett as a baby, so he gave him to Willie and Martha Boucan. The Boucans already had two teenagers, a son and a daughter. They adopted Everett and often took him to their hunting camp. He stayed with them for about two years. When my father sent word that my mother was back from the hospital and that Everett could come home, the Boucan family didn't want to give him back. They had become very attached to Everett, so they headed as far away from Good Hope as they could go, northeast past Colville Lake.

Georgina and Noel Kakfwi with three of their children, Stephen, Everett and Jean (fall 1954). Photo by Rene Fumoleau

The Kakfwi family, in 1955. Back row, left to right: Jonas Kakfwi, Bella Kakfwi, Domitille Kakfwi, Georgina Kakfwi, Noel Kakfwi, Gabriel Kakfwi. Second row, left to right: Everett Kakfwi, Jean Kakfwi, Cathy Kakfwi, Tommy Kakfwi. Front: Stephen Kakfwi. Photo by Rene Fumoleau

That's when my grandfather got involved. Gabriel Kakfwi was running a general store in Good Hope at the time. He was a fur trader and a merchant, so he had the money to charter a plane, an unbelievable expense back then. He took an RCMP officer with him, flew to the Boucans' camp and retrieved Everett.

It was upsetting for everybody, including Everett, but that ill will didn't last. Despite this episode, my grandparents had a close relationship with the Boucan family. Even after Everett came back to our family, he'd often stay with the Boucans; he even lived with them for a few summers when they went to their fish camp along the Mackenzie River.

I have often wondered why the Boucans treated Everett so well whenever we visited them. He would walk in like he owned the place. About a year after Everett officially moved back in with us, the Boucans adopted another boy who was about the same age as me. His name was Frederick Rabesca. His father had passed away and his mother couldn't care for him. He became known in Good Hope as Rabbi, a play on his last name.

Rabbi's arrival caused trouble for Everett. Everett thought he was still the Boucans' favourite, so when they adopted Rabbi, he thought, You're trying to take my place and I'm not going to let you do it. The boys never fought, but whenever they were in the same house there was intense rivalry, which

Frederick Rabesca, better known as
Rabbi. ©NWT Archives/Rene Fumoleau
fonds/N-1995-002: 0512

grew more apparent as we grew up. For instance, if it was time for all the kids to go into someone's house for dinner, and we knew there was a bag of candy to be had, it was usually the son or the daughter of the family who'd ask for the candy so it could be shared. But when we went into the Boucans' house, it was always Everett who asked instead of Rabbi. Rabbi would have to sit back; it was simply what happened.

Their unique relationship has had a profound effect on me, even after they went to the Spirit World. But first, back to my childhood years... Everett was with me when we were taken to residential school.

Chapter Three

The Horror of Grollier Hall

He cried to his father

"Please come and help free me"

Now he longs to be free

Of the wounds you can't see

And he tires of those demons

That keep him from sleeping

Alone in the walls

And the halls of his mind

—Stephen Kakfwi, "In the Walls of His Mind,"
from the album *In the Walls of His Mind*

I was taken to residential school in January 1960, when I was nine years old. My brother Everett, my sister Cathy and I were sent there in the middle of the school year, because my mother was in a TB hospital in Edmonton, and my father, my sister Jean, my brother Tommy and both of my grandparents had been sent to another TB hospital in Aklavik. So, it was easy for the authorities to put the three of us younger ones on a plane to Inuvik. That plane took us to a residential school called Grollier Hall.

Benedicamus domino!

This is what we woke up to every morning. Sister Hebert would shriek it out. It was Latin for "Praise the Lord." She would clap her hands and we would all struggle out of bed, fall on our knees and say, "*Deo gratias.*" Thanks be to God. I said it, too, but each morning I woke up at Grollier Hall I would discover that I had wet my bed at some point in the night. I had never wet my bed before that and I haven't since then.

Many years later, in the mid-nineties, Grollier Hall students were starting to talk about the abuse that they had suffered. At that time, I was the minister of justice in the NWT. I didn't say anything, but they kept asking me, "What about you, Steve? You were there. What about you?"

I'd always answer the same. "Nothing happened to me. I was not a good boy and I didn't listen, so the sister spanked me a lot. That's all."

Then one evening in Yellowknife, my wife and I were having dinner with the federal prosecutor and his wife. They asked me, "So, what's the worst thing that ever happened to you in residential school?"

I thought about it a bit, then answered, "I don't know. I got a spanking with a plastic skipping rope one time."

"What do you mean by that?"

"Well, I wasn't listening and I was misbehaving, so Sister Hebert got angry. She tied knots in this plastic skipping rope and spanked me with it."

My wife, Marie, spoke up quickly. "What do you mean?"

"Well, she spanked me on my arms and on my hands."

"Wait. So, how exactly was she doing that?"

I demonstrated it to them, and as I was going through the motion I realized what I was doing. Marie called it out. "That's not a spanking. That's a whipping. You were getting whipped."

That was a pivotal moment. It was never clearer. Before, I was remembering it the way I understood it as a nine-year-old Catholic boy, who thought nuns and priests and brothers were all God's people. I believed that they did nothing wrong and if they thought someone was evil or bad, then they would know best because they worked for God. So, I had reasoned, I was bad.

I also realized that, back then, I didn't want anybody—not Mum or Dad, not my grandparents—to know that I was so bad that the nun was whipping me, so I said I was getting spanked. But this wasn't true. That nun whipped my arms, hands and back as if I were an animal.

Shortly after that realization, I was on a flight from Norman Wells to Yellowknife and I took out a piece of paper and started writing. I wanted to see what else I could remember. The first line I wrote down was, "I remember the years when they took all the children, and they locked them away and they taught them to pray." Then I wrote down three or four verses after that, all in about twenty minutes. I titled it "In the Walls of His Mind." As I wrote it, it came with a melody; I could hear it. There was a woman I knew on the plane named Violet Doolittle, and I showed it to her. She read it, and then she looked at me and said, "Steve, this is a song. I can hear the song." This would become an important song for me because it helped me realize that songwriting was something I could do. At the time, I didn't want to give my detractors any reason to claim I wasn't fit or qualified for office, so I couldn't come out in an interview and say, "Well, yeah, I had some abuse and I want to talk about it…" Songwriting became my release instead. I guess you could call it my therapy.

One morning, not long after that flight, I was getting dressed for work and listening to CBC Radio. There was breaking news: "John Comeau, a former supervisor at Grollier Hall, has been convicted of indecent assault against students at Grollier Hall."

I knew that man. He used to volunteer to take care of us in the evenings and on weekends. He worked at a bank in Inuvik, or at least I thought that was his job. He was kind gentle and loved to hug us kids. We all wanted to be close to him. He made us feel safe. I always thought, Thank God, we're okay, somebody likes us, there are some kind people left.

That's what I remembered—until that winter. Then it all became clear. I realized that I had not been truthful to myself about Grollier Hall, and also that people were going to know what happened.

I had to be ready to admit that this man used to come into the storage room where I was locked away and sexually abuse me in the dark after all the other kids had gone to bed.

Stephen's sketch of himself locked in the storage room at residential school in Grollier Hall.

Sister Hebert would routinely lock me in a storage room as punishment, punishment for anything: not listening, fighting with other kids, wetting the bed or just being me. The room was in a hallway and had no windows. Sister Hebert would lock me in there, telling me, "You're just like a little devil. You're bad. You're dark."

It was so dark in that room. The only light came in from under the door. This man would come into the room and close the door. In the darkness, he would sexually abuse me. In order to survive, I told myself it was a bad dream, I was dreaming of all the groping and the pain and hysteria and it was all just a dream.

I made this sketch on an Air Canada flight from Ottawa to Edmonton in 1998. It came out of a counselling session, where the counsellor said that I have to change the way I remember things. She told me, "You're terrified and traumatized because you thought nobody in the world knew where you were and what was happening to you. Look at that experience as if your grandfather was always with you, always watching over you, and that he never left you."

I knew that I had prayed many times in my childhood, but when the memories of that time came back to me, I remember praying in that dark room only once. "Holy Mary, Mother of God, pray for us sinners now and at the hour of our death. Amen." I said that over and over on the floor of that dark room where that man abused me, when all I could see was the faint light that came in under the door. I now understand why the whole experience was so confusing to me: I was using the prayer that the church taught me to escape the abuse that the church inflicted.

When I heard that radio program, it was as if somebody put a bunch of pictures on the table and said, "You can't say nothing happened to you anymore, Steve. Something did happen to you. You were alone in that room at Grollier Hall, and this man was not a nice man. He was a pedophile. He just got convicted. So, what is the truth?"

In that storage room I remember wondering, Where is my mother? Where is my father? Am I dark like the devil? Does the nun see the devil in me? And where is God, anyway? Where are the people that are supposed to take care of me? Where is everyone?

I think that the feeling of being alone, forgotten, stuck and with no place to go was too much to bear. I couldn't deal with it psychologically as a nine-year-old, so I told myself it was all a big bad dream. That explanation worked fine until I heard the news. It wasn't a dream: there it was in black and white. It was real. It came back to me in bits and pieces, like a montage sequence in a silent motion picture. You see something happen in your mind and at first you think, Oh, yeah, I got abused. I was groped and a man's hand was inside my coveralls. But later, you remember what it feels like. And then after that, you realize, *Holy shit*, I was on the floor and I had no clothes on and it's happening in the dark and he's sexually assaulting me.

It comes a little bit at a time.

When I first found out that I was going to Grollier Hall in 1959, I remember thinking that it would be the adventure that I had been wanting for so long. I had always wanted to go with the other boys and girls that went to residential school, but my parents and grandparents would never let me, and there I was, finally getting to go. I thought, Here I am in the middle of winter, going to see all my friends. I don't have to wait till the summer. We're going to play and we're going to have fun, like we do every summer.

When Cathy, Everett and I got to Inuvik, we met the priest that ran the school, a man named Father Ruyant. He and some of the senior girls came to the airport to pick us up and then we drove to Grollier Hall.

It was strange. I could see kids I knew, older boys and girls, but we junior boys were not allowed to talk to anybody. Cathy was taken away, so Everett and I ate with the junior boys.

That's when I met the nun who was in charge of us. Sister Hebert. She looked enormous and round. When she stood in front of you, her arms stuck out to the sides and her hands looked like great big pieces of ham.

She made Everett and I strip naked in front of all the other boys, which was frightening for us; we had been raised to be very modest so the humiliation was overwhelming. She threw away all our clothes and we never saw them again. She poured oil onto our heads—to delouse us, I think—and then, using electric hair clippers, she cut our hair down to about a quarter-inch long. I had a cut on top of my head, from what I don't know, that was starting to scab over. I could feel the delousing oil getting in there and it hurt a little bit, but then Sister Hebert tore that scab right off with her hair clippers.

I realize now that this was the first indication of how cruel she was. She enjoyed inflicting pain. She was mad because I was trying to squirm away from her, so to stop me she gave me a couple of cuffs. I was starting to get concerned: this was not quite the adventure that I had in mind.

Once we had our hair cut, she made us stand up—still naked, totally intimidated—and marched us off to the shower room. That's when I had my first shower at Grollier Hall. Huge shower heads, maybe six or eight on each side, stuck out from the walls. She turned on a central large tap and water started flowing from each shower head. We adjusted the temperature and cleaned ourselves with soap and warm water, and then she told us to turn off the hot water and stand under the cold water, and that knocked the wind right out of me. I jumped away from the shower and Sister Hebert flew into a rage. She marched right into the shower room, getting water on her habit, grabbed me by my skinny neck, slammed me into the wall tiles and held me under the stream of cold water. That's when I understood the full horror of my situation.

When we got out, she gave us pyjamas for the night and clothes for the next day and led us to the dorm. From there we went to the recreation room. A lot of the junior boys were cowering but some of them were playing.

One boy, John McDonald from Norman Wells, was having a lot of fun, playing around and laughing. He was running along the wall when he tripped and fell; his head hit the baseboard and he cut open his temple. Sister Hebert tore across the room, raging and with eyes bulging out of her head. She picked him up by the hair and the neck and started to fling him around. He was screaming because there was blood pouring down the side of his face from the cut. She slapped the bejesus out of him and had his blood all over her. The more John screamed, the madder she got. We watched her cuff him until he was quietly whimpering, then she dragged him out by the collar. When he came back, he was stitched up and very quiet.

That was my first night in Grollier Hall.

The next morning, I woke up in shock. I had wet my bed for the first time in my life.

"Benedicamus domino!"

Everybody jumped out of bed at the sound of Sister Hebert's voice. She then went row by row, singling out everybody who had wet their bed. I wasn't the only one, but since I was new she ridiculed me. She made us strip the wet blankets, have a quick shower and then come back and get dressed. I learned at that time what it means to be terrorized, when you're too small to fight back when the people meant to be taking care of you are out to hurt you.

—

I had a needle that winter. I don't remember what the needle was for, but everybody had it. You'd get a scab on your arm and it took a little while to heal. Sister Hebert would stop me in the hall and ask to see it, and often the scab would be stuck to the inside of my shirt because it never got treated. There were no bandages for us. She'd see it and she'd pull it right off. It was incredibly painful. I remember that. Then she'd get mad at me for crying out. I also remember her hitting me on the top of my head, where another scab was, to the point where I was so dizzy I was close to fainting from the pain. I even wet myself once. Sometimes her violence came out of nowhere; I'd be running by and she didn't like that, so she'd grab me by the arm and cuff me with her big meaty hands.

Right from my first day, I think she always reached her limit with me— like that time she grabbed the plastic skipping rope. I just looked at her as she whipped me. I didn't respond or flinch, so she whipped my hands harder, then tied more knots in the rope until it was all lumpy. Likely then I realized she wasn't going to quit, which scared me, so I started to cry a little, but it wasn't enough for her. She lost it. She started whipping me on my head and back.

She did other things to punish me. I was the only kid that had rubber boots that winter: all the other kids had mukluks made of canvas and moosehide. When they made us play outside, we had no choice but to stay out until it was time to come in. My feet used to freeze out there. Everett and my friends used to pull those rubber boots off me and massage my feet, trying to keep me warm while we were outside, and I would look up and see her standing in her second-floor bedroom window, watching us. She wouldn't do anything. When the doors opened and we were allowed back inside, it was a totally different kind of pain as my feet thawed out. I couldn't win: my feet hurt when they were freezing and then I'd be crying because my feet were thawing.

One of the only times I was happy was when I was with the senior boys. Every Sunday morning before Mass we were allowed to skate on the senior boys' rink. It was such a relief to get away from Sister Hebert, so I went there a lot. One guy, Robert Andre from Arctic Red River, befriended me. The senior boys were my heroes. Little did I know, they were having their own traumas as well.

Then there was the tapioca.

I don't know how many times a week they served it, and even today, I don't know what tapioca is. I'd never seen it before and I've never seen it since, but it used to make me gag and throw up. Sister Hebert would watch us during our meals to make sure we ate our food. When it came time to eat the tapioca, she knew to watch me. I'd spoon it in my mouth, and then gag and spit it all out, coughing up tapioca all over my tray. Sister Hebert would come over and cuff me on the head, so I'd eat some more but then I'd throw up everything again, and I'd be crying. So there on my tray was tapioca and puke all mixed up, and she'd grab me, force me to open my mouth and she'd shovel all that in. I'd throw it back up, she wouldn't give up and I couldn't hold it down.

After everybody had left the cafeteria to go back to class, she would finally let me go. I remember the feeling of bliss as I ran back to the school building in the wintertime. Tears were freezing on my face, but I was away from Sister Hebert and I was happy. I didn't know what I hated more, Sister Hebert or tapioca, but I was glad to leave them both behind.

When I got home that June, my uncle asked me about Grollier Hall, and I told him I was always fighting. It was true; I would fight with this kid and that kid, and I was defiant, as small as I was, but what I was really doing was taking all my frustration with Sister Hebert out on everybody else. The more

I was beaten and brutalized, the angrier I got. I was fighting all the time—and so back into that dark storage room I would go.

There was an Inuvialuit boy, Bert Kimiksana from Tuktoyaktuk, who for some reason befriended me. I never fought with him; if I did, I don't remember. We met again by chance in the winter of 1985 at the Eskimo Inn in Inuvik on a Saturday afternoon. I hadn't seen him since Grollier, twenty-five years earlier. I sat down with him and we started drinking, and soon we started talking about Grollier.

One of the things he said was, "I remember that you were always in the storage room… in that dark room." Kind of laughing, he continued, "I think you used to live in there. I don't think you ever slept in your own bed." I remember thinking at the time that he was embellishing the story a bit.

If I was locked up during the day, Bert would often hang around and wait for Sister Hebert to let me out. When she finally did, I'd be sobbing while at the same time trying to stop. I'd wipe my tears and try hard to look like I was okay, you know. Bert would be hanging around and he made me feel good about myself.

Every Sunday night, after we were in our pyjamas and before we brushed our teeth, Sister Hebert would line us up. She'd walk down the line with a big, bright brassy pail full of chunks of chocolate. We had to stand there with our hands open, ready to receive a piece in case we got one. She'd stop at each one of us and tell us what she thought of our behaviour that week, whether we were good or bad. Some were rewarded, some were humiliated, some were chastised.

I never got chocolate from Sister Hebert.

Never.

And I remember the first few times—I mean, we were already traumatized, so any kind of reward or gesture that said "You're okay, kid" would have been enormous. The first couple of times, she passed me by and I got nothing. Sometimes she'd say, "You are very bad. You don't listen. You fight all the time."

The other kids would get these chunks of chocolate and oh, I love chocolate. I've been eating Oh Henry, Crispy Crunch and Eat-More since I was about four years old. A couple of years ago, a doctor said I had to quit my sinful ways so I gave them up, though I still have a little treat occasionally. But here's what happened at Grollier.

It was another night of humiliation for me. No chocolate. One kid, I think it was Bert, got his chunk of chocolate. He knew the rules: no sharing your chocolate with anybody. What you got you were supposed to keep for yourself, because Sister Hebert didn't want any of us who were denied chocolate to taste it. But somehow, Bert passed me a piece of his chocolate. I ate it... and I just about spit it back out.

I knew chocolate with a certain level of sugar in it; this was cooking chocolate! I wanted to gag. "This is not chocolate! This is just a piece of brown..."

The trouble was, I couldn't spit it out or I'd get my friend in trouble. I ate the darn thing, but I never forgot what it tasted like. And that was what we were supposed to be salivating for every Sunday night. I never wanted it again. I lined up and I put my hand out, but I couldn't care less when Sister Hebert passed me by. That's a gleeful little memory that I have.

It mattered to me a lot that Bert was my friend. He liked me and cared for me, I guess. Little confirmations like that—first the conviction of John Comeau and then running into friends like Bert and another guy, John Banksland from Aklavik—helped me realize I was not making this stuff up. When I saw John years later, he said to me, *Benedicamus domino*—that's what they said every morning when they woke us up, *Benedicamus domino*. Be grateful to God for another great day."

Benedicamus domino.

I have since learned more about why I am the way I am. When you experience that kind of trauma day after day your emotions get flattened. They die on you. You don't feel anything. The joy that you could feel is so limited because you don't believe anything anymore. I would think, Well, Mum and Dad love me but where the hell are they?

I grew up with indifference, I guess, a kind of deadening of my emotions. Even after I got married I had trouble sleeping. I was a light sleeper, sometimes waking up at two, three, four o'clock in the morning, and the very second I woke up, I'd get up and get dressed. Marie would ask me why I'd get out of bed, and I'd tell her, "Well, that's just the way I am. It's my nature." But this is learned behaviour. For me, beds are not a safe place. The minute I wake up I think, I've got to get the hell out of here.

Then I prepare myself to face the day and whatever demons are hanging around.

CHAPTER FOUR

SWEET SUMMER OF SIXTY

Marie Wilson and I were married in Quebec City in 1981. We lived there and in Fort Good Hope but we have spent most of our time in Yellowknife.

Marie's parents, Neil and Ellen Wilson, used to come up from southern Ontario and stay with us in Yellowknife for a couple of weeks. They would usually visit in the summer, when all the mining exploration was going on, so there were always many float planes landing and taking off nearby. Right from daylight, four o'clock in the morning, Cessna 207s, Beavers, Single Otters and Twin Otters would start taxiing through Back Bay and Yellowknife Bay.

My father-in-law, Neil, just loved it. He'd walk down to the water and spend an hour or two each day watching the planes take off, thundering as they picked up speed on top of the water, or watching them land, coming in slow. Neil enjoyed it, but I had a different reaction. I always associate the sound of a Beaver or a Single Otter taking off with taking people away: taking my mother away to the hospital or children to their residential schools. When I was growing up, there was no airport in Good Hope. There were only float planes and planes with skis to land on the frozen river in the winter. Sometimes when people were sick, they would leave in a float plane and we'd never see them again. It's an incredibly deep and lonely experience for me to watch a plane take off, circle around, set its sights on its direction and slowly disappear over the horizon.

People might say to me, "Okay, okay, you had a hard time. Get over it." But what kind of things do we have to get over? Something that is triggering to me and many residential school Survivors is just that: the sound of a small plane.

I remember one time when my mother left on a float plane headed toward the TB hospital—again. I was young. It was a nice, sunny day and she was busy making bread. A tractor showed up with a wagon on the back and the authorities took her, put a mask on her, put her in the wagon and drove to the float plane tied up by the shore. We ran behind the tractor, following it to the shoreline, and then watched the plane take off and disappear.

When the float planes were coming to take children to residential school, some parents left town: they took their children and went into the bush. Other parents just stood there and cried. They hugged her kids and stoically watched them leave. Not everybody dealt with it the same way.

Every time a plane came in, half the town would run to the riverbank. "Who's coming in? Who's going?" By the time the plane landed and taxied to a little dock, dozens of people would be sitting on the sloping gravel shoreline. And it was a big event when the mail plane came in. The name for the plane in Dene is *in-eetla-alla*, which translates to "the mail plane." *In-eetla* means "paper"; *alla* means "plane."

At the end of June 1960, after months at Grollier Hall, Everett and I, along with some other children from Good Hope, boarded a Single Otter float plane in Inuvik. We were excited: residential school was over for the summer and we were going home.

We landed on the Mackenzie River, just below the RCMP detachment. We all came piling out of there onto the little dock. There were parents, brothers, sisters, grandparents and other relatives, and everybody was so happy to see the kids.

After everyone had gone, my brother and I realized that there was nobody there for us. We didn't know what to do. Deep down I think we knew that it was likely that Mum and Dad were still in the TB hospitals, so we just stood there with our little bags. I had a pillowcase with some things in it.

Sometime later, Alice Masuzumi—a long-time family friend who was there when I was born—came down to the dock and said, "There's a wedding at the church and your grandparents are there. They're waiting for you."

Up the hill and down the road we went. Once we reached the big church, we joined our grandparents. Paul Cotchilly and Monica Oudzi were married that day, and Uncle Jonas was playing the church organ. Afterward, we went back to my grandparents' house, got something to eat and went to bed on a big couch that folded out. That was great. It was almost like we picked up where we left off the summer before, because we often stayed with our grandparents.

From the very first day at Grollier Hall until the last I wet my bed, but once I returned to Good Hope, it never happened again. I was back home. Everything was okay.

That summer of 1960, our land was our playground. Some places on the land were open, with stands of birch where we could play-fight or build willow houses, lie beneath the trees and look up at the summer clouds. There was a creek, Jackfish Creek, that meandered out of the hills northeast of Good Hope. The creek had shallow pools where we could swim. We fished there, too, with our bows and arrows and spears. There were probably wolves and bears around, but we were lucky, I guess. We were a formidable force: strong, young Dene warriors, sometimes as many as ten of us, heavily armed with spears, bows and arrows, slingshots and pocket knives. I suppose the wolves and the bears knew better than to mess with us.

We had all come from residential school. Among the boys were Walter Edgi, Barney Masuzumi, Edward Grandjambe, Antoine Mountain, Ernie Manuel, Jean-Marie Oudzi, Charlie Tobac, John T'Seleie, Everett and me. All of us were likely traumatized, but we enjoyed the healing powers of the land. Here, we were kings and princes of all we surveyed. We had special swimming places along the creek, like the one we called Fiddlesticks, places to fish and firepits, and we knew where all the gooseberry and raspberry bushes were.

Every sunny day, Everett and I would get up early, eat at Granny's table and then head down the hill to join the others for a day of hunting, swimming and playing. We'd get home late, around dinnertime. I don't think very many of us had lunch. If we caught some grayling and we had some salt, we would cook the fish on an open fire and eat it, but most of the time we were having too much fun to bother running back to town for lunch. At the end of every day, our grandmother would ask us to stand in front of her and she would slowly inspect our hands, fingers, heads, arms, legs, feet and toes for any cut, scratch or bruise. When our skin was dry from swimming in the silty water of the creek, she would get out her bowl of bear grease and rub the grease into our faces and other parts of our body, and we would walk around all shiny. Sometimes she'd give us a single spearmint candy, although that was not a regular habit of hers.

There was one interruption. In August, my brother and I were picked up and sent by plane to Fort Smith hospital for medical tests to see if we had contracted TB like the rest of our family. We were there for a few weeks, and it was a dismal time: we didn't know what they were doing to us and we thought we might end up in the hospital without the chance to go home. For some reason, they split us up for about a week; they put Everett in another wing of the hospital. We were only nine and eleven years old. It was a confusing, scary time. I thought I would never see my father or mother ever again. I could see my brother if he came to the end of the hallway, but they wouldn't let me out of the wing. I did have a Dene Elder in my room with me. He was Edward Blondin, father of George Blondin, and he knew my grandfather and the other Elders in Good Hope. He was a great comfort to me, telling me jokes and funny stories to keep my spirits up. I can still hear his voice.

We eventually arrived back home, and we were happy boys when we got there. We went straight into the bush with our friends again. They had started building willow houses on top of a beautiful hill that had bare ground. We'd cut willow sticks that were about ten feet long and place them upright in a circle, then bend the tips down into a round-topped hut and tie the small ends together. The older boys built much larger willow houses, and they made fires inside and lived there.

When September came, my friends returned to Grollier Hall, but I was saved by my uncle Albert Lafferty. He worked for Northern Transportation Company Limited as a river pilot. My other uncle, Jonas Kakfwi, told me years later that Uncle Albert radioed in from his NTCL tugboat, the *Radium Dew*, and asked that I be kept in Good Hope to stay with him for the winter.

With all the kids back at Grollier Hall, the town felt empty. It was just Everett, me and a few other boys around. There was nothing to do. On those quiet, beautiful fall days, I'd go by myself to a particular stand of birch in a clearing I was fond of, check the willow houses that were still standing and lie under the trees and think about my friends and family. It was a reflective time, and for years I felt that this clearing was a safe place; it was my little retreat, a place I had for myself. When I was there, I never thought about bears and wolves, or nuns or pedophiles.

—

I didn't know Uncle Albert that well. He was a tall, quiet man and he was gone a lot: in the winter he was out trapping, then all summer, from May until October, he was on his tugboat.

Everett was staying with my grandparents. I wanted to be there with him, but my grandparents said I had to go to Uncle Albert's, so that September I spent time with Uncle Albert's wife, Auntie Dora, and my cousin Michel. I was still adjusting to Dene life after my months in residential school. I learned how to help with the wood: I would climb up on top of a log on the sawhorse and sit on it so that Michel could cut it without it rolling around. After he split the wood block, I would fill up the woodbox on the porch and the other box by the kitchen stove.

My other cousin, Peter Mountain Jr., who lived next door, taught me how to set snares for rabbits. One day, he took me down to the creek and cut about twenty straight green willows, then he said, "We're gonna make arrows and we gonna let them dry, so we've got to put them under something flat so they don't get too bent out of shape when they dry."

After we did that, he set some snares. I was so excited. I'd run over to his place every day and get him to come with me down to the creek to check them. At one point he finally said, "Look, it's for you. You take care of these snares from here on. They're your snares now."

So, it became a little thing for me to do.

Auntie Dora was always fond of telling this one story. One morning, she said, "Let's go to church, you and me."

"Just wait," I replied. "I have to go check my snares first."

Auntie Dora answered with a line she often used: "Okay then, but you better hurry up and get smartened up anyways though."

And this is the way she tells the story. I went out the door, still wearing nothing but my long johns; I didn't even get dressed, I just put on my rubber boots and down the hill I went to check my snares. When I came back, she said, "Well, did you get any rabbits?" She was a little annoyed.

"No, but I just about got one. I could see the tracks but it went around the snare."

"Aw, darn it, anyway," she said. "Maybe next time. Now hurry up!"

So that was my snare line—and part of the bonding experience that's supposed to happen between Dene families, which I was getting by chance. Years later, when the pope came in 1987, I arranged for Peter Mountain Sr. to be the Elder that accompanied me on the stage. That was my gift in return to the Mountain family.

When I did go to church with Auntie Dora, I always thought it was odd that Uncle Albert didn't join us. I'd ask him, and he'd always say no.

I was a kid. It wasn't my place to ask why, but it bothered me. Back then, I really believed in the Catholic propaganda. They said, "If you don't go to church, you're going to hell," and I didn't want Uncle Albert to go to hell. So, when Christmastime came, I thought he would come for sure, but he didn't.

Years later, he told me why.

Uncle Albert came to Good Hope sometime in the early 1930s. People moved around a lot then. He worked as a clerk at the Hudson's Bay store. Albert had been to residential school before that, where he was likely smacked around by the nuns, and that's one reason he had no use for the church. But the first two winters he was in Good Hope, there was a bad flu epidemic: people were dying everywhere, and some of the elderly passed on as quick as six hours after they got this flu. If people died out in the bush, their family members would bring them to the mission by dogsled, and Uncle Albert said that sometimes those bodies would be stacked up in the church warehouse, left for the priest to bury. But it was Uncle Albert who would dig those graves, night after night, week after week, month after month, and he said no one from the church would help him. "I never saw a priest or a brother dig a grave," he told me.

So, he spent those two winters burying people because there was nobody else who would do it. Most of the Dene families were out in the bush. After his shift at the store, he'd make himself dinner and then take a toboggan and some tools and go dig graves. When the ground was frozen, he'd take wood so he could make a fire to thaw out the earth. He did this for two years when he was just a teenager.

That stuck with me. Uncle Albert always said, "Stephen, charity is more powerful than prayer. God must get tired of us saying the same thing to him day after day, the same prayers. Charity work is more important and powerful." I've always held that close. I try to teach my children that. It reminds me of a prayer by Saint Francis of Assisi: "It is in giving that we receive."

Chapter Five

My Name Is Gha Fee

Looking at the photograph of my grandfather brings back a lot of things: the sound of his voice, his manners, even how he sat. He used to have these solid blocks of Dixie Smoking Tobacco that he'd cut up and put in his pipe.

Michael Grandjambe told me this story about my grandfather Gabriel. A few of them were out in the bush and my grandfather, in his sixties, lost his pipe. It fell in the water. The other hunters were upset about it because they knew he was a man who loved his pipe and he was likely having nicotine withdrawal. It happened that Michael was a master carver. He found a solid birch root that was buried in the gravel of the creek where they were hunting, cut it out and then cut it in half with a hacksaw. He carved out a bowl and a stem and then put it back together with sinew and who knows what else, spruce gum maybe. He gave it to my grandfather, who immediately stuffed it full of tobacco. "Ah," he said, in a long exhale. He came back to life.

My grandfather was centred all the time; you never saw the old man anxious or upset. He was a man who didn't want anything. He was born in the Anderson River area with a group of Dene who spoke both K'áshog-ot'iné (*Kah-sh-ow-tin-eh*), the Fort Good Hope dialect of Dene, and Dinjii Zhu' Ginjik, the Gwich'in language.

His name, *Gha Fee*, means Rabbit Head in English. Shortly after he was born, his mother passed on and his father refused to give him up, so he raised him on his own. The story is that he raised his son on boiled rabbit brains. If you boil a rabbit head, the brain looks white—like pudding—and they say that's what my great-grandfather fed his son when he refused to give the baby up to a nursing mother.

My grandfather told me that he saw his first white man on the ice of the Arctic Ocean when he was a young boy. It was also the first time he ever tasted sugar. They would take their dog team out to a ship at the edge of the ice on the Arctic Ocean. His father was trading fur with the whalers and in return they got things like guns, knives, pots, pans and sugar.

My grandparents lived in Good Hope and every August they, along with five or six dogs with little packs on their backs, walked down the Mackenzie riverbank for about 20 miles. From there, they would cut inland toward Colville Lake, heading farther north until they hit the Anderson

River, about 150 miles from Good Hope. And they walked it, with all their stuff in dog packs. Every fall, they'd get half a dozen moose and tan the moosehide, and then make moccasins, tents, parkas and new harnesses for the dog teams. It was also a great source of dry meat.

One day, two Elders, Thomas Manuel and Gabriel Kochon, bragged to me about my grandfather. They told me, "Your grandfather was capable of setting eighty-six deadfall traps in one day." A deadfall trap is a log that's propped up and drops if a marten comes along and pulls the bait. But eighty-six in one day? At first I thought they were stretching the truth, but here's how I think he did it.

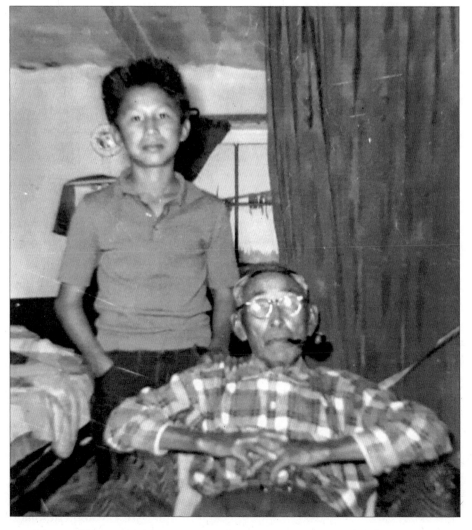

Stephen and his grandfather Gabriel Kakfwi.

Whenever my grandfather got to Anderson River in August, he got enough moose and fish to last from September to December. He never trapped after December; there was something he loved about Christmas, so he always made it home in time. Another important point to this story is that his house was impeccable. He was the only man in town who always had a huge, neatly stacked woodpile. He would say, "If I die today, your grandmother has enough wood for the big stove, the heating stove and the kitchen stove for two years. I always have enough wood for your grandmother." And it was true. Every day that he was home he cut wood for one or two hours. He was cutting wood on the day that he died at the age of ninety-three. His heart started to fail and he passed after his neighbours carried him inside.

When my grandfather went trapping at his Anderson River camp, he did nothing but cut wood for days before the snow came, so he was way ahead of the others when it came time to set traplines. So, when it came time to trap, that was all he did: run along the trail, build it up and set up traps until he had eighty-six of them. He always met his target of pelts before the beginning of December, then he'd spring his traps, shut down his camp and be home for Christmas. Afterward, he'd go work for the church or the Hudson's Bay Company, providing them with fish and meat.

He made a lot of money trapping, but one year he got in an argument with Hudson's Bay. The manager finally said, "Gabriel, if you don't like how we're paying you, then leave and don't come back."

So, he said, "Okay, I don't need you either."

There was no other store in Good Hope, but even so my grandfather left and he never went back. When the spring came, he got a ticket for a steamship and took it down the Mackenzie River and across Great Slave Lake to Fort Smith. Then he went overland to Waterways, a place that is now close to Fort McMurray. From there, he took a train—remember, this is a man that doesn't speak English, although he did bring somebody with him to translate—to Edmonton and put in a huge order for his groceries and supplies there. He took it all back with him on a barge and returned to Good Hope with enough supplies to last a whole year.

He told me that a lot of people started coming to him instead of going to the Hudson's Bay Company that winter. They would go to his camp downriver from Good Hope and say, "Gabriel, trade us some tea and sugar and we'll give you some marten pelts." So, he started trading his goods for fur. He thought he might get in trouble for this, since Treaty Dene were not allowed to trade, so the next summer he went back to Edmonton, voluntarily gave up his Treaty status and asked for a trader's licence. That's how he became a fur trader.

My grandfather soon owned and operated his own general store, Kakfwi General Store, out of his house. He had a sign out front: nothing fancy, just "G. Kakfwi Store." He'd buy fur from people and in exchange he sold them motors and food and all kinds of things. This was back in the 1930s and it lasted into the early fifties. He did it himself for quite a few years, and later on he hired people to run it for him. He couldn't read or write, he couldn't speak English and he never went to school a day in his life, but through sheer tenacity and hard work he became a fur trader and a general merchant.

My grandmother Domitille played the role of the dutiful wife. They married when she was a young girl and she was always in awe of him. He'd tell her stories and she'd sit there and listen, looking mesmerized by the man she married. Even when they were both in their eighties, she'd be sitting there and enjoying his storytelling. A pretty neat little relationship.

I used to hang out with my grandparents a lot when I was young, around four, five, six years old. A lot of the grandmothers used to take their grandchildren to get wood. We did it all year round, but especially in the summer. It was a social thing for them, an afternoon foraging in the bush for rotten wood, which they needed to smoke moose and caribou hides. They also had snare lines, so they'd go check their snares too. You'd never go out and come back with nothing.

When I went along, I was too small to pack anything heavy but the grandmothers filled up my little packsack with dry birchbark because it's got no weight. That's who I was: the birchbark kid. And that's what Martha Rabesca used to call me, *Say-khe-woh-leh*. My birchbark.

—

In June 1964, after my first year at Grandin College, my grandfather called for me. He said, "Of all my grandchildren, you are the one who's going to make my name known across this country. Everybody is going to know my name because of you."

I remember thinking, Why is my grandfather so vain? But it stuck in my head. Later, I understood that he was making a prophecy: "You are going to be well known across Canada, and that's how people are going to know my name. Kakfwi."

One day, when I was about thirteen, he was sitting there smoking his pipe when suddenly he said, "My grandson, throughout your life, things will always be swirling around you. Whatever you do, wherever you go, it's always going to be like that; just like the wind. And whatever you decide to work on, whatever is important to you, focus on it carefully and finish it before you look away."

Stephen's grandfather Gabriel Kakfwi, February 1969. ©NWT Archives/Rene Fumoleau fonds/N-1995-002: 0053

My grandfather never gave me a dollar in his life. I could always go to his home and sleep and eat there, but money was not something he gave to his grandchildren. One time, I asked him if he could give me some because I was going back to Grandin College residential school, and you know what he gave me? A pencil. A beat-up little pencil, probably about three inches long. He said, "That's what you're going to need."

For him, it symbolized the tool I would need. He was telling me, "Learn how to use this, because that's what you're going to need in this new world." He didn't know how to write himself, but he understood that a formal education was part of the answer to the future.

The funny thing is, as a kid I wanted to be a hunter and a trapper. When I was about eight years old, I kept telling my grandparents, "I don't want to go to school; I want to go into the bush and I want to go trapping."

And he kept saying, "No, you've got to go to school."

I wouldn't relent, so one day he agreed to take me out to set some traps. This is going to be good, I thought.

I went to bed early the night before but I could hardly sleep. I was so tired in the early morning that he had to help me get dressed. He said, "We have to dress carefully because we're going to be outside all day."

Then I got excited. I thought, Oh man, this is going to be great. I get to carry a gun!

We had a big breakfast and my grandfather led me out the door. We had a little sled with a packsack full of lunch, a teapot, some traps and an axe. I was carrying the rifle. Down the hill we went, across this creek and up the other side, all the way up the hill. It was about a mile to the top of the hill and then we disappeared into the mainland.

I was prancing behind him: I had a .22-calibre rifle, bolt action, with a string around the barrel and the stock, and I was so happy to be carrying it. About an hour later it was getting heavy, so my grandfather stopped and made a fire and we had something to eat. Then, he started setting traps. He was fast. He'd take an axe, trim the trees, set a trap and go on to the next. I was carrying the rifle again. It's amazing how heavy something gets if you carry it for a few hours. We walked and we walked, I was getting more and more tired, and my grandfather was enjoying himself. We must have made a fire about three or four times that

Stephen's grandmother Domitille Kakfwi, February 1969. ©NWT Archives/Rene Fumoleau fonds/N-1995-002: 0036

day because he didn't want me to get cold. Every time we did, he'd make tea and have his pipe and he was just in his element. Every time I said, "Maybe we could go back now?" he'd reply, "Oh no, we've still got some traps to set."

Well, we set those traps all day. By the time we turned back for home, it was getting dark and I was dragging that rifle. I wasn't pretending that I could carry it anymore. He never took it from me, because carrying it was the manly thing to do, I guess.

Anyway, we got home; I don't know what hour it was. My grandmother had supper ready. I got undressed and put my mukluks up to the stove to dry out, and I don't think I finished eating. I crawled into the bed my grandmother set up for me while they were still eating and went straight to sleep. The next morning, I was pretty happy to go back to school.

That spring, my grandmother took me out trapping for muskrats. It was April and the sun was starting to shine a lot longer each day. There's an island right across from Good Hope with a lot of lakes that had muskrat push-ups—igloo-shaped houses made of twigs and weeds where muskrats lived during the winter. You could cut a little piece out of the side of the house and put the trap inside on the ledge, and that's the way you trap muskrats.

My grandmother and I set traps on three different lakes. It's a lot of work but we took our time, and she didn't make me carry anything; she put everything in the sled. I enjoyed that. She and I would walk across the river, check the traps and throw the muskrats into a packsack. Then we'd drag the sled back to town and take the muskrats to her widowed friend, Martha Rabesca. She's the one who used to call me My Birchbark. She took all the muskrats we brought her, skinned them and kept the fur. She took half of the carcasses for herself and gave the rest to my grandmother.

My grandmother wasn't interested in the fur; she wanted to eat muskrat. And me? I got to eat the muskrat tails, which are sweet and fatty. When you grill the tails on the stove, the skin comes off and you munch on that. It was always delicious.

After I got the hang of collecting muskrats from the traps, they started sending me alone. I was eight years old, just a small kid with a sled, and nervous about it. I remember walking across the river, but that was no problem: it was wide open and you could see if there were wolves or bears or anything. But if it was windy, once you got onto the island everything creaked: the trees were big, many were dead and they were all leaning up against each other. The whole island could groan. I was always relieved to see the first lake. I'd quickly find the muskrat push-ups, check the traps and, if there was a muskrat in it, throw it in the sled, and then reset the trap, put it back inside, reseal the push-up and go on to the next one.

The only real scare I had was on one day in April, when the sun was starting to get hot. That's when the sun starts to melt the top layer of snow over the lake. When it gets heavy enough, the whole top layer of snow drops suddenly onto the ice of the lake below. It can be scary. So here I am, eight years old, walking across the lake feeling pretty happy. Suddenly, I heard a loud *WHOOMPH* as the top layer of snow crashed down. My little legs collapsed and I fell into a heap on the side of the trail, with snow up to my chin. "What the heck just happened?"

I had no idea. I lay there quietly for a while, and when I figured it was safe I made it through the rest of the trip, checking all the traps. I made it back to town and brought the muskrats to Martha.

Whenever I brought her the muskrats, she would always give me some bannock and cook some tails for me so that I kept busy eating while she skinned them. Then I would bring half of the muskrats back to my grandmother. It was a great working relationship for the two women.

I was eight years old, and I was a trapper. I wasn't making any money, but I had all the muskrat tails that I could eat.

—

My grandfather's trading business ended when I was a young man. For years, the government of Canada had been imposing and lifting restrictions and prohibitions on fur and wildlife trade, regulating everything from beaver to marten to moose. Then, in the early fifties, the fur market crashed. It was a brutal time for everybody and my grandfather closed his store. He was already in his sixties and likely ready to retire, but one of my uncles who worked for him said he was devastated by the poverty that came with the crash. Poverty for everyone.

My grandfather was very religious, a devout Catholic. Every winter morning, my grandmother would be the first one out of bed to make the fire and warm up the house. My grandfather would prop himself up in bed and say the whole Catholic rosary. I don't know how long that would take—half an hour, I guess, maybe more. My grandmother would bring him a hot cup of tea, put it beside him while he said his prayers. That was their ritual.

In the spring, when the fish were in the river, it was my grandfather who got up early. He made the fire and the tea, jumped in his canoe and paddled up the river to check his nets. He'd haul his fish up the riverbank to the back of their house, and by then my grandmother would have breakfast ready. While he ate, she'd come out and prepare the fish so they could dry it. They were an interesting team.

CHAPTER SIX

MY FATHER, NOGHA

My father, Noel Kakfwi, was a hunter and a trapper. My uncle Albert called him *Seh Nogha*, which means My Wolverine. For a long time, I didn't know why.

One of the last times Dad went trapping was the winter of 1972–73. He had a camp at a fish lake north of Fort Good Hope, about twenty or thirty miles from town. He was there with my family and the family of my cousin Michel Lafferty. That year my father had no dog team, but my brother Everett did. One day at camp, Everett came back from the trapline and said, "Dad, there's a wolverine on our trapline."

Once there's a wolverine on your trapline, it's a disaster: it destroys all your fur and takes all the bait. You might as well quit trapping. So, early the next morning, when Michel and his wife were just getting up, my father went into their tent and said, "I have an empty sled outside. I have an axe on it and that's all. I'm going out to my trapline and when I come back tonight there's going to be a dead wolverine on my sled."

He didn't even have a gun—just an axe. But when he came back that night, that wolverine was on his sled. He'd killed it with an axe. I don't know how he did it. He wouldn't tell the whole story, but what he would say was, "I saw the wolverine tracks. I left the dogs and followed it on snowshoes. I figured out where it was going and I caught up to it."

My father probably treed the wolverine and then cut down the tree while the wolverine was still in it. Then, he would have walked up to the animal, killed it, tossed the body into his sled and come home. I've never heard of anybody who was able to do that.

When my father passed away, my brothers and I went to see Uncle Albert. He was grieving. That's when we first heard the name *Seh Nogha*. He quietly shared it with us. "That's what I called him when we were alone," he said. "*Seh Nogha*." My Wolverine.

My father was born on the trail, near Anderson River. No one remembers exactly which day he was born, but it was near the twenty-fifth of December, so they just said it was Christmas and called him Noel.

My father never talked about residential school, but we think that he must have gone there because he could read and write, and there was no school in Good Hope when he was a boy. The other clue was that he was almost completely ambidextrous: he was naturally left-handed, but he wrote and did other things with his right hand. And we knew that the nuns said, "To be left-handed is a mark of the devil." They would never let you write with your left hand; you had to learn to do things with your right.

My grandfather raised my father the way he was raised: strict, spartan and independent. For example, one summer, when Dad was around eighteen and still living with his parents, there was a dance in town and he wanted to go. My grandfather said, "Go ahead, but if you're not back by eleven o'clock, the door will be locked and it will never open for you again."

Dad said, "Whatever," and he went, stayed out late, and when he came back, the door was locked. He spent the night outside. When my grandparents got up in the morning, they opened the door and my grandfather said, "Go and get your things. You're on your own now."

Dad replied, "I don't care."

Those men were a different breed of people. Dad left his parents and he went fishing and hunting. He decided to marry my mother, Georgina Barnaby, that summer. That fall, they went to the northern end of Great Bear Lake, spent the winter there and then went to Colville Lake. That's how they spent their honeymoon years.

My father and an Elder named Eddie Cook were the first Indigenous justices of the peace and coroners appointed in Canada. This was back in the sixties. He was very dedicated to that work. Here's an example: In February 1971, my sister Jean passed away tragically and the story was never well explained. She died of exposure under someone's house, and I always thought she was probably trying to get away from someone who was threatening her. My parents were grieving, but a couple of days after Jean passed on, Dad said, "They're asking me if I feel strong enough to get back to work and I told them I could do it." He had just lost his daughter under terrible circumstances and he thought he was calm enough to preside over other people's court cases. That was my dad.

One spring, a seismic company operating in the area was trying to get some equipment across Jackfish Lake when a vehicle went through the ice and a young man drowned. The RCMP, divers and people in the community spent a week or two searching. Every day, my father would get up early and go out to the search. He had to be there, and we watched him get more and more exhausted each day. I remember at one point he said, "You know, that young guy, his mum and dad, they want to find his body and we've got to try to find him." Unfortunately, they never did.

My father was also a boxer. I saw him box once and I was absolutely amazed; it was just bare fists. My dad's younger brother Jonas was staying with us one winter and he got into an argument with Dad and challenged him. So, they stood in the middle of the kitchen, feet planted, and Jonas was throwing punches—body punches, head punches—and he never hit him. Dad blocked every punch and never once hit Uncle Jonas. It was an amazing thing to watch. I was proud of my father then.

My father wasn't so strict with me, but he was clever. When I was fifteen, I was hanging around with older guys and getting into trouble, so he made a plan: in August of 1967 and '68, he sent me to a fish camp with Martha Rabesca. I stayed in a canvas tent on the river shoreline with Martha and her two older sons. I was the only kid at the camp: there were three families there, but everybody was in their twenties and thirties. That first summer, I could see Good Hope from our fish camp but I had no way to get there. I mean, it was right there, you know. I wanted so badly to be back with my friends and the girls, but it didn't matter. The whole month of August I was in the fish camp.

I was helping with the nets and cutting and hauling wood. Martha had a snare line on the top of that riverbank, probably one hundred feet up, and we'd climb up there every two days and check the snares for rabbits. On our way back, we'd pick berries and grab some wood. Martha cooked every night, and we lived on rabbit, duck and fish. She'd roast or boil the fish and fry or roast the rabbit over the fire. She'd also make fresh bannock. It was always a feast. When we ate, we'd all kneel around spruce boughs gathered together with a tablecloth on top. Martha put all the food in the centre and once everything was set, we'd say our prayers and then dig in. We could eat as much as we wanted. The woman loved to cook and she rewarded everybody for their hard work.

One time, though, I was chopping wood and I was getting tired of it. I was a lot rougher than I needed to be and I broke the axe handle. It was made with birch by Martha's son Alfred. Martha didn't make a scene, but after supper, when we'd all finished eating, she said, "My Birchbark, you broke that axe handle. Alfred, he worked hard to make it. So, you must fix it: find a birch, cut it and whittle it down. Find a good birch. Maybe Alfred will go with you."

So, after supper, off we went into the trees, looking for a birch. We found one and I cut it using another axe. I did all the work; Alfred was just sitting there, enjoying himself, telling me stories, and I was working away. He told me how to do it properly.

The second summer, I guess God was merciful because they took me farther down the river where I couldn't see Good Hope, what I was missing. I was always thinking, Why did my father send me away to a fish camp? Why would anybody do that? I only get two months at home each year and

Martha Rabesca at her Dehcho fish camp, where Stephen spent two summers as a teenager. ©NWT Archives/Rene Fumoleau fonds/N-1995-002: 0362

he sends me down to this old woman's place for a whole month.

And he did that two years in a row.

As I got older, I realized that my father wanted to keep me out of trouble. I was hanging out with some wild young guys in Good Hope and starting to drink. Even so, I always carried some anger toward my father. I was angry about the lack of control I had over my life. I blamed the government, the church and my father, and I know now that I was wrong to include him. The result was that I never got close to him; I never spent quality time with him after I was twelve. When I was twenty-five, we were just starting to talk and build a better relationship and that's when he passed away.

There is one conversation that I remember well. It was in the early seventies before the Berger Commission hearings began. I had been hired as a fieldworker and it was a time when our Elders were starting to formulate a vision of how to go forward with the inquiry, questioning what it would mean for our land and our chance to regain control. One day my father asked, "So tell me, what are you going to do?" He had the biggest smile on his face.

I launched into my vision, totally unrestrained. I was twenty-four years old and had probably worked two jobs in my life. I told him, "Well, we plan to take back our land. We're going to take the whole thing back from the government, half a million square miles. We're going to control the activity. We'll get the money we need from resources—oil, gas, gold and minerals. We're going to take over, get rid of the territorial government and set up a new government, a system that's fair and that allows us to make decisions and govern ourselves the way we want, and we're going to rename the whole thing—the river, our communities—the Northwest Territories. We're going to start giving Dene people back their Dene names and we're going to put one of our people in Ottawa as a member of Parliament and in the Senate. Dad, we're going to try to take over the government so we can change it."

I believed it completely. But he sat back and asked me with a smile, "Are you sure you're going to be able to do all that?"

"Yeah, Dad, yeah. That's what we're going to do."

He was curious—and I think inspired, as were a lot of older people— to hear the determined and clear statements we were making.

"That's what we're going to do."

We had support from the Elders, but I still felt that personal distance from my father. Maybe neither of us had any idea how fathers and sons were supposed to get along because we'd both been taken away to residential school. It was no better with my mother. I never had a conversation with her, so the distance that developed only grew. At least when the Berger Inquiry came, we all had something to talk about.

If he had lived a few more years, I could have learned more from him. We could have been closer. My career might have been different, more positive, less tumultuous. I didn't have any daily mentoring from him as an Elder, so I missed him that way.

My father did have a great sense of humour, though. People still remind me of the days when Dad got his hair cut. First he'd go in search of Antoine Abalon, the man known as Old Woman. He was a wise man and people respected him. When he spoke to the Berger Inquiry, he was seventy-four years old. I remember what he said:

> Maybe I'll die tomorrow, but I am here speaking because I am thinking of my children and my grandchildren. This land means so much to us. We live off the land: when our fathers kill something or catch a fish, our mothers feed on the fish and then breast-feed us.

Anyway, this old man was about as funny as anyone I'd ever met. I have always thought, To understand us, you need to understand Antoine Abalon, because that's who we are. In a true Dene person, you see the two sides of Antoine Abalon: the serious and the humorous.

Antoine cut people's hair with a pair of clippers he owned, and whenever my father would go up the road to Antoine's to get a haircut in the summertime, everyone in town would know. "Oh, Noel's gonna get a haircut," they would say. "He's gone to get Antoine!"

Those two would be walking down the hill together, back to Dad's place where Antoine would cut Dad's hair, and people throughout Good Hope would watch them coming. Antoine could tell my father stories that made him laugh so hard he could barely walk, and my father's antics would have Antoine bent over in laughter too. So, all down the hill back to Dad's house, people would watch Noel Kakfwi and Antoine Abalon walking together, laughing. They were the community entertainment.

—

There was only one time when I hugged my dad. He'd brought a friend of his to Yellowknife and he asked me to help that man make his way in the city while my father continued on a business trip to Edmonton. We hugged briefly in the hallway of a hotel when my father left.

Years later, I had a dream about him. It was in the nineties, after all the news of the abuse at residential schools became public. I was dealing with my own memories and always looking for someone to blame, and I realized how much rage I had toward my father.

I think it's a beautiful dream. In it, I am walking down a road and I see a group of people on the side of it, distressed and pointing into this mist. I ask them, "What are you doing? What's going on?"

"There's a man out there in the mist and he's all alone. We don't know if we could find him. Can you have a look for us?"

So, I walk into this fog and wander around. It is a cold, grey day. After a while, I see the outline of a person looking forlorn, with his head bowed and shoulder slumped. I walk up and say, "Hello. Who are you?"

The figure turns around, and it is my dad.

"Dad, what are you doing out here all by yourself? Why are you here? Why are you alone?"

"My son, this is where you left me."

I reached out to touch him, but I woke up as I stretched out my arm. The moment I woke up, I realized what my father must have gone through raising us by himself in his thirties, trying to do the best he could while my mother was away for years, and then losing us to residential school because he got TB himself.

Oddly enough, it was my father's death that helped me discover much of our family history. I didn't know how to handle grief like that, so I was medicating myself, drinking in the Gold Range every day. New Year's Eve came along and I was joined by a friend of mine from residential school, a guy named John Mackenzie. He said, "Why don't you come and spend New Year's with my mom, dad and me in Behchokǫ̀?" So, that's where we went.

The next day was New Year's Eve and I wanted to go off and party someplace. The Mackenzies went to church and John went with them, and around one o'clock, John came back and said, "Steve, some people want to see you; do you want to come with me?"

I thought it would be a party, so I tidied myself up and went with him. He led me to this big log house; I walked in and the whole place was full. There were rows of Elders sitting on the floor or on benches, and John told me that these people wanted to meet me. Me? At the time, I was just a field-worker with the Indian Brotherhood, a slightly hungover twenty-five-year-old guy from Fort Good Hope. John's parents were there and they told me to go shake everyone's hand, so I did. I had to, even though I was incredibly shy. It was hard, but I went around and shook everybody's hand, then I sat down and they started talking. It was early afternoon and they didn't stop talking till about five or six. I sat there the whole afternoon. They were speaking Tłı̨chǫ and I didn't understand the language that well, so I didn't catch everything that was being said. I could tell they valued me as a visitor but I didn't know why. I left Behchokǫ̀ without knowing what that afternoon was all about.

It all became clear, years later, when my daughter Kyla married a young man named Amos Scott. His father is Pat Scott and his mother, Gabrielle, is one of the Mackenzies. When I met Gabrielle, she said, "My father wants to meet you."

Her father, Suzi Mackenzie, was an old man. He told me the story.

When he was a young man, he hitched up his dogs and took off north toward Great Bear Lake with his friend George Blondin. It was hard going: the journey is at least three hundred miles and they often had to break trail with snowshoes, but eventually they made it. Their next destination was Colville Lake and then the town of Good Hope.

Here's what Suzi told me: "When I got to Good Hope, I had one of the biggest surprises in my life, one I will never, ever forget. I walked into Good Hope and what do I see? I see a Dene man who couldn't speak English and who never went to school running his own store. This old man was buying fur and selling boats, outboard motors, rifles and sleds. All that stuff was lying around, and the old man was sitting there smoking his pipe." Then he turned to me and said, "And that was your grandfather, Gabriel Kakfwi."

"Yeah," I replied. "That was my grandfather."

"That's why we knew your last name. We had all heard the story of the Dene man with the store in Good Hope. So, on January 1, 1976, when we heard that a young man named Kakfwi from Good Hope was coming to Behchokǫ̀ we all knew the name and we all wanted to meet him."

That was the beginning of my lifelong association with the Tłı̨chǫ people. And I have my grandfather and my father to thank for that.

CHAPTER SEVEN

FATHER POCHAT

Bishop Paul Piché was the Catholic bishop of the NWT for almost thirty years. He was appointed in 1959, and by then the residential school system had been taking children away from their parents and communities for generations. But the church had a problem: it was losing its hold over the people and it was having an increasingly difficult time recruiting a new generation of priests, brothers and nuns. So, Bishop Piché had a vision of creating a new residential school for select Indigenous children, a place where he could train them as priests, nuns and brothers, but also as the next generation of leaders in their communities.

With support from the federal government, Bishop Piché used the church's resources to create Grandin Home, an institution in Fort Smith for promising young Dene, Métis, Inuit and Inuvialuit children. Bishop Piché recruited kids from across the North in 1962, including my brother Everett and a couple of other boys from Fort Good Hope, Walter and Barney Masuzumi. In 1963, when he came back, I was twelve years old.

The bishop came every summer and it was always a huge event. He'd fly in with his entourage and the whole community went to see him arrive. His entourage wore black cassocks and Bishop Piché had one trimmed in a rich purple. Dozens of us—adults and kids—followed them around as they walked through Good Hope. That was the kind of importance and charisma that he had.

Travelling with the bishop was Father Jean Pochat-Cotilloux, or Father Pochat—a man who would have a significant impact on my life. Father Pochat had been chosen to run Grandin Home, so he and Bishop Piché were both looking for students. Though Bishop Piché made it clear that he wanted to train kids for the priesthood, Father Pochat had a different idea from the outset. He was a firm believer in liberation theology, an approach founded in the idea that the Dene and other Indigenous Northerners were going through a period of dramatic transition; people were starting to move off the land and into communities, which meant that they were not going to be hunting and trapping as much as their parents did. So, he believed that the future lay in building communities to keep our people strong. He wanted to transform his select group of young people into a cadre of future leaders—and if he ended up with a couple of priests, he was okay with that too.

Father Pochat asked for me, so I went to see him. He told me who he was and then asked me about my schooling. The school in Good Hope only went up to grade six and I had just finished that. After our conversation, he invited me to Grandin Home.

I was very excited. I was young, but I felt like I was special and I wanted to go so badly. I had forgotten—literally forgotten—the trauma I had experienced at Grollier Hall just three years earlier. I don't know why; I guess psychologically I had to block out the horrible parts. At the time, I was remembering it as an adventure and I wanted another one. Everybody in my family agreed that I should go, so I boarded a float plane, a small Beaver, and flew over six hundred miles south of Good Hope to Fort Smith with my brother Everett.

Stephen, twelve years old, at Grandin Home, September 1963.

A few days after I arrived, it dawned on me that I had been in a situation like this before and it hadn't turned out so well. During that first week I was often on the verge of tears. I felt as if the full horror of what I had gone through at Grollier Hall—the sexual abuse, the beatings, the whipping and everything else—was all coming back to me. I was realizing what it meant to be away from home for ten months. Everett walked me around, making sure I didn't fall into a sobbing heap, but I was thinking, I'm stuck and this is a great, big mistake.

We went to a public school, Joseph Burr Tyrrell Elementary, and lived in the Catholic student residence called Grandin Home. It became clear right away that I was having trouble speaking. I was very shy, mumbling a lot, and I simply could not read out loud. My teacher requested that I be taken out of grade seven and moved back two years. Instead of doing that, Father Pochat said, "No. Give me a month and I will deal with it."

So, one evening he came into the dining room, where we were all sitting, and said to me, "Steve. After dinner. Seven o'clock. Come to my office."

It wasn't ominous, but I took it as if it was. I was so scared the abuse would start again. Seven o'clock rolled around and I tiptoed down the stairs. It was dark; the whole damn place was dark, right out of a horror movie. I went down the hallway and stepped into his office. He then led me down another dark hallway, right to the end of the hall, and the whole time I was thinking, You know, this is not good.

He walked into a room and turned the light on, and I followed him in. It was a meeting room with a long table, and on the table was this huge reel-to-reel tape recorder. He sat me down and said, "You must learn how to read, otherwise they're going to put you back in grade five. I'm not going to let them do that, so we're going to work on it, every night if we have to, until you learn how to read out loud."

I could have jumped up and… while I wouldn't say hug him… the relief I felt was enormous.

He said, "There's a pile of *Reader's Digest* magazines here. Pick a story, any story."

I remember the story that I picked; it was about World War II tail gunner Nicholas Alkemade, whose plane was shot down by the Germans. Rather than go down with the plane, he jumped, without a parachute, and survived. The article was called "I Fell 18,000 Feet and Lived," and I read that damn story over and over until I could do it flawlessly, out loud and into a microphone.

That was the beginning of my relationship with Father Pochat.

And there was an element of self-discovery in our meetings as well. Father Pochat played the recordings of me reading back to me, and I thought I sounded terrible. Everyone was right. That was a big, big moment for me. After that, there was some trust between me and Father Pochat. There was some comfort. I was thinking, I'm okay. This guy is okay.

There was something else too. I had a typical haircut for a Dene boy, short on the sides and long on the top, but I was too self-conscious to comb my hair. So, one day Father Pochat came down to the breakfast table and said, "Steve, you must comb your hair and be tidy, or we'll do like they do in the army and give you a haircut." Well, I didn't comb it, so a few days later he gave me a brush cut, with two inches left on top. I was too shy to say that I was thankful I didn't have to comb my hair anymore. That became our ritual: every summer, I'd return home and grow my hair out all long and bushy, and within the first week back at Grandin in September, for the next six years, Father Pochat would say, "Steve? Time for your haircut." That was our thing. The fall of 1968, when I was in grade twelve, was the last time he cut it. That was also the year I grew out my hair and combed it down like Ringo Starr.

But I need to tell you more about Grandin because it's important. There were Dene, Métis, Inuit and Inuvialuit students, but we were all Catholic. The students who went there did become leaders: people like James Wah-Shee, who was a Tłı̨chǫ leader for many years, a minister in the 1980s and president of the Dene Nation. Nick Sibbeston was there; he became a senator. Michael Miltenberger became a prominent minister and Ethel Blondin-Andrew was a member of Parliament in the NWT. There were Chiefs too: Jim Thom and Joachim Bonnetrouge from Fort Providence; Jim Antoine, who became a premier and minister and was a lifelong Chief of Fort Simpson; Bob McLeod, who was also a premier and minister for many years; Tony Mercredi and Archie Waquan, leaders from Fort Chipewyan; Chief Felix Lockhart from Łutsel K'e; Chief Gerry Cheezie of Smith's Landing; and Cindy Gilday and Fibbie Tatti from Délı̨nę. Grandin turned out a high number of Northern leaders.

Although Grandin was a residential school, as far as I know there are no reports of abuse—no physical, sexual, mental or psychological abuse. It's the one institution that I know of where we never heard any complaints. There may have been some trouble, but I have not heard about it.

The original Grandin Home was open for a few years before it got too small, so they built a huge brick building that had a gymnasium, probably one of the biggest gyms in the NWT at the time. The old wooden building, Grandin Home, became the residence for the girls, and the new building, known as Grandin College, was built for the boys.

I started to think back on my time with Father Pochat in my thirties and forties. He helped shape me into the person that I am today, especially because my own father was not there for so many years. He was my other father for six years of my life, from when I was twelve until I was eighteen. But I never thought about that then. When I got out of Grandin in June 1969, I couldn't get far enough fast enough: I never wanted to see another priest, nun or brother, I never wanted to go to church again, I never wanted to be anywhere near any of that. When I left, I felt as if I'd been a captive for six years.

Father Pochat left Grandin around the same time I did. He went back to his own parish, what we call today Behchokǫ̀, but back then it was Fort Rae. Father Pochat went back to be with the Tłı̨chǫ Dene. He learned their language and had his own dog team so he could visit people out on the land, because that's where they were. And that's where he's buried now. His parish was his whole life, and the Tłı̨chǫ were his people.

I only recently realized that he was part of the reason why I always had such strong support from the Tłı̨chǫ. All throughout my tenure as a minister, premier and leader of the Dene Nation, the Tłı̨chǫ people supported me. To this day, if I go to Behchokǫ̀ the Elders will come and shake my hand. They remember me, who I am. When I got into trouble as a premier, busloads of people from Behchokǫ̀ rallied around me. There was no obvious explanation for that, but now I know that it was because of Father Pochat's influence. He didn't abandon us after we graduated; all his life, he provided us support and encouragement.

I was the minister of justice in the early 1990s when the allegations of sexual abuse were starting to surface in the NWT. It began with former students of Grollier Hall in Inuvik, and it was controversial. People were angry and afraid to speak up, worried about the shame and the possibility of reprisals. What's more, the church was in denial.

One day, Father Pochat called me and said, "Steve, I have a boss, Father Provincial, the man in charge of all the Oblate priests. Father Provincial knows we were together at Grandin College and he has asked me to arrange a meeting with you as minister of justice. He wants it to be private and away from the government offices. If you could host him at your house he would be very grateful."

"Okay, but what does he want to talk about?"

"He has refused to tell me, but I'll tell you right now, Steve, if Father Provincial raises the issue of sexual abuse of students by Catholic Oblates, I will walk out of that meeting. I will shut that meeting down, I promise you. It's not right and I do not want to be a part of it."

"Okay, I agree."

So, I hosted the meeting at my house in Yellowknife on a beautiful summer day. When Father Pochat and Father Provincial arrived, we sat down, had some tea, hummed and hawed, and finally Father Provincial said, "Steve, you're the minister of justice and you're a former student of Grollier Hall and Grandin College. I'm asking you, as a minister of the NWT, to deny the allegations. These are not substantiated. There's no proof and I want you to stand with us."

Father Pochat got up and said, "Father Provincial, I cannot be a part of this. I told Steve that if you ask him to go against these allegations, I would shut this meeting down. I will have nothing to do with it." Father Pochat got up and walked out.

Father Provincial didn't know what to do. Finally, he said, "Well, can we finish the meeting?"

"No. You cannot ask me. I'm the minister of justice and you cannot talk to me about these matters in private. We will deal with this in court." And I kicked him out.

Once again, that was a moment where I saw the character of Father Pochat. He could have said, "Steve, look, I don't like the accusations against the order, but I'm an Oblate and I want you to defend us." But he didn't say that. He said, "If these things are true, then we should suffer the consequences. If there has been sexual, physical and psychological abuse, then we must deal with it."

You know, you hear about how holy priests are, or ought to be. I never thanked Father Pochat for his intervention that day, but I had a profound sense of what an incredible man he was. I never told him about the abuse I suffered at Grollier Hall, but I'll tell you something: my life in politics was not always easy, and as thick-skinned as I thought I was, there were times when I was licking my wounds, feeling weary and pained. I would jump in my truck on a Sunday, drive the hour-long trip to Behchokǫ̀ and walk into the church while Father Pochat was saying Mass. He'd see me walk in

and nod to an empty place for me to sit. I'd sit there in silence, feeling comforted, and that there, in Father Pochat's church, no one could touch me. I did that for years. Sometimes I'd take my wife, Marie, sometimes my kids, sometimes I'd just go by myself, but he always came over afterward to say hello, invite me to stay for some coffee or cookies.

There was always a big gathering in his mission after Mass; anywhere from ten to thirty people would go. That was the kind of influence he had. I didn't always go, but I did more often over the years. After I retired from politics in 2003 we grew closer, and he got close to Marie too. We renewed our marriage vows with him in 2007.

Father Jean Pochat photographed at his home in Behchokǫ̀, in August 1975. ©NWT Archives/Native Communications Society fonds/N-2018-010: 03034

One morning, Marie and I got a call from one of the Tłı̨chǫ leaders, who told us Father Pochat was on his deathbed. "He wants you to come to see him."

Marie and I drove to Behchokǫ̀, and when we walked into his room we saw that he was surrounded by Elders who were comforting him and praying. He was lying on a simple bed with nothing but a sheet covering him. Marie talked to him in French for a while. You could see that he could hear her, for French was the language of his childhood. Then I took a turn and whispered into his ear in Dene. I told him that before he left this earth, I wanted him to know how much I'd come to appreciate who he was and what he had done, and that I was sorry I never saw it before, but I had been troubled by many things. I thanked him for being my father for six years and for his support, and I told him that we love him, that I love him. I could see tears rolling down the side of his face. He squeezed my hand, so I know he heard me. Those were the words I said to him. He passed away about ten minutes later, so I was one of the last people who talked to him on this earth.

The effect that Grandin College had on the North was immense and Father Pochat was the one who put it all together. He received the Order of Canada for the work he did with us students. To me, Father Pochat was what an Oblate was supposed to be. He took vows of poverty and humility, and he never spoke about himself. He was devout. He lived a simple life and yet his influence was profound.

In 2020, many years after he passed, I took my two grandsons, Tydzeh and Ry'den, to his church in Behchokǫ̀. They were thirteen and eight years old. Before I led them inside, I said, "You know, people might come over to shake my hand. So, if that happens, you stand politely and you look at them and you shake their hands."

We went inside and sat down, and after the Elders had received Communion and were coming back down the aisle to their seats, they all came over to shake my hand and my grandchildren saw that. I explained to them who the Tłı̨chǫ leaders were, who Father Pochat was and why those old people were coming by. It was a good story to share. When Mass was over, we went to Father Pochat's gravesite. I said, "This guy was my father for six years and that's why he was important to me."

Chapter Eight

My Cousin Teaches Me

I was always told in residential school that there was no future in hunting or trapping and that you had to get educated. At the same time, some of the Elders were starting to say, "Steve is getting an education, so he's going to be useful to us someday." So, I was getting a bit of a swelled head. As a young guy, I was different from the other teenagers in Fort Good Hope.

One summer, I went to a party with some older boys and a fight broke out. When they fought, they wrestled instead of punching each other. Once you were down, that was it: you lost. But I stepped in and punched one of the young trappers. He was older than me, so it was a real sign of disrespect. But I was thinking, Hey, you know, that's me: I know how to fight, I'm educated, I'm superior.

As soon as I hit him, my cousin Michel Lafferty, who's six feet three inches, grabbed me, lifted me up, carried me right out of the house and parked me outside. He went back in and closed the door.

A few evenings later, I went to Michel's place. I walked in and saw all those older guys from the party sitting there, smoking, drinking and telling stories. I was just a kid and I walked right into their evening. I didn't know what to do. I couldn't turn around and walk out because it would be too embarrassing, so I just stayed there and they completely ignored me. Turns out this was also embarrassing.

Eventually, my cousin turned to me and said, "Steve, you want to go hunting?" There was a dance going on at the community hall just down the street, so I didn't want to go anywhere, but I didn't want to say no either, so I said, "Yeah, sure."

He said, "Go home and get your gloves and boots, and then we'll go."

When I got back, his friends were gone. Michel said, "Okay, we're going to take two guns. I have my packsack and I've got a packsack for you too. You carry the guns and I'll carry the hunting canoe." It was a homemade canoe: canvas over a spruce frame. He picked it up and we were off. The hunting canoe wasn't heavy but you start to feel it if you carry it for more than an hour. So, I was walking behind him, carrying a couple of guns and feeling pretty happy about it.

It was just after midnight—but on a June evening in the North the sun barely dips below the horizon. When we got to the edge of town he disappeared into a heavy thicket of dark green willows. I could barely see the trail but I went in after him. It was low ground, all muggy and swampy. Then the mosquitoes came out. Millions of them.

Once we got through the willows he passed the canoe to me. My turn. I had to balance the canoe with both hands, which meant I couldn't bat the mosquitoes away anymore, and I had to all but run to keep up with Michel. He was tall and fast. We came to a creek and crossed it, then climbed up the first of a number of hills. The ground then flattened out and we walked for what felt like two hours, through land that was infested with even more mosquitoes. I carried that canoe the whole way. He was going to show me how hard you have to work to be a good hunter and trapper.

Once we got to the lakes, I was exhausted. I said, "I'm kind of tired and I'd like to sleep."

Michel was amused. "You can't sleep. We came out here to hunt ducks."

So, off we went paddling around to shoot ducks. My job was to pick the dead ducks out of the water and throw them into the bow of the canoe, while he sat behind me and did the shooting. The canoe is small and tippy, so we had to fold our legs underneath us and sit incredibly still.

We hunted ducks until the canoe became heavy and was only an inch above the waterline. We landed and again I said, "I wouldn't mind getting a little sleep."

And he said, "No, you can't. We have to gut the ducks."

So, we cut the wings and heads off and then slit the bellies. Reaching in with our hands, we took the insides out and lined the ducks up on a bunch of willows to cool.

"Okay, *now* I can get some sleep."

"No, no, no," Michel said. "We're going out again."

That's what we did, hour after hour. I was beyond exhausted by the end, and while we were gutting and cleaning the last batch of ducks, he said, "We could get more but I don't think you can carry very much, so that's all we're going to get."

I didn't even care about his insult. Thank God, I thought, we can go home now.

We put the ducks in our packsacks, and I know that he took most of the ducks, but he still put enough in mine that I didn't feel like I was making a token effort. He had the canoe, most of the ducks and one gun and I carried the gun and some ducks. It was early morning by then, so the sun was beating down on us and we were just sweating.

When we were close to home we stopped on the side of a hill. "Let's sit down for a minute," Michel said. It was a beautiful little clearing beneath some birch trees.

I fell flat on my back beside him, thinking I was close to dying. Michel pulled out a cigarette and offered me one. I thought, I guess he must still like me.

As we were having a cigarette together, he said, "You're probably wondering why I asked you to go hunting." I was too tired to even speak. He continued, "Well, you've been going to school for years and you think you know everything.

July 1968, Fort Good Hope. Stephen Kakfwi after a day of chopping wood and helping with the laundry.

You think you're educated. Out here, you know nothing, absolutely nothing. All the schooling in the world doesn't do anything for you.

"All these hunters and trappers, they know more than you ever will. They don't teach you stuff like this in school. I think you should learn to respect hunters and trappers."

He didn't say it in a mean way, but as if to say, "Open your eyes. This is the Dene. This is the way it should be."

And that was 1967. I was only sixteen but I always remembered it.

One day, fifty years later, I brought up the hunting trip to Michel. He said, "I always wondered whether you remembered anything I told you."

"Well, I do," I replied. "And I know exactly what you meant. I spent my life learning stuff in school, but since then I have spent a lot of time learning about the land, the legends, the language, the history of our people and our traditions. And I realize that, yeah, I knew nothing compared to most of my people. I was away too long.

"But because of what you did and what you said, I've always had the highest respect for hunters and trappers. During my years with the Dene Nation, I went to war with the European Parliament to protect our right to trap and sell wild fur in Europe, the United States and across Canada. And I instituted guaranteed minimum fur prices for our people when I was a minister of renewable resources. I did those things because I knew what you meant that day."

Michel says he's always amazed at the things I remember, but I owe it to him. That day hunting was one of the first times I realized that I needed to relearn how to be Dene.

CHAPTER NINE

MY PSYCHEDELIC SHIRT

The December of 1968—the year we were all walking around with mop-top hairdos, vests and bell-bottoms, inspired by the Beatles—my parents were able to buy me a plane ticket so I could be in Fort Good Hope for Christmas. I hadn't been home for Christmas in six years, since I started at Grandin Home, and I'd been asking for this every year. It felt too good to be true!

Herb Lafferty, a friend of mine at Grandin, had a navy-style peacoat that was too small for him; he couldn't return it, so he gave it to me. That was a big boost to my confidence because my clothes were pretty shabby. I wanted to make a good impression when I went home.

Inspired by my wardrobe upgrade, I decided to order something from Eaton's too. Their catalogue, *The Christmas Wish Book*, was out, and I liked a colourful Carnaby Street vest shirt with a psychedelic paisley pattern. I ordered it and it arrived just before Christmas, so when I packed for home, I put that shirt in my suitcase and away I went to Good Hope.

As excited as I was to get home, it was not to be a happy homecoming. Good Hope did not have an airport: you had to land in Norman Wells and then make your way to Good Hope either on a small plane or by driving along a winter road. So, I stopped in Norman Wells and stayed with my aunt Bella, my dad's youngest sister. I liked her a lot. She helped raise me; she was the one who introduced me to birthday cakes. She loved to celebrate like that.

There were a couple of days when the weather was horrible, so my flight was delayed. It was very dark: there are only a few hours of daylight in December and the only plane that could fly out of there was a Beaver on skis. Aunt Bella was kind enough to let me stay with her until my rescheduled departure. One night, Bella went out partying and she never came back. No one knew where she'd gone. They found her on the river ice. She had died from exposure; she likely wandered off the riverbank through deep snow and onto the ice after leaving a party in some cabin. The people there said they thought she had left to go home, but I think she ran away from somebody.

We had a funeral for her in Good Hope. That Christmas was very heavy. It was an awful time for my grandparents and Dad was heartbroken. Bella was his baby sister.

I had forgotten what Good Hope was like at Christmas. Everybody was visiting, sharing fish, moose meat and caribou, as well as their grief for Bella.

People hadn't seen each other for a long time. I have a lot of relatives there and I was close to a lot of the Elders, people like Peter Mountain Sr., a huge Dene man who came out of the mountains. He was six feet four inches, very tall for a Dene, and he was married to the smallest little woman in Good Hope. She must have been just under five feet, and everybody called her Granny Mountain.

One night we went to a concert, which was just a bunch of kids singing Christmas carols. The place was packed with people who had just come off the land: they had their bush clothes on—mukluks and beaver mitts—and some of them hadn't had a decent haircut in months, so there were these huge tufts of black hair sticking out from under their hats. They were beaming and all packed inside this huge community hall. This is one of the only places in the world where you could get an audience like that.

There was this good-looking girl in the audience who'd caught my eye. It was the first time I saw Suzanne. I was wearing my peacoat and the Carnaby Street shirt underneath. This was going to be my chance to strut around a little bit. Even with the wood stove on, though, the log house was cold—too cold to take the peacoat off. She never got to see my new psychedelic shirt. Nobody did.

There was a lot of socializing throughout the holidays: we'd party one night at my uncle's place and the next night it would be at my auntie's place. We partied with Peter Mountain Sr. and his wife, then they'd party at our house. In the course of all the partying, I noticed that some things were missing from my luggage. I wasn't sure what was gone, but I knew that my suitcase wasn't as full as it had been.

After New Year's Day, everybody stopped partying. People began cleaning up their houses and getting their dog teams and sleds ready to head back to their traplines, back to the life of hunting and trapping. Everybody was busy. I was helping my parents clean up the house and get our woodpile stacked up.

My mother said, "Steve, go over to Granny Mountain's and ask for her small axe."

It was a break from cleaning up the house, so off I went to Granny Mountain's house. She was sweeping up her floor and it was kind of dark: there was no electricity, just a glow from the wood stove and a faint light from the window. I looked at her and wondered, What in the world is she wearing?

She had long hair, and like most Dene women she had a colourful kerchief over her hair and tied around her neck. When I stepped up closer, the light hit her—and here was Granny Mountain wearing my psychedelic Carnaby Street shirt.

The log homes of Fort Good Hope in the winter of 1968. ©NWT Archives/Rene Fumoleau fonds/N-1995-002: 0139

She's holding a broom and she's looking at me almost defiantly, you know, like, *What do you want?*

"Granny, Mom asked if she could borrow an axe. And hey," I added, "where did you get that beautiful blouse from?"

"Oh," she said, "your mum. She loves me so much. Your mum gave me this a few days after Christmas and I just love it."

She already had a couple of little safety pins pinned to the front of the vest, the place where Dene women keep pins for diapers, even though she hadn't been a mother for about twenty-five years.

I took the axe and I went home. I asked my mother why she had given away my psychedelic shirt and she was so surprised, then she just started to laugh when she realized what she had done. Finally, she said, "Well, we didn't know whose it was. We thought some woman had left it behind." She started laughing even harder. "It looked just like a colourful Dene woman's kerchief."

And she was right. It had the same kind of pattern, in bright pink, yellow, gold and purple—the colours were all there. They had no idea this was the rage in London, England, half a world away. In Good Hope, in Christmas of '68, it looked just like an old granny's blouse.

CHAPTER TEN

LEARNING FROM MY ELDERS

When I was growing up, we were still getting almost all our food off the land. This was our traditional food and we had traditional ways of sharing it. There were no grocery stores with chicken or pork chops. I have some beautiful memories of meals I remember well; they were opportunities given to me as I was trying to relearn my Dene culture.

One happened during the winter of 1968. My sister Jean woke me up early one morning and said, "Steve, get up. Mom and Dad want us to go check the loche hooks."

Our parents had set hooks under the ice on the other side of the river, across from Fort Good Hope along the shallow part of the shoreline. They were for a bottom-feeding fish called loche, or burbot or ling cod.

Jean and I got a fire going and had a piece of bannock, and away we went. We each had a packsack and as soon as we stepped outside, my sister sprinted ahead of me. It was dark and cold. Her mukluks made almost no sound as she flew across the snow. We headed west and ran straight across town, down the steep bank and onto the Mackenzie River.

The river is always colder than anywhere else because it's the lowest part of the land and it collects the cold air. There was no moonlight and we didn't have a flashlight, so it was pitch-dark. I was so happy following my sister as we flew through the cold air across the river. We got to the hooks and used a chisel to chip through the ice. There were three or four loche, all different sizes, and Jean was happy because we were going to bring something home to our parents. We rebaited the hooks, put them back in the water and covered up the ice hole with the chiselled ice that we'd scooped up. That way it refreezes right away. Then we turned around and ran all the way back to our house, with the fish freezing in our little canvas packs.

When we got home, it seemed as if our parents knew we were going to bring something home: the house was hot, the gas lantern was on and Mom was making bannock. And we had the happiest Mom and Dad. The land provided what they wanted to eat and their children went and got it for them. They cut it up right there, threw the liver in the pan—when fried, a delicacy—and fried up the rest of the fish. It's a firm- and sweet-tasting fish; some people call it the poor man's lobster.

That's what we had for breakfast. You might say it's the farthest thing from a bowl of cereal or bacon and eggs, which I'd eaten for years in residential school. That's what made it so memorable. At residential school we had electricity, showers and oil furnaces. My meals were all provided for. I'd get up, go wash and go to the cafeteria and my tray was there with my plate already on it. But in Good Hope, we had to sprint across a river for breakfast. Sometimes, we'd have rabbit or caribou or whitefish. In many ways we were poor, but I don't know how many southern Canadians could have afforded the wonderful selection of meat that we had at our disposal on any given day: rock ptarmigan, spruce grouse, rabbit, caribou, moose, whitefish, loche or trout. Nobody down south could afford that and we could have it every day. We just didn't have salad. I remember this time with my parents so well because I was able to properly experience what life in Good Hope during the winter was like.

—

Another memory I have is of a meal called Granny's Dish. My siblings and I really connected with my grandmother, Domitille Kakfwi. She helped raise us. When she had a piece of meat and there wasn't enough for everybody, she would dice it up into the smallest pieces, put them in a frying pan or a pot and then add water and oatmeal. Instead of adding sugar or honey, she would salt it. That would become our meal, which we all affectionately call Granny's Dish.

My sisters Rita (NeeNee) Kakfwi and Ruth (Yogi) Kakfwi, February 1969. ©NWT Archives/Rene Fumoleau fonds/N-1995-002: 0032

She really knew how to stretch it. It was such an affectionate thing for her to do, to add some oats to a dish so we could all enjoy it. We would gobble it up, and we love the dish to this day. I still make it, and my children, Kyla, Daylyn and Keenan, know that dish and they all love it. And all four grandchildren too: Maslyn, Sadeya, Tydzeh and Ry'den. We all still call it Granny's Dish.

If a grandparent gave us a piece of rabbit, ptarmigan or spruce grouse, they would make sure we ate every morsel of meat off the bones. They would teach us how: you take it in your hands and nibble at it until the bones are clean. It's mostly because they don't like to waste anything. No one is allowed to take three bites out of that piece of meat and then throw it out. Whatever they give you, you have to eat it. We learned to do that as kids, so most people my age, if you give us some spruce grouse, we'll eat it until there's nothing left but the bone. That's how we were raised.

When my grandmother was young, people could starve to death if they got stuck in the bush, three or four days away from food. And it happens. There are times when there are no moose or caribou, so every little morsel counts. People have also said that there were times when they ate nothing but fish for a month because they simply couldn't get anything else, and you can't live on just ptarmigan or rabbit. Eventually you starve because there's not enough nutrition. It was a fact: sometimes the Dene had no food. We know what it's like to be hungry.

—

We all have our biological grandmothers and grandfathers, but every other grandmother or grandfather in Fort Good Hope was our grandparent too. We call them *Ah-sohn* and *Eh-seh*. We were always told to respect our Elders. Some lived in log cabins or tents, and some stayed in tents year-round. For those that lived in tents, my parents or grandparents would often say, "Go visit those Elders and make sure they have kindling and wood that is cut and split. Make sure they have birchbark or spruce boughs to get their fire going in the morning, and make sure their water pail is full."

In the winter, they'd add, "And make sure they have some ice and crystal snow." Tea tastes better with crystal snow. You never make tea with tap water: you make it using the snow that has turned to crystal under the top layer. It's better like that.

When the Elders became too old to live on their own, they were often taken into people's homes. There was no old folks' home in Good Hope when I was a kid. It was not uncommon for a grandmother to move in with another family; you'd walk in to visit a friend and there would be an elderly lady by the door with all her things around her, her pipe and maybe some sewing.

The family took care of her and fed her, and often these older women would be the storytellers in the house. They were always cheerful because they had to add a positive atmosphere to the house, wherever they were.

Speaking of cheerfulness—there was an Elder in Good Hope when I was young named George Big Ox, but everyone called him by his Dene name: *Deh-Fee-Weh-Khe*, the Old Man Who Shot Himself in the Head. The story I heard was that he was out hunting caribou. He was carrying his gun and running on snowshoes when he fell, the gun went off and he shot himself in the head. They thought he was going to die but he surprisingly regained consciousness. He was blind in one eye and paralyzed from the waist down, but he was totally happy to come back to life. Rather than be burdened by his disability, for the rest of his life he was as exuberant and happy as anybody you could meet.

When I first met him, I was around five or six years old. He and his wife were living in a tent and a group of us kids would often visit them. He loved playing games with us. One of them was to pretend to hold Mass. He started doing that because when we all lined up at the foot of his tent, he was reminded of people lining up to receive Communion in church. So, he would pretend to say Mass... except it wasn't real Latin. "Ah, baba, dah, babba dah babba da..."

Then, we'd respond to him like we were in church answering the priest's prayer: "Abba, dabba, dabba, dabba..."

We would all laugh and laugh. He was having so much fun. He'd pretend to scold us, then he'd wave his hand to the four corners of the cross and bless us all individually. "Abba, abba, dabba, you, Stephen, abba, abba, dabba, dabba, dabba..."

And we were just as happy as sin. Afterward, we'd get up and run out, having survived another mass with the Old Man Who Shot Himself in the Head.

He had to go to the store every once in a while. He'd say, "I need my dog team!"

We'd all pretend to be his dogs.

"*Yah-hah-tee*!" he'd say. Bark!

At the foot of his tent, we'd all be barking. His wife would go get his toboggan, a little one, maybe four feet long, with a rope at the end. We'd pretend to attach ourselves by holding that rope, one kid on each side. He'd get himself propped up on the toboggan with his legs folded underneath him, and up on that toboggan he was the happiest man in Good Hope. He'd start yelling, "Gee!" To the right! Then, "Jaw!" To the left!

When there was snow it was easier for us to pull him along; in the summertime, he'd still get onto the toboggan and we would start pulling, but we couldn't run very fast. We'd be kicking up clouds of billowing dust. We were quite the spectacle: a bunch of kids dragging an old man on a flat sled several hundred feet to the Hudson's Bay store. People would watch and laugh. We had so much fun with the Old Man Who Shot Himself in the Head. He was a Dene man who knew that it was always better to laugh.

—

Another Elder I knew also taught me about food. Chief George Kodakin of Délı̨nę was a powerful traditional Dene Chief, and he was still serving after younger Chiefs like Paul Andrew, Jim Antoine, Joachim Bonnetrouge and Jim Thom came and went. When Chief Kodakin met Justice Thomas Berger before the Berger Inquiry, he said, "You want to have hearings in my communities? You're not going to learn very much, even if you visit each one. The only way you can learn anything is if you come live with me. So, I want you to come live with me in Délı̨nę before you start hearings."

Berger agreed, but he didn't go himself; he sent his legal counsel Michael Jackson instead. So, Jackson travelled throughout the communities and got to know them. Chief Kodakin knew it was the only way they could be taken seriously by the locals. He was that kind of guy: a visionary, tough and very clear-headed.

When I started working as a fieldworker in 1974, I was drawn to Chief Kodakin like a magnet. He was my mentor. I'd go to Délı̨nę just so I could listen to him talk. He had meetings with his councillors at his house and he would invite me. Sometimes, they would ask me to say something—they didn't care what—but I had to do it in Dene. In the quiet and security of that gathering, I would stumble and hesitate and find words and put them together. Eventually I got confident enough to start speaking my language in Délı̨nę, then in Tulita and then in my own town of Good Hope. It was their mentoring and coaching that got me there, so I hung around with Kodakin and his councillors for years. I got as close to them as anybody from the outside could.

This one time I was in Délı̨nę for a weekend. My departing flight was on Monday and Chief Kodakin sent Mary, one of his daughters, to find me. She said, "My father wants you to come by this afternoon."

So, in the early afternoon I went there and his wife, Elizabeth, met me at the door. She was dressed up to go out. She had her colourful kerchief on her head and her coat on, and she said, "Come. I want to tell you something."

She led me to the back of the house and said, "What you're going to have is something very special, because he doesn't invite anybody to share what he's going to share with you. Once a month he does this and it's always by himself. This is his alone time and it's always very special. Just so you know." She turned around and left the house.

I had no idea what she was talking about, but I found Chief Kodakin alone at the dining table, so I joined him. We had some tea and we talked for a long time. Finally, he said, "Since I was little, I watched old people do this. Some of them, they have no teeth or don't have enough teeth to chew meat anymore, and some of them don't want to eat the meat that should go to younger people, so they collect bones with little scraps of meat and tendon on them. They put it in a big pot and they boil it for a whole day. That's what I asked you to come and share with me."

He took this big pot off the stove. It was full of bones, like leg bones from caribou. Everything had been boiling for so long that the meat and tendons were just falling off. He put the pot on the table and said, "Let's pray now and then we'll eat."

I sat beside him at the table but these Elders are more accustomed to sitting on the floor of a tent, so he was perched on his chair with one leg up and the other folded underneath him, as if he were on the ground. I sat there with Chief Kodakin and he told me stories as we ate. There is a certain way you are supposed to eat: you take one piece of bone and with a sharp knife cut off a piece of meat that's hanging off the bone. Then you take the marrow out, eat the marrow and have some bannock. The pieces of meat and tendon, they're all soft. The tendon has turned to a kind of jelly. For Dene people it's very delicious. To this day, when I'm offered meat, I always say, "I'll take the bones." My kids, I always amuse them when I tell them, "I'm going to have my bones this week."

Chief Kodakin lost two of his sons in October 1977. They drowned in Great Bear Lake. From then on, he lost his power and his strength. He wasn't the same person that he once was. In the early nineties he got sick. His family was gathered around him in Yellowknife when he sent for me. In front of everybody, he said, "I'm not going to be here much longer, maybe a day, maybe two. Steve, I don't want to worry about my wife, so can you promise me that she will always be okay when she comes to Yellowknife?"

I said, "Yes, I will do that." And for years after that I looked after her whenever she came to Yellowknife for a visit. That was something I did for George Kodakin.

My last story about eating with Elders takes me back to Good Hope that Christmas of 1968. Some of the Elders were curious about me, this young man in his last year of high school, so I was invited to share some food with a group of grandmothers. They were slow cooking a caribou head at Leoni Orlias's house. Madeline Jackson was there, and so was Marie Shae,

Angelina Taureau, Mrs. Chinna, Madeline Boniface and one of my grand-mothers, Martha Rabesca.

These Elders were under the impression I'd been sent to Fort Smith to become a priest or an Oblate brother. Of course, this was the bishop's plan with Grandin College and I never said otherwise, so these grandmothers wanted to know what I, a future priest, was like. I wasn't that crazy about going, I was taking care of some other Christmas business at that time, but I went anyway. I thought, Well, what the heck. I'll go, have a quick meal and that will be the end of that.

There was bannock, the caribou head and other goodies, all traditional food. We sat down on the floor; they said a prayer and then started passing around the food. They asked me what I wanted and I said I'd have some tongue and parts of the jawbone. They gave me that, and they also threw in one of the caribou eyes. "Here, you eat this too."

I didn't want to eat the caribou eyeball; it was sitting in my dish look-ing at me. I knew what it tasted like because I had tried it when I was a kid. Some people like it and some people don't, and I wasn't particularly crazy about it. It was boiled and it does become a little harder when it's boiled, not as liquidy, but the centre is… well, the idea of an eyeball squishing around in my mouth was an idea I wasn't crazy about. I dared not say anything, so I just pretended. "Yeah," I said. "That's okay."

We started eating, and I was really focussing on the tongue and the other meaty parts of the caribou head on my plate, knowing I'd get to that caribou eye soon enough.

They started asking me questions—and a lot of them. "How many more years are you going to go to school? Are you going to be a priest? What are you going to do? What do you do when you get up in the morn-ing? What is your day like? What do you do at night? Do you pray every day? Do you go to church every day, or just on Sunday? What do you do when it's time to play? What do you do at night? What do you do on the weekends?"

They were right into a serious interview; it was like they were having a hearing! I was answering them the best I could. It went on and on, but at some point or other they started talking among themselves. Right at that time, I took the caribou eyeball and started cutting it out of the small piece of skull it was still attached to. I cut off the meat and fat around it, because that's yummy stuff, and when I thought they weren't looking, I quickly popped the eyeball into the pocket of my fancy peacoat. No one noticed, and that was it. The night went on, and I had a great evening with that group of beautiful grandmothers.

That caribou eyeball, it turned out, was not finished with me. In a strange way, it became a symbol of my first love, and that's something I never forgot.

I never got to see that girl from the Christmas concert again that trip home. One of my sisters said she had run into the girl's mother and the mother told her, "My daughter was sure impressed with your brother. She saw him on the stage the other night."

So, I thought, Hey, I've got an inside track! I figured if I couldn't see her this winter, I'd make sure I saw her in June, and I'd ask her to be my girlfriend then.

When I returned to Fort Smith it was late evening. I was unpacking my stuff at Grandin College when this dried-up, black, brown and white piece of… *something* fell out of my bag and onto the floor. I picked it up and I couldn't for the life of me figure out what it was. It looked like a miniature of Saturn, with a black core that had a ring around it and all these stripes of lighter colours. I realized suddenly—*it was the caribou eyeball!*

And so there I was with this petrified caribou eyeball. I left it sitting on my desk. Sometimes during study time, which was for two and a half hours every night, I was bored stiff and I'd get to looking at this thing. One night I thought, You know what? I could make something out of this.

I got a knife and I cut away any fat and meat still around it. It looked interesting: blackish, brownish, yellowish and hard. As I cleaned it, I thought, This is probably the only dried caribou eyeball ever kept by anybody in the history of the world. So, what am I going to do with it?

I took that eyeball (and now I was thinking about it as a kind of token or amulet) and I carved a hole in the edge, threaded a piece of caribou string through it and made it into an amulet. I wanted to give it to that blond girl in Good Hope in June. I'd impress the bejesus out of her by saying, "This is the only time in the history of the world where anybody has received a gift this unique: a dried caribou eyeball."

The very first day I was back in Good Hope that summer, I was having a few beers and my friends dared me to go to her house. So, I did; I went up to her house and I introduced myself and I told her, "I want to go out with you. I want you to be my girlfriend."

She said, "Oh you do, do you?"

I gave her that caribou eyeball, and that's how we met. Her name was Suzanne and she eventually became my girlfriend. Like most first loves, it was both fun and heartbreaking, and I never forgot her. I remember thinking that summer, Somebody loves me. Somebody loves me, totally and unconditionally.

CHAPTER ELEVEN

A YOUNG DENE IN RESIDENTIAL SCHOOL

Although I was raised in a remote Dene community, I was profoundly influenced by what was going on elsewhere in the world. Much of the news that caught my attention in the 1960s came from the United States. The heroes of the civil rights movement and the growing defiance of young Americans came to me as it came to many of the other young men and women I knew in the North, through newspapers and *Time* and *Life* magazines. We read about the assassination of the Kennedys and Martin Luther King Jr., the Vietnam War protests, the American Indian Movement and the push for the civil rights of women and black people.

I started reading as a young person. The Federal Day School in Fort Good Hope had a library with many books. My father was the school's janitor, so if I couldn't find my friends or it was raining, I would wander up to the school and look for him. He'd be busy working, so I would go to the library. That's where I stumbled on a series of books on American heroes, like Davy Crockett, Daniel Boone, Paul Revere, John Paul Jones and Zachary Taylor. I always wondered where the Canadian heroes were. It never occurred to me to ask what a hero was.

But I really liked these characters; they were daring and strong, and even though a lot of them killed Indians, they were famous—famous Indian fighters. This was my first encounter with what you would call propaganda, but I read all the stories and, because of the way those stories were told, I cheered for the cavalry and the cowboys who killed the Indians, because they were the good guys.

I remember seeing a movie about Crazy Horse and when they killed him, his Spirit rode his horse up to the sky and disappeared. I was thinking, He didn't lose. He's free and he's strong and he's beautiful and he's in the Spirit World now.

The reality though was that in Good Hope, we didn't see ourselves in that kind of conflict. We still thought that the land was our land, that we had our community and we were independent. We didn't see thousands of white people invading our country and taking the land; these stories happened in the United States hundreds of years ago. Of course, you couldn't find anything in those books about what was happening in Canada.

At home, we had a radio and my father always listened to the news. The first time I saw my father riveted to the radio was in October 1962, during the Cuban Missile Crisis and the Cold War. When we had to practise hiding under our desks at school, I was conflicted: the idea of a nuclear war seemed scary, but it was also too far away to be real. We had wolves and bears to fear.

I went to Grandin College the following year and I went to the school library there too. I was homesick and looking for things to read about the North and Dene people, but there was nothing there. It was like we didn't exist. I did, however, find a copy of Treaty 11, so I read that. I told my grandfather about it the next summer, and I think he just about pulled me out of school when I asked him why he sold our land for five dollars a year.

I often wondered who put that copy of Treaty 11 there. Maybe it was Father Pochat, because he always believed in Dene people, that it was our land and that we should be in control of our lives and our communities.

I read everything I could in that library, including stories about the fight over the Holy Land between the Palestinians and the Israelis. At the time, I could never figure out why they were fighting; why couldn't they just share the land? I read the Bible, too, and I always wondered why, if people believed in God and Jesus and "loving thy neighbour," no one could share. I read about George Wallace, who was fighting to deny black people the right to vote and black students the right to attend universities.

I also read about John F. Kennedy and I remember thinking what a fairy tale it all seemed to be. Before he was elected, we'd see pictures of old presidents like Eisenhower and Truman; then suddenly here's this young, articulate and eloquent president with a beautiful wife. Two months into my first year at Grandin, he was assassinated. I remember seeing pictures of state troopers at the scene and seeing no sign of compassion in their faces.

I also remember reading the Declaration of Independence and thinking it was beautiful. "We hold these truths to be self-evident, that all men are created equal, that they are endowed by their Creator with certain unalienable rights, that among these are life, liberty and the pursuit of happiness." But I was also thinking, They said all this beautiful stuff—why aren't they doing it? It was my first inkling of racism. The world, I was starting to see, was not perfect.

—

My first year at Grandin, I was younger and smaller than everybody. I was homesick, so I was trying to find things that I could feel good about. And right around that time, along came Muhammad Ali. Father Pochat used to let me read his copy of the *Edmonton Journal* and I read about this outspoken fighter who had dark skin. He caught my eye because boxers were never quoted in the paper. He became one of my heroes. That's what I wanted to be like: I wanted to be tall, strong, defiant of everybody and able to talk confidently.

I was not the only one at Grandin who paid attention to characters like Ali, King or Malcolm X. We all followed that stuff. There was nothing else to do but read. I think even Bishop Piché was caught up in the social revolution of the sixties, and he saw the direction things were going. That's what made Grandin College so unusual. Father Pochat kept telling us that we were

Stephen at Grandin College, after his annual haircut with Father Pochat. School photo by Walter Masazumi

leaders and the most important resource for the North. Do you know how many students graduated Grandin and joined the Catholic Church? No one. Not one.

We had a strict program: we got up every day at seven o'clock and it was lights out at eleven. In the mornings, we'd do our exercises, then shower, dress, clean up, have breakfast and do our chores. Everybody helped with that. We kept the building clean ourselves. We had two and a half hours of supervised study every night, from seven to nine thirty, and on the weekends it was five hours. That's when we did our homework, read and researched.

We had no clothing allowance and that meant a lot of hand-me-downs. Some students had extra clothes to help each other out, but I know in some pictures you can see me running around with pants that were too short or shirts with missing buttons.

We had a sports program, so every day after school, we'd play hockey, basketball or volleyball. We had that large gym at our disposal. We had teams and we competed in territorial basketball and hockey tournaments; we won the basketball tournament a number of years, beating Yellowknife, Inuvik and Hay River.

We were also all going through our teenage years and had to navigate the mixing of boys and girls, and that was a lot harder than it should have been. Good Hope was in the middle of nowhere and we all had strict Catholic and traditional Dene upbringings. Boys didn't talk to girls; it just wasn't done. Single men weren't allowed to talk to single women unless it was pre-arranged. And because it was so strictly Catholic, it was assumed that if you were talking to a girl, it must be for sexual reasons. If you're going to talk to a girl, their logic went, then it's because you're interested in them, and if you're going to have a relationship, that means you must get married first. That was kind of beaten into us and it made for a lot of turmoil, anguish and stress. Some of us had a hard time with it.

There were coed events like dances. Sometimes they were just for Grandin kids, and other times there were high school dances with kids from town. If you look at pictures from my first few years at Grandin, from grade seven to nine, you can see all the nuns in attendance in their full habit, watching the girls. That meant that if you went and you were waltzing or slow dancing with the girl of your dreams, the nun would make sure there was always about six inches between you. But we also played volleyball and had picnics together, and the college had a log cabin, about fifteen miles out of town, so we used to go there on the weekends and camp and play music, so that was good. Even still, some of us just couldn't relax around girls.

There was a group of four of us from Good Hope at Grandin. One was Richard McNeely, who later became the president of the Métis Association. At Grandin, Richard had an intellect unmatched by others around him. He was tall, pale and anxious to be well liked and grew increasingly confident. Another one was John T'Seleie, who became a lifelong Dene leader and activist. He was our academic of the group: very studious and a bit of an introvert. The other member was Antoine Mountain. He was the artist and comedian. He had a good sense of humour and was always upbeat and positive. He was popular and always ended up with girls around him.

The four of us always sat together at a table in the cafeteria. It was a table for four and we kept it like that. We didn't allow anybody else to join us. Sometimes one of the senior girls would try to join us and it never turned out well; we just didn't want to socialize.

I think some students made the best of Grandin, but I remember the six years that I was there as an incredibly lonely time. I was never completely convinced by the claims that we would all become leaders. If I had stayed in Good Hope, I would have always known my language, culture, land and people and I would not have had to relearn everything. And I wouldn't have suffered the trauma of being away from my family and having my family fall apart. That trauma is what marked so many of us. Many of us were socially awkward, introverted, angry and incapable of having a healthy relationship with our own families, with women, with people generally. My whole life has been marked by that. There's an awkwardness to everything.

But there is one story about Grandin that's important, and it's how I started to become influenced by music. We heard the Beatles, but their songs didn't stick in my mind like one song by Bob Dylan did. There was a publication we could read at Grandin called the *Hit Parader* that published the lyrics of all the top hits. There wasn't much to reading the lyrics of songs like "I Want to Hold Your Hand" or "Love Me Do"; they are pretty well on the light side. But one day I read the lyrics for a song called "Mr. Tambourine Man." I'd only heard it once and the lyrics were hard to understand, and I remember thinking, What the heck is Bob Dylan doing writing commercials for tambourines? Then I read the lyrics and they blew me away. There's a verse that's all dark and gloomy, talking about foggy ruins, haunted trees and misery, but it ends with the image of someone dancing and waving at the sky. I imagined it as a guy on a horse with one hand in the air. I wrote those lyrics down on index cards and carried them around with me. I wanted to be that guy reaching for the sky.

When the June of our final year rolled around, we were all ready to leave—most of us with no idea of where we were going or how we were going to get there. At the graduation ceremony, the valedictorian gave an address for the ages. I still remember it. "Let each of us be the best we can be; if you are a mountain, be the best mountain in the valley, and if you are with the lowest shrubs in the valley, then be the best shrub in the valley."

I remember saying jokingly to my friends, "We want to be the lowest shrubs in the valley, but by God we'll be the best shrubs." John, Antoine and I found a lot comfort saying that: "Yes, we are the shrubs of the valley."

But confidence is everything, even if you are a shrub, and at that age I wasn't confident until after a couple of beers. Beer was the medication I needed to become a laughing, confident, handsome devil—or so it made me feel. It's important to say this because it helps explain the role that drinking had in my life.

I said farewell to Grandin College at the end of June 1969 and hopped on a plane. I figured I was going home, but that summer there were forest fires all over the Sahtu Region. The Mackenzie Valley was burning up and we were smoked out, so we landed in Inuvik instead. And where would I have to spend the night on my way home from six years of residential school? Grollier Hall. I did not see Sister Hebert, but I wasn't looking for her either. Thankfully, all my friends from Good Hope were there because they couldn't fly either. That night we probably slept a couple of hours because we were too busy talking. The next morning, we all got on a plane headed for Good Hope but it was too smoky to land there so we diverted to Norman Wells. It was turning into a bit of an adventure. We were all prepared to settle in for the night in Norman Wells, but later that day my uncle Cassien Edgi and his friend Wilford Jackson arrived by boat from Good Hope. They singled me out; for whatever reason, they had decided to take me home on the river with them. So, we left at midnight that night. It doesn't get dark in June that time of year. I was so excited to be on my way at last.

I'll never forget the journey. Even though it was daylight, the smoke on the river was so thick that sometimes we could barely see. The riverbanks were blazing and we could see trees on fire, tumbling down the tall banks into the river. In places the smoke over the river was a deep purple colour. As we headed down the river, the sun was climbing higher in the sky and the smoke started to thin out. I think there must have been a wind from the west that was clearing the air. Around five o'clock in the morning we came around the last bend—what we call the Ramparts, these 150-foot limestone cliffs—and there was Good Hope sitting in the sun. The smoke was gone and there was that big, white wooden cross on the riverbank beside the church. The whole town was still sleeping. It was the most beautiful thing I'd seen in a long time. I still remember it so clearly. June 29, 1969. I was home, finally. No more residential school. No more reasons to leave.

Chapter Twelve

The Road to Activism

Northern boy meets a girl

Got together, were going out

Northern boy asked the girl

Do you know what it's all about?

How far will I fall when I fall in love?

And where will I fall when I'm falling out?

—Stephen Kakfwi, "How Far Will I Fall?,"
from the album *Last Chance Hotel*

When I landed in Fort Good Hope that morning, I remember thinking, Nobody is ever going to make me leave home again. It was very simple for me: I'd get a job that kept me in Fort Good Hope.

Life was always beautiful in the summer at home. We went swimming. We connected with family. My grandparents, parents and siblings were there, so it was like one long picnic. I slept on the couch at home. I didn't care. Life was good. And I was in love: Suzanne was my girlfriend. The world will remember that July as the month when Neil Armstrong stepped on the moon, his giant step for mankind; I will remember it as the first month that I was free and in love. I was over the moon.

When fall came, the other kids went back to school and I stayed in town. It was getting cold and there were only about four or five jobs in town, so Suzanne and I asked for work at the regional airline. We'd sell tickets and meet the

Suzanne, in her house by the river.

plane and do the manifest and all that. The manager gave Suzanne the job. It made me feel as if he had a choice, and he gave the job to the white person.

At the same time, it was becoming clear that there was no room for me in my parents' house. I didn't have a job or any work experience. There was no work in Good Hope and I didn't really want to go hunting and trapping or live in a house where I had to collect wood every day. I didn't want to run across the ice and check my loche hooks in order to eat breakfast. I had no way to support Suzanne if I wanted to marry her: I was broke and unemployed and had nothing to offer. At first Suzanne and I didn't care; it was all just fun. We were holding hands and going for walks. But I was beginning to realize that I didn't want to live in Good Hope and I couldn't see much of a future for us. The fairy tale of my first love was coming to an end, and I was caught between that fact and the wish that it wasn't happening.

It all came to me one cold, cold night. It was close to fifty below and I was walking home from Suzanne's place around two o'clock in the morning. The whole town was sleeping, the sky was clear and the stars were out. I was going back to my house knowing that it would be just as cold inside as it was outside. Then, I thought I heard something. *Shooh, shooh.* I stopped to listen. I didn't hear it, so I kept walking. I heard it again: *Shooh, shooh.* I thought it was my boots, but then I realized that it was my breath. It was so cold that my breath was crystallizing each time I breathed out.

I got home and went up to my bed, crawling under the covers with all my clothes on. All I had was a piece of canvas and a summer sleeping sheet. I saw then the stark reality of how poor we were. I couldn't stay in Good Hope and honestly say, "You know what? Next year is going to be better." There was no future. My parents were drinking more often and they didn't have jobs. It wasn't the home I left when I went to residential school and it wasn't the home I had made it out to be in my mind. My parents were different. I was different.

I would realize only much later that the fact that both of my parents had been to residential school was a part of all that. There was very little affection. Nobody checked in on anyone. Everybody was operating at an almost comatose level and the drinking was getting worse. And I was right in there, partying with my parents, and then I would go out and party with friends. Because my parents drank a lot, I figured it gave me licence to do that as well. I realized it wasn't doing me any good. It was no way to live. It was painful for me to realize, but unlike my friends who were getting married and settling in Good Hope, living what were often difficult lives and taking the odd job, I wanted to have a career and a nice life where I could make money and have my independence. That was hard to say, so all I said was,

"You know what? I've got to get out of town and get back to school."

Soon after that, I said to Suzanne, "I want to go back to school to train as a teacher. I don't want to be a truck driver and I don't want to go trapping." She didn't know what she was going to do herself but we knew our relationship was coming to an end.

I remember time with Suzanne as the first time in my life that I loved someone and someone said "I love you" to me. But when I saw Suzanne eighteen years later, she said, "I don't remember you ever saying you loved me, and if you did you had a strange way of showing it, because all you ever did was leave. I remember what you used to say; you'd say it jokingly after you'd spend an evening with me. 'Okay,' you'd say. 'I think I better leave now before I decide to stay.'"

While Suzanne was the first person to say that she loved me, she was also the first to see the cold and unfeeling side of me. She didn't understand it and neither did I. Our relationship was all wound up with my romantic ideas about returning to Good Hope to make a life there, and we both discovered that wasn't going to last.

—

My plan was to go to teachers' college in Alberta, so in the spring of 1970, I needed to start earning some money. I got a job with a company that was drilling a deeper channel in the Sans Sault Rapids about seventy miles south of Good Hope. On a day in early May, I was back in town and I went to have breakfast with Uncle Albert. I found him very distraught. I walked into his house and he said, "*Deewin*"—calling me by my Dene name—"*Deewin*... the Americans are shooting students at the university. Four students are dead."

On May 4, 1970, the National Guard had shot students who were protesting the Vietnam War at Kent State University. I was nineteen years old, the same age as those students, and they were shot by soldiers for voicing opposition. My uncle knew I was planning to go south to university in the fall, and he said, "It's not safe, *Deewin*. I don't think you should go."

I had read about the Ku Klux Klan and the lynching of black people in the United States, but at Kent State they were shooting the white kids, their own kids. And if they did that to white kids, what would they do to me? This event had a big impact on my thinking. The government had the power to be violent toward its own citizens. Rather than going south that fall, I chose to study at the teachers' college in Fort Smith.

While I was at college, I received tragic news: my sister Jean passed away from exposure. She froze to death one night after drinking with friends and it was ruled an "accidental death." No one knew the full story, but I think she was scared of somebody and hid under a house. It was winter and very cold. These days, after all the talk about Missing and Murdered Indigenous Women, maybe someone would have tried to figure out what happened to her—and my aunt Bella three years earlier—but back in the late sixties and early seventies, it was like it didn't matter, or they didn't matter.

Around that time, I had one of my first experiences in politics. In the winter of 1971, there was a territorial election and a Dene leader by the name of Ed Bird decided to run. Ed would go on to become a prominent Dene leader, but in 1971 he wasn't even a Chief yet. He was just Ed Bird. He came to the teachers' college and asked to see me. He wondered if I would campaign with him around Fort Smith and particularly on a road trip to Fort Resolution. I didn't know what else to say, so I said sure. The instructors gave me some time off and I spent two days travelling with Ed. Even today, I don't know why he asked me.

In later years, Ed got into a confrontation with the RCMP. He stepped out of his trailer one day while he was drinking and the RCMP thought he had a gun. They shot and killed him. I still think about him.

—

In the spring of 1972, I was back in Good Hope teaching adult education. I got pneumonia and was bedridden for a few days. A few weeks after that, my grandparents called for me. "We want to check you out and make sure you're okay," they said. "Can you lie down on the bed?"

I really didn't want to do it. I wasn't a boy anymore; I was twenty-one years old! But I went along with it. My grandfather sat beside me and put his hand on my chest. My grandmother was watching like the student of my grandfather's that she was all her life. After a few moments, he said, "Okay. Come and sit down and finish your tea."

We sat down and he said, "There's an illness in your lungs and your chest. Right now, there are two holes in your lungs about the size of the end of a pencil, but if you go to the hospital, the doctors can fix you up and you can be home by Christmas." I said thank you, drank my tea and left. I was thinking, I sat there listening to that for two hours? At the time I was still skeptical of these kinds of insights.

In early June, some health-care professionals came to Good Hope to do our annual chest X-rays for tuberculosis. They called me because of my family's history with TB, so I went and I didn't think about it again.

Later that month, I went to Edmonton to study at the University of Alberta. I was to spend the summer semester working on my teaching courses. That's when I got a call from the Charles Camsell Hospital in Edmonton requesting that I come in because of my X-ray results. I didn't go, but then I got a second call. "Are you going to come or are we going to have to come and get you?"

So I went, and an older doctor, Dr. Romanowski, called me into his office. He put the X-rays up on the wall, and there they were, two little holes in my lungs. I was so surprised. "You know what?" I told him. "My grandfather told me I had two holes in my lung in May."

"He was right. You can see them right here. I believe what you're saying about your grandfather. I've been at this hospital for many years now. I've met Inuit, Blackfoot, Cree, Lakota... people that never spoke a word of English in their life. Traditional people, Medicine People, Healers. I have seen a lot of strange things in my life, so I'm not surprised by what you're telling me."

"Well, he also told me that if I get treatment, I can be home by Christmas."

"I don't know about that, but you are sick. Your TB is active, so we can't let you out. If you hadn't come over, we would have had to send the police after you."

They wanted me to move around the hospital and go for walks, and I didn't like the idea of wandering around in one of those hospital gowns. I asked Dr. Romanowski if I could stay in my regular clothes and thankfully he agreed.

While I was there, I got into painting. Each week I was finishing three or four landscapes, sometimes portraits, and the nurses were buying them for fifteen dollars apiece. Then this young woman came along, her name was Cena LaBarge, and she said, "Give me two of your best ones and I'll see if I can sell them downtown."

She came back the next day with $300; she'd sold each of them for $150. And she told me, "Don't produce so many. Just work on a couple of good ones every week and I'll sell them for you." She became my very best friend at that time.

I recovered in the hospital and, true to my grandfather's prediction, I made it back to Good Hope in December. I went to see my grandfather once I was back. He knew that I had been in the hospital and he just chuckled. "I told you, but you got medicine and everything is okay now."

But I didn't stay in Good Hope for Christmas. Three days after I got back from the hospital, I moved to Hay River to teach as an intern. For some reason, the department of education wouldn't give me my licence, even though I was qualified to teach on a provisional basis. If I had a licence, I could have been a full-fledged adult educator with a full salary, but they said that since I didn't have all my qualifications, I had to stay in the trainee position. I was making so little money that I lived on a diet of fish, rice, ground meat, macaroni and Cheez Whiz.

In Hay River I had another chance to see what politics was like. Four fieldworkers from the Indian Brotherhood showed up to organize a meeting. Chief Daniel Sonfrere, of the Hay River Band, had just set up a reserve, the only one of its kind in the North, and the fieldworkers wanted to inform the people about why they should fight against its establishment. They saw it as conforming too much to the Indian Act.

I invited the fieldworkers to stay at my place. I came home on my lunch break one day and I remember one of them getting up off my couch and saying, "Come on guys. Let's get our shit together."

They didn't have a plan. They were just going to go to the reserve, call a meeting and try to get people to kick out the Chief and kill the idea of the reserve. When I came home from teaching around five o'clock later that day, they were back in my trailer, looking like they just took an ass kicking. They went into the hall where a meeting was already taking place; as soon as they walked in, the Chief told them, "You've come here to cause trouble for me and my people. You're not invited and I want you off the reserve." The RCMP escorted them off. They were unceremoniously dispatched by a cagey and organized Chief who knew exactly what he was doing. I felt badly for them, but I also knew they didn't have any kind of plan.

I understood what they were talking about. They discussed Treaty 11 and I thought I was probably the only one in the room who actually knew what was in it. They were talking about rights and self-government and I understood that stuff, but they seemed disorganized and ineffective to me. I thought, I could do this kind of work.

This was also a time when some of the first copies of the *Native Press* were floating around. I read the *Edmonton Journal*, but here was news about us written by reporters in the North. Stories by somebody reporting out of Fort McPherson, Aklavik, Kakisa, Wrigley or Fort Norman and about people we knew. We all wanted to read it. "Hey, you have a copy of that?" It was starting to make a difference, and it was part of my shift from teaching to politics.

In the spring of 1974, I went to Fort Providence for a few months to teach elementary school. While I was there, Jim Antoine invited me to an Indian Brotherhood Chiefs' meeting in Fort Rae, now Behchokǫ̀. I took time off to go.

It was the first time I heard James Wah-Shee speak. He had a deep, clear and resonant way of speaking and he could speak Tłı̨chǫ and English. He was both young and charismatic.

The people were listening and the Chiefs were all over him. In the meeting he talked about politics, elections, land and community. I was becoming interested in this kind of work. I think I was already on the list of people marked as potential troublemakers and who were being watched by the RCMP and the government.

I was still not ready to give up teaching, though. I found it frustrating that I couldn't get my licence. That summer, I went to the University of Saskatoon to complete some more courses. When I came back, the adult educator position in Hay River was vacant, but the department of education was dead set against giving me my licence. They thought there already was a lot of what they called "subversive activity" going on.

There was a draft dodger in Hay River at the time, and the superintendent of education, Mr. Graves, was a big, tall Texan with a lot of sympathy for him. Mr. Graves hired him to be the adult educator, although he had no background in teaching. Mr. Graves told me, "Well, I hired this man to be the adult educator, so that job is no longer available—but you can still be a trainee, or you could you teach him some material, because he doesn't know…"

A woman out of Yellowknife named Echo Lidster oversaw special and continuing education. She was an advocate for me and didn't want me to quit, but she couldn't figure out why I couldn't get a job anywhere in the Mackenzie Valley. She found one job opening in Eskimo Point, along the Hudson Bay coast. I looked Eskimo Point up in the library and once I found out there were no trees there, I said, "No way, I'm absolutely not going."

I felt like they were trying to get rid of me, send me as far away as possible, so I resigned. I never talked to them again, though they called me a few times. I packed up my stuff and hopped on a plane to Yellowknife.

I didn't realize the extent of their determination to keep me from a position of responsibility until some fifteen years later when I was the minister of education. An older bureaucrat in the department of education came to see me and gave me a rolled-up piece of paper. "Here," he said. "This has been in our office since the seventies. I don't know why you never got it or why it was never sent to you, but my apologies. This belongs to you."

It was my provisional teaching licence. It seems somebody had intervened to make sure I never got it.

—

I was looking forward to seeing what everyone else was up to in Yellowknife. I had some friends there and I was aware that interesting things were happening.

People were on the move. For example, there was a group called the Company of Young Canadians that had come north in the early seventies and had recruited young Dene, like Georges Erasmus and fellow Grandin students Joachim Bonnetrouge and Charlie Charlo. Jim Antoine was in Yellowknife, too, where he was working with the Indian Brotherhood. He had actively tried to recruit me the year before, so when I got to town, I went to the Indian Brotherhood office. Georges Erasmus was the director of the community development fieldworker program and James Wah-Shee was the president.

Georges had a job for me. "You want to be a field worker?"

I said sure. I liked that I could work from Good Hope because I was planning on returning. He explained the land use mapping project, which was researching the historical use of land by Dene hunters and trappers. Other people, like my old classmate John T'Seleie, were working on that in Good Hope already. Before I left Georges's office, he said, "Why don't you be the regional coordinator for all the fieldworkers in the Sahtu? Keep an eye out on what they're doing and send us a report once a month." So, I got the job, then I got a promotion within the hour.

Georges's program was about community development based in the ideological belief that we have rights and we must struggle to keep them. There was a lot of socialist rhetoric about decolonization, along with stuff from Tanzania, the teachings of Mao Zedong, the American Indian Movement and a little bit from the Black Panthers. I liked that. I thought it was going to be exciting work.

Many of us had just come from residential school. For the first time in our lives, we were free from the grips of the church and the government, in a sense. The church was still powerful—even though that power was waning—and the government was powerful too. Oil and gas companies were also influential, having their way with our land with minimal resistance. The government and the oil companies had their line: "This land was given up. It's part of Canada. We will decide what goes on here." At the time, our people were weak and unaware of the corporate and colonial forces that were around us. We were not asserting our rights and challenging the government.

We knew about people who'd made their commitment to the civil rights movement and the American Indian Movement, and we knew how hard they had to work. But where did I come from? A community with 350 people. The enormity of the challenge ahead of us was staggering. We were starting to wonder, How are we going to survive? What should we do? You could survive by succumbing to the colonizing forces and becoming a benign citizen. But did we want to live full lives as Dene? We were thinking, This is our land. They're saying that we have no land, but this is our land.

They're saying we have no rights, but we have all our rights.

This was the growing sense that we had. Some of us were willing to say, "No, you won't have the final word on this land, because it's ours, we're living on it, we're hunting and trapping and making a living as we have for thousands of years, and we're still going to do that." And that's where we came up with the determination to move forward. We knew we were never going to win, but we could fight, and the freedom is in the fighting if we are fighting to assert ourselves, to have a presence, to project our own ideas of what we wanted for ourselves as a people. That's freedom; the freedom is in the fighting. We would never win everything, but we would fight so we didn't lose everything.

Stephen at Carcajou Ridge on the Mackenzie River (1978). Photographed by friend Bob Overvold

We were the next generation of leaders. We talked about making choices. Many of us went back to our communities and relearned our languages, learned how to drum and sing traditional songs, how to hunt and go out on our land. We talked to our Elders. We worked at becoming as Dene as we could.

CHAPTER THIRTEEN

THE BERGER INQUIRY

I arrived back in Fort Good Hope and was getting myself set up when I got a call from Georges Erasmus. "Um, Steve," he said, "when we hired you, we didn't know you aren't Treaty Dene, so we can't have you working for us."

When my grandfather chose to give up his Treaty status to open a store, that affected my Treaty status as well.

"It's what we have to do, because that's what the government of Canada told us: we can't hire non-Treaty people."

So that was the end of that, and it was upsetting because Georges had just pumped me up with all this rhetoric. "We're Dene and we want to be in control and we're a self-determining people." Then the government said, "No, you can't hire non-Treaty people," and the Indian Brotherhood simply accepted that.

I got another call later. They said they could transfer me to the Métis Association, which would take non-status people like me. According to the government of Canada, I wasn't legally an Indian—but I wasn't Métis either. Bob Overvold, the executive director of the association, was willing to work with me. This wasn't an attractive proposition, and it was confirmed when I went there. I met with the president, Rick Hardy. He said, "Look, we're in the business of working for Métis. We're Métis people and we've got our own rights, but we end up getting stuck with people like you, non-status Dene, and we have to take you in."

I felt sullied; the whole thing felt sullied. But when I met with Bob, I got into it. Bob and I were friends: we went to university together and we both taught in Hay River, so when we started working together it turned out well. We stayed friends all our lives and worked together for many years.

Bob, Georges and I began preparing for the Berger Inquiry. The government of Canada commissioned Justice Thomas Berger to report on the potential impact of the proposed Mackenzie Valley Pipeline, and we wanted to inform everyone of what this pipeline would mean for us environmentally and culturally. This meant giving people basic information about the size of the pipeline, what natural gas was, where it was coming from, where it was going and the impact of the construction. I travelled to communities whenever I was requested. I was eager to learn and to travel, to Aklavik, Trout Lake, Fort Liard, Fort Smith—any community. I wanted to be everywhere. Every time I went to a new community, the first thing I did was meet with the Chief and let them know who we were, what we were doing and why we were doing it, and how long we were going to be there.

The Berger Inquiry was going to start hearings across southern Canada, so we organized ourselves and went on two tours across the country, to cities like Victoria, Vancouver, Edmonton, Calgary, Winnipeg, Toronto, Ottawa, Montreal and Charlottetown. We met with churches and universities, anyone interested in learning about the Dene and the North. Debbie DeLancey, who was in charge of building southern support, travelled with me. The tours were exhausting. I started to forget what city I was in, and I was so tired that I couldn't remember what I had said and what I hadn't said. Despite this, we built strong support in the south. We were a small group of people with limited funds, but we were prepared. We were ready to take on Canada.

James Wah-Shee hired a group of people who became important resources. Gerry Sutton was a lawyer who filed a historic case: known as the Paulette caveat case, it gave the Dene their first legal claim to some four hundred thousand square miles of traditional land.

Then there was Peter Puxley. He was a young former Rhodes scholar looking for something to do. He liked what he saw in these communities and got to work as an adviser for the Indian Brotherhood. He oversaw the early stages of the land use mapping project, which he then turned over to Phoebe Nahanni, a young Dene activist. This project had an incredible impact on Ottawa: it was an official (and indisputable) document that mapped

Left to right: Gina Blondin, Stephen Kakfwi, and Chief George Kodakin, preparing for the Berger Inquiry at a meeting in Déline, 1975. ©NWT Archives/Rene Fumoleau fonds/N-1995-002: 9398

our land and our knowledge of it. Steve Iveson also came up in the early seventies as a volunteer for the Company of Young Canadians. Wah-Shee hired him to set up the community development program for the Indian Brotherhood.

Finally, there was Wilf Bean. Wilf had been hired by Commissioner Stuart Hodgson to organize municipal councils for the government of the NWT, but in the end he found it contrary to what he believed was common sense—which was that the Dene already had a system of governance. Wilf resigned and the Indian Brotherhood hired him as an adviser. So, we had Steve Iveson, Peter Puxley, Gerry Sutton and Wilf Bean, and with their help we weren't just standing there saying, "It's our land!" We proved that it was. We proved that we were self-governing Dene.

Some members of the NWT Council at the time—like David Searle, Dave Nickerson, Tom Butters and Stuart Hodgson—were critical of the help we were getting from non-Indigenous advisers, suggesting we couldn't talk for ourselves. The charge was always that we were being manipulated by these smart left-wing socialists. We heard it, but we weren't bothered by it because we knew the resource group, Gerry, Peter, Wilf and Steve, were working with us, aligned with what leaders like James Wah-Shee, Georges Erasmus and George Barnaby were already thinking. The group was helping us carry the message to the media, so they were great to work with.

For example, Wilf often travelled with me to the Mackenzie Delta. We visited people in Arctic Red River, Inuvik, Fort McPherson and Aklavik, and we went house to house to house. We sat around with the Chiefs, and if they needed help, we provided it. It was the same in the Dehcho and Sahtu Regions. Steve Iveson married a Dene woman, Fibbie Tatti, and they were living in Délı̨nę, and Wilf was writing songs about the North. I felt that they were a part of our community, our people. Our community was united under the belief that we were struggling for basic human rights and the right to take back what had been taken from us.

I worked with Chief Frank T'Seleie and his brother John to prepare Good Hope for the Berger Inquiry, and we realized we didn't have much time. We needed someone who had good rapport with Elders to help so we hired Alice Masuzumi. She was one of the women who brought me into the world and she was perfect for the job. She understood English, she could read, she spoke wonderful Dene and she was incredibly compassionate and friendly. Everybody loved Alice. She was a single mother of four children. She had to get her own water, provide her own wood and feed her kids. In fact, she would always feed anyone who visited her. "Steve," she would say, "have some bannock. Have some tea. Have some fish."

When I asked her if she wanted to work with us, she was at first reluctant about fieldwork. "What does it mean? I'm not going to tell people what to think."

I explained that somebody had to tell them what the pipeline was about—like the size of it, whether it's going to be buried or above ground—and answer questions people have. Eventually she agreed, and she worked very hard. We went to Colville Lake together in the middle of the winter. We found a log house and the Chief found somebody to get some wood for us, so we had a fire going and we had some fish and meat from the local people. Alice made some of her bannock and soon all kinds of people were visiting. We stayed there three or four days and we had people visiting steadily. We thought they were coming to talk about the pipeline, but they were probably coming for Alice's cooking.

Alice did many of her "home visits," as she called them, alone because she often felt more comfortable that way. She'd say, "Stephen, you always want to start talking about the pipeline right away. Not everybody wants to talk about that pipeline, you know. They want to talk about the things they care about, and then later they'll ask you, 'What do you want to talk about?' That's when you start. You can't just walk in and start with the pipeline." So, Alice was teaching me some things about fieldwork.

Uncle Albert never wanted his picture taken or to be recorded throughout his life, but after six months of visiting with Alice, he agreed. She didn't use the recordings for the Berger Inquiry, but she said she wanted proof that she wasn't making anything up. She was quite the lady.

I was struck by how well thought out and meticulous the planning was to make sure that there was a hearing in every community. We gave people support so they were adequately prepared to speak publicly. These were not people that would normally speak to an inquiry like this, so we helped them rehearse and made sure the things they said were factually solid. The media would come to see that.

More than anybody else, though, it was the fieldworkers and the Chiefs that prepared the Dene for the Berger Inquiry. And the resource group was part of that: any time we needed research or help preparing, they were the technical team that helped.

Alice was the most nervous person in Good Hope during the two weeks leading up to the Berger Inquiry. We had been encouraging people to come to the inquiry to speak, but she worried. "Of all the people that I talked to, is anybody going to go forward and say something? Are they going to say something wrong because I told them something wrong?" But we were well prepared and everything fell into place.

On August 5, 1975, Chief Frank T'Seleie took his seat in front of the cameras, microphones and Justice Thomas Berger.

We do not want to have to fight and struggle forever just to survive as a people. Your nation has the power to destroy us all tomorrow if it chooses to. It has chosen instead to torture us slowly. To take our children from us, teach them foreign ways and tell us that you are teaching them to be civilized. Sometimes now, we hardly know our own children. You have forced us into communities and tried to make us forget how to live off the land, so that you could take the resources from where we trap and hunt and fish... Five hundred years from now, someone with skin my colour and with moccasins on his feet will climb up the Ramparts, look over the river and feel that he too has a place in the universe. He will thank the same Spirits that I thank, that his ancestors have looked after his land well, and he will be proud to be a Dene. It is for this unborn child, Mr. Berger, that my nation will stop the pipeline.

He spoke defiantly and clearly. It was the presentation of his life and his address made the national news. Like so many of us, he had worked a long time preparing for the inquiry.

I also spoke at the Berger Inquiry. Many people said they liked what I had to say, but I wasn't sure if I should. I wasn't elected. Chief T'Seleie had the authority to speak. I talked to him about it and he said, "Well, speak on the day after me. It will work out." So, I addressed Justice Berger on August 6.

Alexander Mackenzie came to our land... My people probably wondered at this strange, pale man in his ridiculous clothes, asking about some great waters he was searching for...

The Traders came... They brought new things with them, new clothes, food, guns, whisky. My people liked their bright clothes, their flour, sugar and tea... their guns and their whisky. So, they traded.

The Catholic Church came... They brought their religion with them. They spoke of truth, love and charity... Their sincerity led my people to think that their religion was good for them.

The Government came... They brought their teachers, nurses, Indian agents, area administrators, social workers and others with them. They spoke of better housing, health-care plans, social assistance, better schools, a better standard of living. Their determination led my people to believe that they knew what was best for all.

Our reality is that this is our land, we are a nation of people and we want to live our own ways...

Our reality is that there is a very simple choice: Dene survival with no pipeline, or a pipeline with no Dene survival.

Once the inquiry was over, Alice was no less nervous. She was running around talking to all the people that had testified so she could thank them. When we met later that day, she was crying, then laughing with relief. She couldn't believe how well everything had turned out. She talked about how much it meant to her, that this was probably the most important work that she'd ever been involved in.

One of the first times I was quoted by the CBC was when they covered the inquiry. I went down to the CBC office in Yellowknife and asked for the transcript of that story. Whit Fraser, the senior editor of the newsroom, said, "Don't you know what you said?"

"Yeah, but I want to see the text." So, he went and got it for me. I wanted to hold the script in my hand, because otherwise I felt that my words were just blowing in the wind. I wanted to believe it by having the text. I was realizing the incredible power that the media had.

On June 9, 1977, we got the long-awaited results from Berger: there'd be a ten-year moratorium. No pipeline.

I've always said that the Berger Inquiry was a magical time. We were never caught blindsided. Everything that happened, from beginning to end, was perfect. We were in control and we were flying. We stayed on message, our people were well informed about the pipeline and the implications of it, and we were well organized. We celebrated the victory. Commissioner Stuart Hodgson and the people in his office weren't making all the decisions in the North anymore.

CHAPTER FOURTEEN

SWEET MARIE

It was a magical time for another reason. I met Marie Wilson on the last of my many tours across Canada while we were preparing for the Berger Inquiry. I had travelled all night and arrived in London, Ontario, at six in the morning, and I was so exhausted I fell asleep, sitting up, on my hotel bed soon after I checked into the Holiday Inn. A guy named Brian Louckes called to get me going because he had arranged meetings for me with students and other people all day.

Later that afternoon, after a long series of meetings, I was ready to collapse—but then Marie walked in. She woke me up. I think it was her good energy; something about her appearance was good for me. In addition to this, ours was not an ordinary session. I didn't have to give all the basic statements—that we're a nation and we're self-determining—because she knew all that stuff. She knew about colonization. She had taught in Africa for a year and went to school in France, so she knew a lot more than most people I was talking to. Her questions were sharp. I couldn't brush them off. Some people were so nice that if you didn't answer their question, they didn't ask you a second time. Not Marie. She would say, "That's not the question I asked you." She was finishing her master's degree in journalism at the time and she wanted to make a presentation to Justice Berger.

Our session finished, but I wanted to keep it going. Brian knew Marie and he thought she might show up at the big meeting we had scheduled in a church basement that night. So, at the meeting, I'm the guest speaker and I'm pretty distracted, because I'm speaking but the whole time what I'm really doing is watching the door, hoping to see her walk in. She arrives late, after I've finished my opening remarks. At the end of my presentation, she comes over and says hello, but then she's off again.

I ask Brian about her again, and he says, "Well, I'm having a party tonight and I've invited her and her friend to come over, play guitar, have a few beers."

I thought, Great. I'm going to see her again.

If Brian hadn't told me about the party I would have crawled into bed, but off I went to his place. At three o'clock in the morning, I was still hoping she would show up. At four o'clock, I headed back to the hotel. I slept for a couple of hours, then hopped on a plane and went back home. I was in a bit of a trance, I guess. I was thinking, God, that was a big deal. Or was it a big deal? Am I just making things up? Maybe I am just too damn tired...

Marie's mailing address was on the list of people that I had met, so I sent her a postcard with a picture of the Ramparts on the front. Never heard a peep out of her. I wrote to her a couple more times, but still nothing.

Georges Erasmus often sent me down south for speaking engagements. Not a lot of Dene were interested in travelling south; who wants to jump on a plane headed to Ottawa for a one-hour presentation and then fly all the way back the next day? It was gruelling but I always said yes.

I was in Edmonton on one of those trips and I decided one night to head to the Cecil Hotel. The Cecil Hotel was kind of like the Gold Range of Edmonton, where everyone I knew would hang out. I was cutting across the parking lot when I ran into a guy from Yellowknife. "There's a bunch of people, including your Chief, from Good Hope in a church basement just over there; are you on your way?"

I was feeling guilty about heading to the bar, so I said yes.

"Well, you're going the wrong way. It's over here."

Once inside, I sat down and started chatting with the people I knew. And who should walk into the periphery of my view but Marie Wilson. It was a big surprise. When the meeting finished, we spent the rest of the evening talking. We found some time in the coming days that we both had free in Edmonton and we spent it alone together, walking all over the city and down by the riverbank. We went to the airport together the next day—November 7, my birthday. I was twenty-five years old. Marie was flying back to London, Ontario, and I was flying to Yellowknife. When I arrived back home, I thought, Well, I guess I'm in love.

For many years, my grandmother, Uncle Jonas and I thought my grandfather was organizing all this for me from the Spirit World. We believed that he had sent me on a mission to do this kind of work, and that he wanted me to have a family, a partner, some stability and to not be alone doing this work. I felt like he was saying, "Okay, here she comes, this Marie Wilson. You better pay attention, because this is the one I want you to spend your life with."

I invited Marie up to Yellowknife for Christmas, and when she landed I had a surprise gift for her. "Yellowknife's interesting," I said to her, "but there's an even more interesting place you'll get to see, and that's Fort Good Hope, where I come from." So, I brought her to Good Hope.

I didn't tell Marie then, but it wasn't easy to arrange. At that time, the people who were managing the community were strong Catholics. I knew my grandparents' house was empty because my grandmother was living with Uncle Jonas. So, I called my brother Everett and I said, "I need a place to stay because I'm going to have my girlfriend with me. Can you ask Grandma if I could use her place?"

Everett thought I was crazy for even suggesting it, but to everyone's surprise, my grandmother said yes. "He can stay in the place with Marie because that's what his grandfather wants for him." And so in a town that had no available housing, I got to have this house all to myself with Marie. It had an oil and wood stove and a bed and everything.

We landed in Good Hope and settled into the house, and the thing that was so striking was that my whole family came to meet Marie—all the aunts and uncles, Albert and Dora, Agnes and Charlie, Sarah and Jonas. Even our next-door neighbour, Norbert Caesar, came in from his trapping camp and brought his wife, Monica, and their kids to meet Marie.

Uncle Albert came on Boxing Day at nine o'clock in the morning and he stayed until eight o'clock that night. He was there eleven hours! He's never done that before and he's never done that since. He came in and settled down, Marie made us breakfast, and then they started talking and they didn't stop. This was the beginning of Marie and Albert's lifelong friendship. She wrote a song about him called "Proud Albert." It's on my CD *New Strings on an Old Guitar*. Years later, she was with him when he was on his deathbed.

It was a different Christmas; you could feel the warmth. I think the way people saw it was like this: my grandparents' house had been empty since June, when my grandfather passed away and my grandmother had moved in with my uncle. So, all that fall there was no light or warmth in that place. Then, suddenly, just before Christmas, to everyone's joy and amazement, there were lights on and smoke coming from the chimney. I think people were happy to see that house come to life again.

She stayed about a week and then she went back to London to finish her master's. I visited her a few times; I was still going on speaking gigs, so once I booked my flight to Toronto, I'd book a train or bus ticket to London so I could see her. That's how it started.

⁓

Marie got a job with CBC North and moved up to Yellowknife in 1977. It was still that tense time after the Berger decision to delay the pipeline, and at one point someone left a voice message on the CBC switchboard in Yellowknife and threatened to kill her. They claimed that the reports she was giving were too sympathetic toward the Dene Nation. The Berger Inquiry polarized the North; there was anger and huge backlash. I used to walk into a restaurant called the Miner's Mess in the Yellowknife Inn, and there'd be a whole table full of non-Dene people sitting there, and they'd turn to look at me and size me up. Although I was just a staff person at the Dene Nation at the time, I was a recognizable spokesman, so the anger was deep.

Marie could feel it, I could feel it and we felt it when we were together. We never went anywhere together. She was a journalist and I was an Indigenous political activist. It felt impossible. If we wanted to go to a movie, she would go in first and then I would go in after, sort of wandering in, and say, "Hey! Hi. Can I sit beside you?" After the lights went out, we'd sit there together and share a popcorn, but that was how polarized it was.

It was a difficult time. Thankfully, we made it through.

CHAPTER FIFTEEN

ANOTHER PIPELINE

After the results of the Berger Inquiry were published, reality was quick to set in. We asked ourselves, "What are we going to do now? What state is Fort Good Hope in? We have no jobs, no plans for our people. The Chief doesn't have staff or an office; there's not even a telephone. Where's our self-government? Where's our business arm? Do we have any money?"

I don't even think that the band had a bank account, so we had to do something about that, build community capacity and get ourselves organized. And, if we were to follow the socialist rhetoric we'd been repeating, we had to decolonize and we had to do it on our own. We didn't want anything to do with the territorial, colonizing government.

But that rhetoric wasn't enough for the Chiefs, especially those from the smaller communities. Their people were starting to move off the land and into town, and they needed houses. They needed garbage systems, roads and running water or water delivery.

Around that same time, we Dene were having our own troubles planning and organizing. In 1979, the year after Berger's recommendation, Georges Erasmus fired Gerry Sutton, Peter Puxley, Steve Iveson and Wilf Bean, our talented resource group. Georges wanted to get moving on some plans, but the group couldn't agree to begin work on something unless it was thoroughly discussed and everybody agreed on a plan. It was almost like a group of architects saying, "Well, we can't start planning our building unless we know how many nails we need, how many sheets of plywood."

I remember the time when they were all let go. A group of us were in Prince George, BC, taking a course in log house construction. Georges called me to help him make an administrative decision. That's when he told me he wanted to fire the resource group because he couldn't get anything done. I told him that he was the president: he decides who works for him and who doesn't. So, he went ahead and let them go.

At this time there was already talk of another pipeline, this time an oil pipeline from Norman Wells going south. Georges was taking a position against it, but we weren't organized for that one: our opposition wasn't well thought out and there was no mobilization. Many of us were already back in our own communities and focussing on making them stronger.

Were we successful in fighting against the Norman Wells oil pipeline?

The answer is no. We tried to rally support and we didn't do well. That pipeline went ahead. We needed a good working team, and part of the team could have been that resource group.

I also felt that we did the resource group a disservice. We could have told them that we were grateful and appreciative, but we were restructuring and had to let them go. I remember the glee among our critics in Yellowknife, who figured that they got rid of those socialist outsiders and that now the Dene would start "behaving" again.

One of the tasks I faced at this time was relearning my language. A lot of us young leaders had spent too much time in residential school and we hadn't been speaking Dene. I could only give a speech in English, but I was relearning the language primarily by spending time in Déłı̨nę and Tulita. The Elders didn't laugh at me and they coaxed me along whenever I was struggling to find the right word. I learned it under the mentorship of Chiefs George Kodakin, Paul Wright and Paul Baton.

In 1978, there was a big Dene assembly in Tulita and I went and gave a great speech—in English. Everyone applauded, but there was no one there to repeat the speech in Dene. Over the PA system, I heard my aunt Mary Wilson say, "Steve, you've spoken so well in English and everybody is happy with what you said. Why don't you talk in Dene now?"

I didn't know what to say, but I tried anyway. That was the very first time I spoke in my language in public. It wasn't eloquent, but it was coherent. My aunt said later, "You were never going to do it unless I forced you. And you did okay. You did okay."

CHAPTER SIXTEEN

TALKING FISH CREEK

In 1978, we formally changed the name of the Indian Brotherhood to the Dene Nation. In those early days, people like Jim Antoine, Frank T'Seleie, François Paulette, Georges Erasmus and I had built up high profiles. We were often invited to meetings and conferences across the country. Indigenous people asked us to speak about our vision of nationhood. We were creating a good national profile for the Dene Nation.

From the beginning, the Dene Nation was meant to include all the Treaty Dene in the NWT and all people of Métis origin or those who culturally identified as Métis. At one point, we thought it would make sense to have all Métis peoples sign a book called *The Declared Dene*, which would mean the end of the Métis Association in the NWT. Some of the Métis peoples were okay with that: they were already in our communities and they didn't see it as a threat. Other Métis were deeply offended. They felt that we were asking them to give up their Métis identity. This turned out to be a serious error on our part, and one that I think needs an apology. The leadership of the Dene Nation thought it was a good idea. This was during Georges Erasmus's time as president, but I was there too. We should have said that we were wrong to ask them to do that and that we apologize for the offence. We eventually scrapped the idea, but we lost a few years with that mistake.

The other part of our vision was to get rid of the territorial council and replace the legislative assembly with a new form of public governance, one mandated by the Chiefs and Indigenous people themselves. Unlike us, the Inuit knew they could use the existing government structures: they had such an overwhelming majority of Inuit on their land that they'd still have all the Indigenous control they wanted. Ottawa had already agreed to it. Things were a bit different for us in the west.

We came close to creating a constitutional framework for a public Indigenous government through the work of the Bourque Commission. It took its mandate from Inuvialuit, the Dene Nation, the Métis peoples and the legislative assembly. The commission was led by people like Rick Hardy from the Métis, François Paulette from the Dene, George Braden from the NWT government and Les Carpenter from the Inuvialuit. Under the chairmanship of Jim Bourque, a Métis leader and former deputy minister, the commission came up with a blueprint for something like a confeder-

The year after the Berger Commission report, Stephen Kakfwi addresses the Dene National Assembly in Délı̨nę (April 1978). ©NWT Archives/Rene Fumoleau fonds/N-1995-002: 0506

acy of regions. The regions would include those of the Inuvialuit and the Sahtu, as well as the Gwich'in, Dehcho, Akaitcho and Tłįchǫ First Nations. The non-Indigenous centres, towns like Fort Smith, Hay River, Norman Wells, Yellowknife and Inuvik, would also have their place. This confederacy would replace the legislature. Every year, MLAs representing each region would come together and make decisions on legislation and budgets.

It was a beautiful plan, but due to different priorities among different peoples and regions, and perhaps some political positioning, it slipped away from us. When James Wah-Shee was president of the Indian Brotherhood, he said that he saw the Dene as a confederacy of peoples: the Gwich'in were a tribe, the Tłįchǫ were a tribe, and the other groups form regions of people. He saw our future as a confederacy of Dene agreeing to work together on certain issues, but there wasn't unanimity on that. Georges Erasmus and the rest of us believed we were one people, one nation, and that we had demonstrated that. I see now that Wah-Shee's statement was more practical. Our perspective was a little heavy on ideology. We became divided and that was unfortunate.

In the spring and early summer of 1980, Georges was still president of the Dene Nation. I had been working there with Bob Overvold for over a year by this point, and Bob and I didn't have much of a salary. We ended

The Dene National Assembly in Fort Good Hope, 1980, where Stephen challenged Georges Erasmus for the presidency and was defeated. ©NWT Archives/Rene Fumoleau fonds/N-1998-051: 1820

up staying on because we believed in the work, and we spent the winter travelling as much as we could, because travel at least gave us cash for meal allowances and our hotels were covered. So, we lived in hotels and saved our meal money. It was a strange thing to be poor and visit a place like Inuvik in the seventies. Everybody was making money working on the offshore rigs and we were there, almost destitute. Those were our "lean times." Of course, we were also young and not as responsible as we became later.

Eventually, Bob, Rene Lamothe and I had this of idea dividing up the leadership work at the Dene Nation office. We felt that there needed to be better administration to prepare for the land claim negotiations and to improve our relationship with the Métis leadership. We suggested that there be a chief negotiator, someone to lead the administrative body and someone to lead the research. The plan was close to creating a new organization.

We thought Georges could be the chief negotiator, Bob would be the administrative manager, I would become the Dene Chief, or the Dene president, and Rene Lamothe would head up the research for the negotiations. We had it all figured it out. But there were problems. First, we never bothered to discuss it with Georges. We also failed to realize that the Métis peoples would never agree to have Georges as chief negotiator.

It's clear in hindsight now. When we brought the plan to him we offended him. He dismissed it after a brief conversation with us and there was no public discussion. He was the elected head of the Dene Nation, so he had the last word. And because he did not agree with us, we resigned and left.

I didn't know it then, but what seemed like the end of something was the beginning of my own move into leadership.

—

I decided to run against Georges for the presidency of the Dene Nation in protest. We had no time to prepare. There were about three weeks before the assembly in Good Hope.

Bob and I were unemployed and we didn't have the money to fly to Good Hope, so we travelled there by boat, from Fort Providence down the Mackenzie to Good Hope. The election did not go well. I lost and Georges was re-elected. The CBC had just offered Marie a job in Quebec City, so she was leaving too. Bob and I stayed in Good Hope for a couple of weeks.

I was at a crossroads. I didn't know what to do. I was angry and a little wounded. I could look for work in Yellowknife or Good Hope. I could forget about trying to find some leadership role for myself and go back to teaching, or I could go to Quebec City and spend some time with Marie to decide whether we were serious about our relationship.

Chief Frank T'Seleie, Charlie Barnaby and my cousin Michel Lafferty saw how I was struggling and said, "This is a good time to go hunting." They took me hunting up what they called the Ramparts River. We went up the river for about five days. It was supposed to be three days, but I didn't want to go back. Frank kept asking me when I wanted to go back, and I kept saying, "I want to keep going."

One night, it was just Frank and me awake in the boat. The sun was going down and the river was calm. It was still relatively warm in the daytime, but in the evening it was cold. We went past a ravine on the right side and a blast of cold air hit me. Frank said, in Dene, "*Lugeh-Godeh-Leline.*" This is Talking Fish Creek.

Talking Fish Creek. The name struck me. It's an ancient name; nobody knows why it's called that. I thought it was one of the catchiest names I'd ever heard.

It was a nice, quiet moment. I was sitting there with Chief Frank T'Seleie and he had one hand on the tiller of the outboard engine, probably a forty-horsepower. I'll never forget that moment, because it became clear to me then what I was going to do. I had to make a decision, and the decision I made was this: the first thing I had to do was go to Quebec City and decide whether Marie was the woman I wanted to marry and have a family with. Once I settled that, everything else would fall into place. That was the gift—and the power—of Talking Fish Creek.

That night, I told everyone my plan and that I was ready to go back. Everyone seemed happy about that.

CHAPTER SEVENTEEN

MARIE ON THE MACKENZIE

Just love his gentle heart
Stay close, get past his guard
So the child knows where to turn
Let your love like a candle burn
'Cause sometimes the wounded child
His sorrow drives him wild
Just take him in your heart
What love he has for you

—Stephen Kakfwi, "Don't Take It to the Heart,"
from the album *New Strings on an Old Guitar*

On my way to visit Marie, I was realizing that there was something different about me. I didn't pay much attention to money, material things or having a place to stay. I was an activist and dreamer.

I was also starting to think once again that I didn't have a lot of feelings. Either I felt too much or I felt nothing at all. I had a hard time with affection. I know now that I was living a life numbed by residential school and all the trauma that my family went through, but back in 1980, I was unable to let myself feel things and my conclusion was, "I'm just like that. I was born like that. It's a handicap. I'm different."

All I knew was that Marie made me feel safe. She was straight, honest and deeply compassionate. She had insight into things and she always wanted to get beyond the veneer. I thought, She sees everything inside me and she likes it; whatever the hell it is that she sees, she must like it. It was a comforting thought.

So, after I'd been in Quebec City with Marie for a while, I asked her to marry me. She recalls me saying something like, "Marie... uh... one of these days... maybe... sometime... we should talk about... the possibility... you know... that we could talk about getting married?" I was beating around the bush for miles. Thankfully, she said yes.

When I was in Quebec City, I thought I'd have nothing to do with my previous work, or with Georges Erasmus or the Dene Nation. After all, I had challenged him as the president. Nevertheless, to Georges's credit, the work always came first. He knew I was in the south and he knew I could be useful. We had our differences, but we also had a lot of respect for each other's skills. He called me one day, late in the fall of 1980, and said, "Can you work with the Chiefs? We're sending Chiefs to Ottawa for a big conference and there's lots of controversy about the constitution." Georges offered me two contracts and I took them.

So, I spent a week in Ottawa. The Chiefs were motivated to fight for and protect their rights in the constitution. There were rumours that there was a constitutional caravan going across the country; the Chiefs said they wanted to join it and take their concerns to the United Nations in New York, so at the conference, that's what I said. "The Dene Chiefs are solid with all the other leadership across the country. We will go to New York."

But the day after the conference, there was not one Dene Chief in Ottawa. Everybody had gone back home, and I was standing there thinking, Who's going to go to New York? I called Georges, and he said, "Well, I can't make them. Can you go?"

"I don't want to go alone. I'm with Marie now and I'd like to invite her along."

"That's a good idea. Go ahead. Send us your expenses."

Georges was my friend again. He gave us a trip to New York, our first one together. We didn't have a credit card, though, so we were living on hamburgers and macaroni. That was December 1980. While we were in New York, John Lennon was shot.

⁓

We spent that Christmas with Marie's family. That was new for me, meeting all the relatives at once. I memorized the names of all her aunts and uncles beforehand.

In January, we set the date of our wedding: March 27. I went to see the Quebec government officials to sign some paperwork for our marriage and Marie gave me the address. I thought that she told me I had a meeting with a woman named Marie Chaville.

So, I walked into this government building and up to the receptionist, and she asked if she could help me. I said, "Yes, I have an appointment soon with Marie Chaville. Is she here?"

"No, she isn't, but I'm sure she should be along shortly."

I sat down and waited for a while; people were coming and going, so about fifteen minutes later, I got up again and I said, "So, where is Marie Chaville? She's supposed to be here. I was supposed to meet her fifteen minutes ago."

The lady was very polite. She said, "Well, I'm sure she'll be along shortly." She must have been thinking, This poor guy is getting stood up by someone called Marie Chaville.

I waited another fifteen minutes, then I stomped up to her again and said, "You know, half an hour ago I had an appointment with Marie Chaville. Is she here or not? Where is she?"

"I don't know... maybe she's late."

"You don't know where she is?" I turned around and stomped down the hall to cool off, thinking, I can't lose it, I got to make these arrangements.

I calmed myself down and went back toward the office door. For the first time, I noticed a sign above the door that said "Mariage Civil."

Mariage Civil.

All this time I thought I was looking for somebody named Marie Chaville, but Marie had said, "Go to this office. Look for Mariage Civil."

I made the arrangements despite myself and we got married on March 27, 1981, in Quebec City. Marie's parents were there and Bob Overvold was my best man. I had a new grey suit with a vest, the whole bit, but I didn't know how to tie a tie. I'd made it a point of honour to not dress like that, but this was different, so my father-in-law, Neil, helped me. Neil, Bob and I were all in the hotel room getting ready, and I realized that the labels were still sewn onto my suit. Neil had a little knife, probably about an inch long, and I asked if I could borrow it.

So, he walks up to me, flips his knife open—this teeny-weeny little thing—and steps up to me. He's really close. He holds it up to my vest and says, "Hey you—have you been fooling around with my daughter?"

We all had a good laugh.

Bob brought Bonnie, my niece, to the wedding, and that was his wedding gift. He flew Bonnie all the way from Fort Good Hope to Quebec City. Bonnie was special to me. Her mother, Jean, was my sister who passed away back in 1971.

Bonnie's a grown woman now. She had a son in 1988. She already had two young children and their father was not there to help, so she wasn't sure she could give this little boy the proper care. She offered him to us in a traditional Dene adoption. We gave him the name Keenan, which means "without arrows." In Dene its *Kee-hey-nee.* We felt he had a strong spirit and power so he was not someone who needed weapons.

The spring after our wedding, Marie and I moved to Good Hope. She was on strike from her CBC job in Quebec City and she was pregnant with our first daughter, Kyla. Even now, Marie says those were some of the best years of our marriage.

We moved into the log house that I had grown up in. My grandmother lived next door at an old folks' home and Uncle Albert, Peter Mountain, little Granny Mountain and my aunt, Mary Wilson the interpreter, all had houses nearby, too, and that's where we lived.

It was a log house, maybe twenty-two by twenty-two feet. It had electricity and two wood stoves—a barrel stove for heating and a wood stove for cooking. We had two forty-five-gallon barrels by the back door for water. We didn't have a television or a telephone, but we had a radio. You can't get much more basic than that, and that's how we started.

I built an unheated log addition to the house so we could store equipment and a little bit of wood. Once the winter came and everything started freezing, we put all our fish, moose meat, caribou meat, spruce grouse and ptarmigan back there. You can get tired of this stuff after a while, so you want to have some variety. I had a snowmobile and I showed Marie how to set snares to catch rabbits, so Marie had a snare line going for a good part of that year. She'd jump on the back of the snowmobile and we'd go across the creek and up the other side of the hill, and she'd check her snares. That was all part of the joy of our honeymoon year in Good Hope. I mean, a snare line is a snare line and it is work, but with Marie it became like everything else, a joy. There was joy in the mundane things that we did.

In the summer and fall, we went for a walk every evening. Marie had a little basket full of hats—toques, baseball caps, rain hats, all kinds of hats—and the Elders used to love to look out for us and see what hat she wore that night. We'd walk by and they'd laugh and say things in Dene like, "Oh, I like her hat," or "Her hat is beautiful." Our neighbours Leon and Jane Kelly would come out and laugh with us. "We were wondering which hat she would wear today."

That was one of the many little things we did. The changing of the hats, you might call it. But nobody could make a hat come alive like Marie.

We had a honey bucket for a toilet, just a pail with a lid. Marie didn't like the idea of going through the whole summer using that, so when she went travelling to Inuvik around her birthday, I built an outhouse on the bank of the creek. It faced east, so when the sun came up in the morning it would shine right into the outhouse. You could leave the door open because there was nobody to see you anyway, so you could sit there with the sun shining down on you—a great way to start the day. It was made of rough sawn spruce planks and I sanded the seat smooth like a park bench. I thought it was an awesome outhouse, as far as outhouses go.

I went to Inuvik to join Marie and we flew back to Good Hope together. I tell you, this woman is sharp. She doesn't miss a thing. We're flying over the river, and as we're approaching the town, she looks down and says, "Oh, what's that? That's a little outhouse!"

I wanted to surprise her when she got home, but she spotted it before we had even landed.

Anyway.

I mean, who else would give their bride an outhouse as a gift?

Marie was learning how to cook with the wood stove. It was one thing to get it started, but you also had to keep it going. When I got home from work one day, she was sobbing. God, what awful thing has befallen her?

"I tried to surprise you," she cried. "I spent two hours out in the bush swatting mosquitoes while I picked raspberries to make a pie for you. I put it in the oven, and just when I thought it was done half an hour ago, I opened the oven and the oven door fell off and the pie fell out and it spilled all over. I tried to salvage it but I couldn't save it."

That really did it to her—she started crying all over again. It was a tender moment, and we laughed about it for years.

But even while we were in Good Hope, times were changing. The year 1981 was the year that TV came to Good Hope. There was a big community discussion about it beforehand. The community was split. A lot of us, including Marie and me, thought the radio was all we needed, and we were worried about the television's impact. In the end, CBC was the only channel broadcast in Good Hope. Everybody rushed off to the Hudson's Bay and bought television sets, mostly big ones. Marie and I discussed it and decided not to buy one ourselves.

Chief Frank T'Seleie bought a humongous TV. When he went trapping in October, he said to us, "I don't want my TV to be sitting in my house frozen. I spent a lot of money on it and I wonder if I could store it in your house so it will be warm. You don't have to use it," he laughed, "but can I leave it with you?"

We put that TV upstairs in our little log house, but after a few weeks we brought it down and plugged it in to watch the news. Soon we were watching *Mork & Mindy*.

After Kyla was born, on September 11 of that year, I bought Marie a little puppy from Yellowknife, half terrier, half husky. We were trying to come up with a name and Robin Williams solved the problem for us by saying, "Nanu nanu." Our dog became Nanoo. We had that beautiful dog for years.

There were funny little moments... there was an old man who had spent the better part of his life in a psychiatric hospital, and he came back to Good Hope as a senior to live in the old folks' home. He was the last member of his family that we knew of and he had a French family name: Sangeteaux. I said to Marie, "You know what? When that old man dies, his name is going to die with him, but let's keep his name alive. Do you mind if I call you that?"

She agreed, and she got used to me saying, "Hey Sangeteaux!" To this day, that's what you hear. We're honouring that old man.

Marie's mother, Ellen, came to Good Hope when Kyla was born and she stayed with us a couple of other times. She was probably thinking, My poor daughter! You couldn't get further into the sticks than this, and you can't get more basic than living in a log house with two wood stoves, no water and no phone. Many people might see this as living in poverty, but Marie's parents never said anything. They honoured her choice. And that's where we raised Kyla for her first year.

Marie's father, Neil, also came to visit. He wanted to know all about the place and the people and our lives. We took a lot of boat trips together and he went hunting with me several times in the winter. Once, in Yellowknife, I shot two caribou with him. It was cold. Forty-four below zero. It was just the two of us and he was worried about the cold. He wanted to get back, but I told him we had to skin the caribou where we were. "That's how we do it. We don't throw them in the truck and bring them home to the garage."

"Well, hurry up, then."

I took the two caribou and I said, "I know your son is a doctor. He knows a little bit about the body and stuff. Me too, I'm a surgeon—watch me!"

I took my skinning knife and started to cut up the caribou. I went up through the belly, took off the legs and then I took out the heart, kidney, liver and stomach. I separated all this stuff—trying to be as neat as possible—and every once in a while, I'd lean back and say, "See, Neil? I told you, I'm a surgeon."

Neil was still worried about the cold. "Warm up your hands, son!"

I was cutting with my bare hands and it's true that your hands would freeze at forty below, but when you cut open the caribou, it's hot and it just steams. You warm them up that way. That's how we did it.

CHAPTER EIGHTEEN

FORT GOOD HOPE LEADS THE WAY

I mentioned earlier about my attempt to challenge Georges Erasmus for the leadership of the Dene Nation. What happened after that was crucial to the political development of the NWT and would have huge implications for the Dene people. It was then that I learned that change must happen at the local level.

We were all mindful of the fact that the Berger Inquiry had set a ten-year moratorium on development, giving the Dene people ten years to get our business in order, figure out self-government and resolve the issue of who had control of the land and resources.

In Fort Good Hope, we wanted to make the Chief and Council our primary decision-making body. We wanted to use our Dene traditions and history and govern ourselves at the community level. Chief Frank T'Seleie, John T'Seleie, Bob Overvold, some other leaders and I had this dream of community government. George Barnaby had been vice-president of the Dene Nation and later became a member of the territorial council. He had moved from Good Hope to Yellowknife, but he was primarily a hunter-trapper and life in the city didn't suit him; he resigned, moved back to Good Hope and would help us create a new level of community government.

Unfortunately, the NWT government had already gone through each community and methodically put housing, health care, water-delivery systems, schools, curriculums and teachers under its control. The NWT commissioner, Stuart Hodgson, tried to replace our Chief and Councils with new settlement councils, which were to run all the municipal services—roads, sewage, garbage, water delivery. The settlement council would be elected but answerable mainly to the territorial government and bureaucrats in Yellowknife.

We thought we would do something about that. We wanted to abolish the settlement council. We began by encouraging all the people in the community to refuse to vote at election time. The first time it happened, the territorial government thought it was a matter of bad timing and rescheduled the election. Again, nobody showed up. They realized then that this was a conscious decision, a protest by the whole community.

For a few years, the government said, "It's very obvious the people in Good Hope are not mature enough to take care of their own affairs," so instead of the settlement council they said they would administer Good Hope from their offices in Inuvik. That's two hundred miles downriver, but people in Good Hope didn't seem to care. The street lights burnt out and the sidewalks were in disrepair, but everyone left town at the end of September to go trapping. People were still eating fish and caribou meat. They didn't need a lot of stuff from the store and they didn't care about the street lights and sidewalks.

At that time, in the fall of 1980, the Chief and Council had no office or telephone, not even a filing cabinet. So, when Bob was hired as band manager, Chief T'Seleie told him that if he wanted to get paid, he had to find the money. This motivated him; he went to work and secured core funding for the Chief and Council and band meetings from Ottawa. He got an office set up in Good Hope, plus a salary for himself and the secretary. This type of organization was starting to happen in other communities as well.

The other thing that tied everything together was the work of James Wah-Shee. He was on the territorial council as the minister for municipal affairs and we started to have meetings with him so we could tell him our vision. Chief T'Seleie led those meetings, and then Bob and I followed up and eventually James Wah-Shee, much to the chagrin of his own bureaucrats, recognized our Chief and Council as a provisional community government.

We made it work because we offered a compromise on elections, saying that anybody who lived in Good Hope could run for Chief or Council and that you didn't have to be Dene or Treaty to run. We made this offer because we knew the demographics of Good Hope: we would always have a majority of Dene on the council, so we set aside one seat for a non-Dene resident and then promptly appointed an Inuvialuit member of the community who'd married a Dene woman.

Chiefs and Councils had been running Good Hope for generations. Back in the early fifties, for example, the Chief and Council decided to build a community hall. They probably had some money from Indian Affairs, but the Chief decided that all the young people had to go out, cut logs and bring them into town, and in the spring they would use them to build the hall. It was a volunteer effort, but the Chief held that kind of authority: when he said something had to be done, that's what the Dene had to do. So, everybody in town found the time to get four or five logs. They ordered some roofing material, doors, windows and a hardwood floor, and they built the place.

The Chief gave the keys of the hall to one of the Elders named Paul Chinna. Paul never had a day of schooling in his life, but he had a knack for building. He built some of the first log homes in Good Hope and he worked without measuring tapes or electricity. Everything was done by hand. My brother

Everett used to say, "When Paul measured things, he grabbed whatever was around, like a stick, and he'd use that to figure out how wide he had to cut a window opening on the wall. These houses were better than anything built since." Some of them are still standing, sixty years later. When we set up the first provisional Indigenous public government in 1980, we knew that we could trust the traditional ways of a Dene community to get the work done.

We also decided to change the curriculum at the local school so our children would learn about Good Hope and their families, leaders, land and landmarks. We initiated a group to spearhead that work and we hired Cindy Erasmus, who worked with a group of Elders to create the material needed to develop the curriculum. That idea spread to other communities and to this day we have a government in the NWT that consistently supports curriculum development. It's now mandatory for all high school students to take a course on the history and culture of the North from a Dene, Inuit, Métis and Inuvialuit perspective. The curriculum also covers Northern geography and demographics, so by the time a student graduates, the student knows where Tuktoyaktuk and Trout Lake are, as well as where the Inuvialuit live. More recently, the history of the residential schools was added to that curriculum.

Another major achievement was how we helped the people take control of their own housing. We wanted to create a home ownership program that was not social housing, something provided by social services. We wanted our people to build their own home and to own it and be responsible for it, independent of the government.

In the mid-sixties, some government administrator delivered a whole load of prefabricated homes—three bedrooms, furnace, the whole bit. At first, everyone thought, Hey, you're gonna give me a house for free, great! But they weren't ready for it. They soon found out that they weren't the owners: they had to pay rent to the government of the NWT, and although it was a low cost, they lost their independence that way. Before they could change their minds, their old log houses were demolished by a bulldozer, which pushed the homes over the riverbank.

The government housing was also an abrupt change in lifestyle: suddenly there was electricity, oil furnaces and a water-delivery system. It sounds like creature comforts, as people no longer had to haul water or cut wood, but the people found they didn't want the changes imposed on them. They wanted their wood stoves back and they wanted their kids to haul water as they had for generations. When the government tried to ship more houses in, the people in Good Hope said no.

Eventually, Chief T'Seleie, Bob, a guy named Tom Erger and I came up with an innovative home ownership pilot project. We were the first community to encourage the movement away from social housing and toward home ownership. Our plan was to provide seven hunters and trappers with the resources to build their own homes for their families. We budgeted approximately $100,000 per house.

I was on the board of the NWT Housing Corporation, and when I pitched the idea to the board, they immediately shot it down. They implied that we had no experience and that they couldn't trust us with that kind of money. It was typical, but still insulting. Chief T'Seleie talked to James Wah-Shee, who supported the plan, and then I met with the minister of housing, Arnold McCallum. He'd been my high school principal at Grandin College just a few years prior. James had probably spoken to Arnold before our meeting, but I was still surprised by what Arnold said: "I remember you from high school. You were always feisty, but here it is: I'm going to take a big chance. I'm going to get the Housing Corporation to write you a cheque and I'm going to get the chairman to give it to you today. They're not going to be happy, but I'll do this."

As he was walking me out, he said, "Steve, don't fuck it up. I'm taking a big chance on you. Don't make me look like a jackass."

"Of course not. We'll build those seven houses."

I went back to the Housing Corporation, and when the chairman handed me the cheque he said, "We don't want our name associated with this. It's going to be a disaster. Money is going to go missing and you're not going to get anything done. It's a complete waste of money and time."

I took that cheque and said with a stony expression, "Thank you very much." And I left.

We hired an architect and Tom Erger, our project manager, was also our carpenter. The community selected seven people to have their homes built; some of them didn't speak English, but they managed that $700,000 and divvied it up among themselves. Once the blueprints were made, we ordered all the material, the people started harvesting spruce logs and we brought the logs into town either by dog or by snowmobile. We wanted to instill pride in the homeowners so they could say, "I got the logs, then I peeled and seasoned them, and then I put those logs up. I built my house with lots of help, but I worked on it." The community was humming. Everybody was working and felt good.

I wanted a house too; Kyla was less than a year old and our log house was too cold. I wanted any kind of house, even a staff house, but Chief Frank T'Seleie felt that we couldn't start serving ourselves. There were other people more deserving.

He laughed. "Look at my house," he said to me. "It's nothing but old plywood and a beat-up foundation, but you don't see me crying about housing."

It was a great success at the local level. The Chief, Bob, Tom and I were so proud. I think there might be four of those houses that are still being used today.

Frank and Bob also started planning to build a new community hall because the one built in the fifties was of no use anymore. They wanted to combine a community hall, where meetings could be held, with an office space. We put it right on top of the most prominent hill in Good Hope, and there was tremendous pride in it. The log building itself was beautiful and the location was great. There was a big feast and drum dance the first night it opened. Chief T'Seleie brought in the NWT's commissioner, John Parker, for the official opening, and he did it by starting up a chainsaw and cutting up a log. No busting champagne bottles here.

We also knew we had to create jobs. Most of our people were working in the oil and gas sector in the Mackenzie and Beaufort Delta regions, but it was always outside the community. The Good Hope leaders knew we needed an economic development plan so that we would be ready for the kids when they graduated high school. So that became my job, and I worked with the Chief, Bob and John T'Seleie.

We considered everything. We thought about the idea of a hotel and a small store, and we looked at buying out the local contractor. We studied the economy, including how much people made from hunting and trapping each year, the approximate value of our food and how much it would cost our people if they had to live off store-bought food. We even looked at the role that card games played; we did a survey and found out, much to our amusement, that there were three or four people in Good Hope whose main source of income was from playing cards. They were good enough that they made enough money to eke out a living. When one of them would win a jackpot, the winner would redistribute the money back to all the people he or she had borrowed money from. There are still people in Good Hope who do this today.

Eventually the community did build a hotel, but we learned that community ownership of something like that was not the best way to go. We hired staff, but nobody really owned it; instead, everybody owned it, so it wasn't well managed and eventually it fell apart. What came out of it, though, were two or three privately run bed and breakfasts and they still operate to this day. We never did build a competing store to the Hudson's Bay Company or Northern, but the community built a co-operative instead and it's been in existence for twenty-five years now.

The fact is that some of our people were happy to have year-round jobs and some were not. There are people who will work three or four months and then quit because they have enough for a snowmobile or a truck. They prefer to hunt and trap and be independent from a nine-to-five job. It's still true today.

———

The ten years Justice Berger gave us was too long; I know now that we could have done everything we needed to prepare for self-government within five years, but the enormity of what we had to do was beyond my little mind then. One thing that was good about his deadline, though, was that it forced us to face our opponents.

As I mentioned earlier, there was great polarization after the Berger Inquiry decision. The gas pipeline project was dead, the business community was very upset, some of the Métis were also upset, people in communities with non-Indigenous populations like Hay River, Norman Wells, Inuvik and Yellowknife were upset. Tom Butters, an old journalist from Inuvik, was pro-pipeline and against the idea of the Dene Nation. Red McBryan was a right-wing conservative and spokesperson for non-Indigenous people in Hay River. Politicians like Don Stewart, David Searle and Dave Nickerson thought we were a bunch of neophyte socialists. That's what they called us. At that time, I was emerging as a young politician, giving a lot of speeches and travelling south for media events, and I think a lot of those men thought, This guy, what the hell does he know?

So, there was anger and resentment in the North, but at the same time there was new leadership emerging. George Braden was elected to a leadership position we would call the premier today. He was young, and Dene like James Wah-Shee and Richard Nerysoo came with him into office. George knew something had to be done about the polarization, so he called for a constitutional conference and invited the Chiefs, non-Indigenous business people and the Dene Nation to share their opinions. He was basically asking, "What is the future of the NWT?"

Chief T'Seleie, Bob, John, a few others from Good Hope and I booked ourselves into the Explorer Hotel in Yellowknife. I was ready to roll up my sleeves and go to battle; if they were angry, I was ready to show them that I was angry too.

The first day I arrived, I was standing in the hotel lobby and I saw this big red-faced non-Indigenous guy walking right toward me. It was Red Mc-Bryan. He was a no-nonsense, take-no-prisoners kind of a guy, so I thought, Okay, if you want to get it on, let's get it on.

"Steve Kakfwi," he said to me. "I was in Good Hope when I was a young guy. I worked on the barges. I know your family. I know your uncle Jonas, your dad, Noel, and your grandfather Gabriel."

Right away, he tried to disarm me. He continued, "Look, I've heard you on the radio, and I don't know what the hell you're talking about. I decided to come here and spend three days listening to you guys, so I can try to understand what the hell it is you guys are talking about."

I said, "Okay, well, that sounds good. We've come here to tell you what we're talking about, so we're going to do that. Thank you."

I shook his hand, and for me that was a turning point at the conference. A guy that conservative reached out and said, in less than flattering terms, "I don't know what the hell you guys are talking about, but I'm here to listen." I thought that was about as good as it could get.

As it turned out, in his later years Red became a good friend of mine. His wife, Bertha, loved music, and she would call me up and ask that I mail her my new CD or visit her the next time I was in Hay River and sing for her. Red and Bertha's son, Joe, started Buffalo Airways. I still stay in touch with him; he's a friend. Joe also knew my dad and Uncle Jonas, and he could rattle off the names of people in Good Hope all along the valley because he flew all over the place. Every time I saw Joe, he would come up and talk to me. When I was under siege as a premier, I got a letter from "Buffalo Joe," Joe McBryan of Buffalo Airways, explaining that he supported me and wanted me to stay premier.

I often think about how important it was that people on both sides of the divide chose to reach out a hand. I can take some credit for that, but it was mainly people like Chief T'Seleie, George Braden and Red McBryan who showed us the way.

CHAPTER NINETEEN

KOH YEH LEY GHO DENE

Chief T'Seleie had an older sister named Christine. She came up to me one day in Yellowknife in the late seventies and she said, "You know, Stephen, you shouldn't worry about people doing anything to you. They can't do anything to you."

I thought she meant that if I had political critics I shouldn't listen to them, but she went on to say, "People can't do anything to you because, you and I, we are both Fire-Carriers." She said it in Dene: *Koh yeh ley gho Dene.*

"We are the Dene who come from the people who carried the fire for their people," she explained. "We are the ones who carried the fire to the next place that our people were going to camp. We're the ones who went into the night with the fire, who showed them the way and found the place where people would be safe, where they can catch fish and get meat. Stephen, those are the people we come from. We always go ahead of everybody. We're always alone, but always leading."

I was captivated by that. I felt the same way that I had when I heard the name of Talking Fish Creek for the first time.

"Certain families have that person who is always up early, restless and on the go, who never rests or works as a group," Christine went on. "That person is always a loner or an introvert. They carry the fire and they light the way so people can follow them. The fire itself is the comfort. The Fire-Carrier would say, 'When you catch up to me, I will have a camp ready for you and the fire will be burning.'"

At that time, I didn't ask her any questions about it, but I always had that recurring nightmare of me hurtling through the universe, through fire, smoke, steam and lights. With time, I came to understand that one reason I couldn't sleep well was because of the sexual abuse I had suffered at residential school. I was scared to be alone, scared of the dark and scared of being in bed. I'd always sleep on a couch if I could; something about having my back braced against the couch gave me more comfort. If I heard the smallest thing in the night I'd jump up, and the second I'd wake up, I'd bolt: get up and get the hell out of there. A bed was not a safe place for me. You'd think I was a troubled man! But Christine's words about being a Fire-Carrier gave me comfort. I liked that better than thinking I was sexually abused so badly that I couldn't sleep.

Many years after Christine told me that, I asked an Elder about it. At that time, Gabe Kochon had just turned ninety and was the oldest guy in Good Hope. He was revered for his Traditional Knowledge. He said, "Stephen, your family, they come from those kind of people. Certain families had the Fire-Carriers; not every family had them, but your family, your grandparents, they were part of that people. That's why you are the way you are. You're always doing something, Steve: working for people, watching out for us. You never sit still. That's a mark of a Dene who carries fire."

Once, Gabe stood up during a public meeting in Good Hope and said, "We talk about *Koh yeh ley gho Dene*. Well, there's one sitting right here, right in front of us." And he was pointing at me.

I felt good about it. I even thought of setting up an award for kids who show Fire-Carrier behaviour.

So, that's one explanation for the way I am.

Sadly, Gabe is no longer with us. In the summer of 2021, he became the first person in the NWT to die from COVID-19.

CHAPTER TWENTY

A PROMISE IS A PROMISE

In 1982, the year before Georges Erasmus left the Dene Nation, the Gwich'in held an assembly in Fort McPherson. It was raining and cold and people were not happy. It was a long way to travel from places like Fort Smith and Fort Resolution, and Georges sometimes let the assemblies go on until midnight or two o'clock in the morning because he never cut anybody off.

These were tough times for the Chiefs. Negotiations were shut down, our relationship with the Métis peoples was broken and we were facing the Norman Wells pipeline proposal. It felt like we had no resources and so much work to do.

I travelled to Fort McPherson for the assembly, and one night some Dene Chiefs and other delegates came to see me and asked if I would stand for nomination if they passed a motion to remove Georges. The assemblies were going very late and they were fed up. I wasn't a delegate or anything; I was just up there hanging around with Marie and Kyla, so it was very uncomfortable. I told them it was too short notice and that I wasn't interested. I didn't even know if they had the numbers to do it and it wasn't going to make anything better. Marie had to stay to cover the assembly, but I left the next morning with baby Kyla.

There was a lot of criticism about how we at the Dene Nation had stalled on several issues, but the patriation of the constitution was creating a lot of excitement among Indigenous people across Canada. We were all aware of this great opportunity. We were thinking, What if we could get a self-government clause in the constitution?

At this time, Georges was frequently hiring me for contract work and he had appointed Bob Overvold as the chief negotiator. After a constitutional conference in Ottawa, Bob and I started talking about the direction of the leadership within the Dene Nation, as we knew Georges would step down soon. I wasn't sure yet whether I wanted to run.

That spring I was flying to a meeting in Iqaluit (which was still called Frobisher Bay at that time), but we got weathered out and ended up landing in Kuujjuaq in northern Quebec. I checked into a hotel, and I don't think I had been in there more than an hour when the phone rang. It was the front desk. "There's a Charlie Watt here to see you." I was surprised. No one knew

I was coming. I had met Charlie. He was one of the chief constitutional nego-tiators for the Inuit. So, I went down to the front desk and there was Charlie Watt. He insisted on taking me for a ride in his huge monster of a Jeep, a four-by-four with tundra tires, parked in front of the hotel. So, I climbed into the truck.

We drove out a couple of miles, and then we stopped among the trees in the middle of nowhere. It was getting dark; I figured he was going to make a fire, but he didn't. Instead, he marched out into the trees, sat down and said, "Look, Steve, I've got something I want to talk to you about, and here it is. We are fighting to get some things in the constitution and we need our best people. I know you're going to run for the presidency of the Dene Nation and I know you're going to get elected, so, when you get elected, I want you to promise me that you will do everything you can to make sure Georges stays on the constitutional file."

I thought about this and said, "Well, thanks, Charlie, but I haven't de-cided whether I'm going to run—"

"Steve." He cut me off. "You're going to run and you're going to get elected, and when you get elected, I want you to get Georges appointed to represent the Dene on the constitution file, because we need him."

I agreed with Charlie that Georges was our best guy for that. He drove me back to the hotel and the next day I flew on to my meeting in Iqaluit.

Sometime that summer, I decided to run. The Dene National Assem-bly was in September. I wasn't sure whether I would have enough votes and I didn't have the money to campaign. At that time, the Dene Nation's vice-president, Herb Norwegian, was the other candidate. He was a great friend and would go on to serve the Dene for over forty years.

So, here's what happened. The Dene Nation executive wouldn't let me into the closed sessions of the assembly because I wasn't a delegate. In re-sponse, I set up my campaign table outside the doors of the assembly and whenever the Chiefs would come out for a break, they'd see me. "Steve, what are you doing out here?"

"I can't go in. They won't let me."

And they would say, "Why the hell is that?"

That worked in my favour and I think it got me some votes. That Sep-tember, I was elected as the president of the Dene Nation.

Once I was back in Yellowknife, I was settling into my new office at the Dene Nation when I got a call from Charlie Watt. He was calling to see if I'd be keeping my promise to let Georges continue as our representative on the constitution. We knew that Georges was the best man for the job, but there was a problem. Under the rules of the Assembly of First Nations, it was Yukon's turn to take on the role of the regional vice-Chief. Georges had already been the regional vice-Chief, so now his term was up. I tried to explain this to Charlie and he had a fit on the phone, so I said, "Okay, I'll talk to Harry Allen in Yukon. I'll see if I can get him to agree that Georges has to stay on that file."

So, I had a long talk with Harry. He was happy to hear that I was elected. I told him why it would be better to leave Georges on the constitutional file, and he said, "You know what? I don't know if the Yukon Chiefs are going to agree. Give me a week."

Finally, he called back and said, "You know, Steve, there was not one Chief that disagreed. They'll take their turn next time. So, yeah—you nominate Georges or I will. We'll do it together."

The rest of it is constitutional history. Georges was one of the leaders on the constitutional team.

I think the last time I saw Charlie was just before he retired. I asked him, "Charlie, did you ever tell Georges how we got him to continue on the constitutional team?"

"Never told him." Charlie had a big smile. "He doesn't know."

So, I might tell Georges one of these days.

We have a complicated history, Georges and I. People said that we were rivals. I look back on it now and I understand how that could have been the public perception, but I worked well with Georges on many things, including the division of the NWT, the Berger Inquiry and the campaign to get rid of the extinguishment policy.

When Georges finished his term as head of the Assembly of First Nations, Chief T'Seleie, Bob and I decided we were going to give Georges a gift. Bob and I had made a point to live in the community and become more Dene: we lived in Good Hope, we travelled on the Mackenzie River together and we learned how to hunt. We did all that together and we thought Georges should be encouraged to do that too. One way you do that is by giving gifts. We thought that every Dene had to have a gun, so we decided to get him one. Bob, Chief T'Seleie and I were all very knowledgeable about guns, so we decided on a Browning .308 lever-action hunting rifle. It's easy to carry, it's good-looking and it's versatile: you could use it for caribou, black bear and moose.

So, I bought the gun and the case and got it all prepared, and the three of us went to the assembly in Winnipeg. When people started presenting their gifts we got in line, and when it was our turn, Chief T'Seleie gave Georges the gun and said, "On behalf of my people and my community and the Dene, I'm giving you this gift, this beautiful rifle, for you to use in your retirement." Of course, Georges wasn't retiring; he would work for many more years in various roles, such as co-chair of the Royal Commission on Aboriginal Peoples, head of Aboriginal Healing Foundation and chief negotiator for the Dehcho First Nations.

A funny thing happened at that assembly. Everyone was going up to the microphone, sounding sad and saying things like, "Georges, we're going to miss you. You were great. You're wonderful. Who can replace you? What are we going to do?"

Then Simon Lucas from BC, a huge man with a deep voice, went to the microphone. "Geooooooorges!" he bellowed, almost sobbing, and the whole place went quiet. "Geooooorges! You were good… you were good… for NOTHING!"

He looked around the hall and he started to smile and then he chuckled, and the whole place cracked up. Of course, Simon was a great supporter of Georges, so it was a great joke and perfectly delivered.

CHAPTER TWENTY-ONE

LYNDA SORENSON

In September 1983, I moved into my new office at the Dene Nation. I was just getting used to the title and the job when a couple of the secretaries knocked on my door. I don't know why there were two of them, maybe they were nervous, but they said, "Steve, there's a woman calling you from Vancouver… she says her name is Victoria Douglas. Do you know anybody by that name?"

"Oh yeah," I said. "That's my kindergarten teacher. I'll talk to her."

I don't think they believed me, but they put the call through.

I guess she had heard my name on the news, but I didn't know what to say. And though I often went to Vancouver, I never arranged to meet with her. I don't know why.

Then one morning, many years later, I heard a man being interviewed on the radio. He had worked with the United States Army Signal Corps in Fort Good Hope back in the 1950s. I remembered that Victoria Douglas's husband, Jim, was also with the Signal Corps, so I tracked the man down and he told me that Jim had passed on but that Victoria was still in Vancouver, though she had Lou Gehrig's disease, or ALS.

The next time I went to Vancouver, I visited her at the hospital. The nurse told me to keep the visit to a half hour because she'd be too tired, but three hours later, we were still talking. There was too much to talk about. We talked and talked about Good Hope and the people we knew, and she was holding my hand and kept saying there was just one more thing she wanted to ask, just one more thing she wanted to say. She couldn't let me go. As I spoke with her, I realized that she was a very liberated woman, even when she lived in Good Hope. She was interested in the Dene, justice, the rights of Indigenous Peoples and the role of women in society.

Each time I visited her, she was weaker than during my previous visit. One day, I don't know why, I asked if I could take a picture of her. She didn't answer for a while, then quietly, because she was losing her voice, she said, "Yes, you can take my picture, but I need to get ready."

I didn't know what she meant at first—she was bedridden!—but it was amazing to watch her. She had a little mirror and she spent a lot of time fixing up her hair and getting her scarf just right. Finally, she said, "You can take my picture now."

So, I have her picture. This woman came into my life when I was four and a half and here she was again, decades later. I brought my family to meet her before she passed on.

~

In my early years with the Dene Nation, the NWT commissioner was like a benign dictator. He would fly around the North on his annual tours, handing out schools and health centres and other infrastructure projects like they were goodies for little children—because that's how the territorial government saw us. In our fight for self-government, we regarded these territorial politicians as the opposition.

There was division among the Dene over what self-government would look like. I disagreed with getting our people into the territorial legislature. I was one of the leaders who said it was best to separate Dene leaders from the colonial system. "We'll never join forces with the territorial government. It's like dancing with the devil."

That's when I first used that phrase. If you dance long enough with the devil, you become seduced; sending our people into the legislature was going to compromise the views we held. I preferred the traditional leadership of our Elders, Chiefs and Indigenous associations—but this was starting to change, and the change was coming from our Chiefs. They said, "Our people want running water. We need roads. Let's get our people elected as ministers. We want people who share our vision and understand what it is we're asking for."

I disagreed, and it created a problem. When I was elected to lead the Dene Nation, the NWT had one of its first Dene premiers, Richard Nerysoo. The two of us did not get along. We never had a meeting. Two Dene leaders, at odds.

One day a woman named Lynda Sorenson called me. She was a Yellowknife MLA (member of the legislative assembly) at the time and a supporter of Nerysoo. She thought she could be a peacemaker. She wanted to fix the division between the Dene Nation office and the territorial government. She asked to meet with me.

When I first met Lynda, I thought she was like Queen Elizabeth: one of the whitest women on earth. And I don't mean that in racial terms; I'm talking about her high heels, her fine clothing, her long fingernails and her perfume wafting twenty feet in every direction. Though she lived in Yellowknife, she appeared to me as one of those southern people who lived in the North with no idea that she was on the land of the Inuit, Inuvialuit, Dene and Métis peoples. I didn't know it then, but Lynda would become an important person in my political life and, oddly enough, a crucial player in the political evolution of the North.

But during that first meeting, we didn't get anywhere. At one point, she stood up and went over to the window. She was standing there staring off into whatever she was staring off into, and I remember looking at her and thinking, Why does she care? Why is she doing this? She left my office, and Richard and I kept our differences.

Lynda was a big wheel in the federal Liberal Party. She was friends with people like Pierre Elliott Trudeau, Paul Martin, John Turner and former finance minister Marc Lalonde, but that didn't translate into support or a positive profile for her in the North. She got herself elected as a Yellowknife MLA in the early eighties, but then she had to resign when she decided to run as the Liberal candidate with John Turner in 1984. She came third. After that, she found herself nowhere to go. Then, to my surprise, she called me one day in the fall of 1984.

"I need to have something to do," she said to me, "and I'd like to work for you at the Dene Nation. I don't need to get paid. I'll volunteer."

Some of the Chiefs simply said that it was my decision who works for me, but others wondered about her politics and whether it would be a good idea to have a high-profile person in the Dene Nation office. So, I told her I didn't need any help—but the truth was, in my first two years as president, I'd had two executive assistants who left because there was too much stress and too much work, so I did need a skilled assistant.

The following spring, I ran into Lynda in the parking lot of a grocery store. I had a change of heart, so I called out to her and asked her if she was still looking for work. We scheduled a meeting and she agreed to volunteer, but we both had conditions. For example, I was trying to imagine what it'd be like if she walked into the Dene Nation office dressed to the nines. "Hey, I'm Steve's new executive assistant." It just wouldn't fit, you know? So, I asked her, "Do you always have to wear a dress, high heels and perfume?"

And she just bristled at that. "I will dress exactly as I please, thank you very much." And that was the end of that inquiry.

Lynda and Ethel Liske, the Dene Nation's executive director at the time, found a way to have a good working relationship. Lynda said she would keep a low profile and she was true to her word. The work was totally overwhelming, but Lynda never once said she was too tired to get the job done.

On one of our first trips to Ottawa, I had the opportunity to ask her why she wanted to work for me. We were on a Northwest Territorial Airways flight, heading home. "Is it about your political beliefs?" I asked.

"No, I'm a Liberal," she answered. "I'm practical. The NDP will never be in office. I prefer the Liberals to the Conservatives, and I think you do too."

"Do you just want to be close to the Dene, then?"

And she said, "Well, working for you gives me access to Ottawa. Like I said, as long as you let me do my Liberal thing once in a while, I'll be a loyal, hard worker."

"This is not a nine-to-five job," I replied. "If you want to work nine to five, I don't think it's going to work. I want to know how committed you are."

She looked at me and said, "Just watch me." She started laughing and then we were both laughing, because she was quoting Pierre Trudeau's famous line from the imposition of the War Measures Act in 1970.

Lynda made good on that promise soon after the plane ride. It happened on her day off.

Richard Nerysoo was trying to get funding from Ottawa for Aboriginal language programs and I took issue with that because I thought that funding should come through the Dene Nation. I didn't like that the Dene Nation was being left out of what we thought was an Indigenous issue. Of course, everyone wanted the premier and the president of Dene Nation to get along, but I wasn't ready. I was young and belligerent, and I wasn't backing down. I didn't do the social chit-chat. I don't stand around "with the boys," slapping each other on the back and performing that "We're all friends, we're all in this together" kind of thing. It didn't go with me. I never wanted to be a part of that.

That September, the Dene Nation organized a meeting where the Chiefs could speak with the Métis peoples. It was a high-level meeting and I didn't want Lynda to be there; I wasn't comfortable with having her around when I was dealing with the Chiefs yet. Lynda made it easy for me. The night before I left for the meeting, she called me up and said, "Look, I want to take a day off. And just so it doesn't offend anybody, you should know that Richard has invited me to come to Norman Wells. It would be on my day off, so I'll accept his invitation, if that's okay with you."

I was blunt. "You're taking a day off. What you do with your time is your business."

The meeting's agenda included negotiations on claims, working with the Métis peoples and Richard. We'd invited him to speak to the Chiefs and the Métis leaders as premier. So, Richard flew in on an executive plane with some of his staff, and with Lynda.

All the Chiefs were aware of my quarrels with Nerysoo and they wanted us to get beyond it. It was petty stuff for them. They didn't care; they just wanted to see the premier and the president getting along.

Lynda Sorenson serving as NWT MLA, November 1979. ©NWT Archives/ Native Communications Society fonds/N-2018-010: 06600

When Lynda got off the plane with Richard, I saw that something had changed. Lynda stepped back and Richard stepped forward to greet me. He was smiling and holding out his hand to shake mine. His manner was completely different and everyone saw it. Everyone saw that there were suddenly friendly relations between Richard Nerysoo and Steve Kakfwi. We were chatting it up. During the meetings, he sat beside me and talked to the Chiefs and the Métis.

I always gave Lynda credit for it. I never said thank you, but I always figured that whatever good relationship she had with Richard worked its magic that day. And all I know is that many Chiefs from up and down the valley and the Métis leaders were grateful for the change.

When we embraced the idea that the Dene Nation and the territorial politicians had to get along to do the best work for the people we claimed to represent, it was a big moment of change. I look back on it now and think that's just the stuff you learn. You know, Richard and I were both thirty-three. We were young and brash and had a little too much ego. But Lynda was the one who, right from the beginning, thought that it could be and should be better, and she worked at it.

Lynda is also one of the people who helped me see that my carefully cultivated stoicism—my disdain for anything social—wasn't always appreciated. She had probably been working for me for about ten years when she invited me to dinner with her family in Victoria. I said sure, not thinking too much about it, but the next time we had to be in BC, she arranged the dinner.

During our stopover in Edmonton on our way to BC, I was sitting in the Air Canada lounge thinking, Oh, God, I don't want to do this. I do not want to have one of those *dinners*.

So, without really thinking it through, I said, "Hey, Lynda, how about if I don't come for the dinner, I just show up for the coffee and the dessert?"

She looked at me and blew up. "Okay, sure! I'll call and I'll cancel everything! I'm sorry I even asked you!"

Just then, the boarding announcement came on. I skipped out of the lounge ahead of her and walked hurriedly to the gate. I had never seen her angry before.

I got in line at the departure gate and I was looking at the window and watching the reflection of all the people behind me so I could see when she walked by. It was winter and we were wearing our heavy coats. Soon, there she was, taking these big strides, her big red coat just flying. She was so angry. I didn't dare turn around. I kept looking out the window like I wasn't watching anything, and then she disappeared. What the hell? I looked around. She was gone. The first door in the hall was the men's washroom, the second one was the women's washroom, and I was sure that she disappeared before she got to the second door. Did she or didn't she just go into the men's washroom?

I decided to check the men's washroom. There were two cubicles beside each other in the washroom, and over the door of the first cubicle was a big red coat. She was in the men's washroom all right, and there was a man in the cubicle next to her and two men at the urinals.

I thought, You know what, I don't want to be around for this one either. So, I turned around and walked out.

I was way ahead of her in the lineup, so I boarded and then took my seat. Eventually, she got on board and took her seat across the aisle from me. We didn't say anything.

About twenty minutes after takeoff, just as we got over the mountains and levelled off, I leaned over and said to her, "So, how was it?"

"How was what?"

"You know, the men's washroom."

"Oh, God... don't you ever miss anything!"

We burst out laughing and we laughed about it all the way over those mountains, and everything was okay again. We got to BC, and we had the dinner with her family as she had planned it. It turned out okay, but it took her crashing the men's washroom to make it happen.

~

Lynda went back to work for the NWT's department of health once I finished my work at the Dene Nation in the summer of 1987, but she came back to work for me several months later when I was elected to the legislative assembly as the MLA for the Sahtu and almost immediately appointed to a position in the cabinet. Four of my cabinet colleagues told me that I was entitled to hire my own staff, but they all said, "Don't hire Lynda Sorenson."

I asked why and they all gave different reasons, but none of them made sense to me. It was just that they didn't like her politically. I finished my meetings with them and I thought, Who do they think they are to tell me who to hire? They're picking on a woman who doesn't deserve to be picked on.

I called her that day to offer her the job as my executive assistant, and a few days later, she accepted the offer.

She was with me from 1987 to 2001 and it worked well for me. She kept me grounded and well organized.

CHAPTER TWENTY-TWO

JOHN PAUL II

"I affirm the right to a just and equitable measure of self-government, along with a land base and adequate resources necessary for developing a viable economy for present and future generations."

—Pope John Paul II, September 20, 1987, in Fort Simpson

In 1984, the Vatican released an announcement stating Pope John Paul II wanted to visit Canada. I thought right away, It's going to be Halifax, Montreal, Toronto, Winnipeg, Edmonton, Vancouver and that will be it. And yes, Indigenous people will be included here and there across the country but only playing a small token role on someone else's stage.

My idea was, if the pope had a special interest in the Indigenous, Aboriginal and First Peoples of Canada, why not organize a meeting exclusively for Indigenous Peoples?

I wasn't interested in doing this because I was a devout Catholic. I'm not. I did it because I wanted our Elders, grandparents and parents, who are devout Catholics, to see that anything is possible. I wanted to bring Pope John Paul II here so they could have the comfort and the honour of seeing the head of the church come to our land. I wanted to tell them, "We are going through hard times and we'll probably continue having difficult years for a while, but here's something for you. We're bringing the pope here so you can see him, and he's going to bless our land, our people, and be with us in prayer."

I wanted the world to see the Dene and other Indigenous Peoples hosting a world figure. The world would see us onstage with the pope, and it would help our push to get our land back and our right to self-government, which was the big goal at the constitutional talks.

I also thought that he might have a very hard time saying no.

At that time, the constitutional discussions had been going on for the past year. Georges Erasmus, still the head of the Dene Nation, had been working with people like Jim Sinclair of the Native Council of Canada, Smokey Bruyere from the Métis, John Amagoalik and other Inuit, and Charlie Watt and Mark R. Gordon from Quebec. They were all trying to make changes to the constitution before it was patriated.

The Assembly of First Nations was headed by David Ahenakew, who was not as much of a team player as Georges Erasmus. Ahenakew always saw Treaty Rights as special and separate from the Inuit and Métis peoples, so many of the Indigenous leaders preferred to work with Georges. They didn't like that Ahenakew was saying, "We're different because we have Treaties and you don't."

Ahenakew knew that Georges was going to run against him for the leadership of the assembly, and that election was not that far away. So, when I was elected to lead the Dene Nation, Ahenakew was happy that he didn't have to deal with Georges anymore. I used this to my advantage.

The first time I went to Ottawa as president, Ahenakew asked to meet with me. He was so happy to see me. He asked, "What can I do for you?"

"Two things," I said. "First, I need support starting up Indigenous Survival International, which will help us fight for our right as Indigenous Peoples to hunt and trap and sell our fur on the international stage."

He said, "You got it. I'll give you a mandate and you can hold the international portfolio. What else?"

I said, "I need money and a mandate to work with the Vatican and the Canadian Conference of Catholic Bishops to persuade the pope to visit Fort Simpson during his trip to Canada next summer. There's a highway and an airport in Fort Simpson, so I think that'd be a good place to host him."

"You got it." He gave me $15,000 for each of the requests as start-up funding. The meeting probably lasted fifteen minutes and I got everything I wanted because of his rivalry with Georges.

Georges wasn't that comfortable seeing me all cozy with Ahenakew, but Ahenakew was still the National Chief. But I worked with Georges, and I had a good relationship with the Inuit leader John Amagoalik and others. The Métis leaders Jim Sinclair and Smokey Bruyere endorsed me as the national host for the papal visit to Fort Simpson.

I think the leaders were distracted with other issues at that time or they thought it was a long shot, but the general opinion seemed to be, "Yeah, go ahead. Do it if you can."

I was young, just thirty-three. I was a bit naive, but that didn't limit my ambition and my confidence to say, "It's doable and I'm going to do it."

It was a formidable job; I had to deal with the government of Canada, the Conference of Catholic Bishops and the bishop in the NWT and, of course, I had to take on the Vatican. I went into full battle mode, doing public and private discussions with everybody. I was saying, over and over, "We want to invite the pope to a place of our choosing to meet with the First Peoples of Canada."

Jim Antoine was the Chief in Fort Simpson at the time and he shared the vision and helped put the plan together. I let Bishop Piché know what I was doing and then planned some meetings with the Conference of Catholic Bishops and said, "This is what I'm doing and it'd be nice if you could help me, but I'm going to go anyway." I worked with the government of Canada and put in a request through the papal nuncio to the Vatican through the representative in the Ottawa. My request said, "I am the designated national host for the papal visit in Fort Simpson and Chief Jim Antoine and I have hand written an invitation for the pope. I want to deliver it personally, so I need a meeting."

We got a letter back from the Vatican telling us to come in February.

Right from the beginning, the Canadian Conference of Catholic Bishops and the Canadian government kept telling us that it could not be a political meeting. Our response to that was, "You don't start telling us what kind of meeting we are going to have."

They were almost pleading with me to say it, that it wouldn't be political, so they could reassure themselves and everyone else, but none of us said it. Although we were all baptized as Catholics, most of us discarded it the second we got out of residential school, but of course we didn't say that. I wanted it to have the appearance of a meeting for Indigenous Peoples. It was a political meeting—but we didn't say that either.

Jim Villeneuve, the mayor of Fort Simpson, Jim Antoine and I had a meeting with Pope John Paul II that February during the day. It was an official kind of meeting with his staff hanging around and he never looked at us. He'd listen and talk to us, but he wouldn't look at us. I think it was one of the ways he dealt with having to meet with so many people: he just talked and looked away.

We were invited back to see him in the evening in a private room high up in the Vatican. There he was personable and easygoing, and he looked straight at us while we talked. He told us about growing up in Poland and how he spent his childhood. He wanted to know what it was like in our land and what our relations with the government were like, and he kept coming back to the same questions: "What do you want? What's the most important thing for you?"

"We want our land back," we said, "and we want you to support us in our quest to get our right to self-government in the constitutional talks that we're engaged in."

We told him that we wanted him to come to our land, say the word *Denendeh*, and recognize our place in Canada and acknowledge that all the land was the homeland of the Indigenous Peoples, the Dene and the Métis.

"You have to go someplace special," we explained. "There will only be Indigenous people there, no bishops or white politicians. We're not going to share the stage with anybody. This is our stage. We'll give you some Dene words, and when you speak to us, if you could use our language, since you speak so many, that would be great. And if you want, we can design garments and a special chair, made by our people for you."

He listened to all that and he seemed amused and pleased. We were supposed to have fifteen minutes with him, but Jim Villeneuve timed the meeting and said it was forty-eight minutes that we had with him, completely in private. That made us feel charged up and that he was taking our request seriously.

I had called Whit Fraser at CBC about a month before the meeting and told him what we were going to do and that we wanted media coverage. He came to Rome with a cameraman, and while he didn't go to the private meeting, he covered all our comings and goings, and that made all the difference: Canada could tune in to *The National* and see Steve Kakfwi, Jim Antoine and Jim Villeneuve striding around the Vatican, having just had a meeting with the pope. When we flew back to Canada and stepped off the plane in Toronto, even the customs people knew who we were and where we'd been.

We started organizing right away. It was an ongoing struggle because the Canadian Conference of Catholic Bishops felt they had to be at the meeting. In fact, they wanted a big delegation of bishops from across the country to go. We said no, and then they asked for a smaller delegation, and we said no again. In the end, we settled on two bishops: one from Yukon and Bishop Piché, our bishop, whom I was fond of but not close to.

Around this time, I encountered someone whom I had hoped to never see again.

It was the spring of 1984, a few months before the visit. Bishop Piché said I should meet with his nephew, Father Piché, his designated spokesman on the papal visit preparations. Father Piché was stationed in Fort Providence and one night he invited me for dinner. I drove over from Yellowknife, and when I arrived Father Piché welcomed me in. We had a chat, and then he said that dinner was ready. And who should walk in to serve us dinner? Sister Hebert from Grollier Hall, the nun that had beaten and abused me back in 1960 when I was nine years old. She walked in the room and I looked at her, then immediately turned away and ignored her. But Father Piché said, "Steve, you must know Sister Hebert from your time at Grollier Hall."

I don't remember whether I said anything, but I refused to acknowledge her. And Sister Hebert says, "Oh yes, I remember Steve very well. He was one of my best students."

Again, I ignored it.

She served us dinner. It had been twenty-four years since I'd last seen her, and now I was the head of the Dene Nation and the national host for the papal visit. She was so nervous that she spilled a glass of orange juice. It was pure agony... she felt so bad.

I have thought about that encounter since that meeting, but back then I didn't have time to dwell on it. We had so much work to do. We were constructing a big teepee out of logs. The architect, Douglas Cardinal, designed a concrete monument representing the four directions of the drum. We also had to figure out how to feed people and where to set up camps.

It all happened quickly after that. We were confident it was going to happen.

The day we expected him in Fort Simpson was beautiful: clear and sunny. But once the cold air from the night started warming up from the sun and the air from the river moved in, a thick fog formed. So, we waited, hoping that the fog would clear; the pope's plane had been diverted to Yellowknife, and they were waiting too. Eventually, they decided they had to stay on schedule and move on: they had a Mass in Vancouver later that day. For us, it was a huge disappointment. Some people had spent their last dollar getting to Fort Simpson, and others had come from as far as Tsiigehtchic, Fort Good Hope, Tulita, Bear Lake and Délįnę. Many were elderly.

I was the national host, so Chief Jim Antoine and I had to decide what to do. We called Father Pochat. "Father, we need you to talk to the bishop. Where the pope was supposed to say Mass in Fort Simpson today, can you ask the bishop to come say Mass instead and have a celebration for all these Elders?" He called us back a couple of hours later and said the bishop would do it.

I felt good that I had been able to ask Father Pochat for help. I had fights with just about everybody on the way to Rome and back: the Oblates, the Canadian Conference of Catholic Bishops, the Jesuits. But I had no problem going to Father Pochat and saying that I needed help.

So, on the grounds where the pope was meant to hold Mass for our people, Bishop Piché celebrated Mass instead. That evening we had a big feast and drum dance, but even so, people were disappointed.

We got a message that evening: the Holy Father invited some of us to see him in Ottawa. They had arranged a chartered plane direct to Ottawa, but Jim Antoine and I made the decision right away. We declined the invitation. Jim said emphatically, "I'm not going. My people are here and I'm staying with my people."

I agreed. "I feel the same way. We brought everybody here and we're not going to have a private meeting with him."

We were not being disrespectful; we were respecting our own people by saying if we're in this together, we're not going to accept special treatment.

A couple of days later, Marie and I were watching the pope leaving Ottawa on the news. On the tarmac, there was a microphone so he could say some final words before he boarded his plane, and he said something to this effect: "I regret very much not being able to visit with the Original People of this land; perhaps Providence will allow me another opportunity." And then he looked up with this little smile on his face and said, "Excuse me, I think I have just invited myself for a second time."

I fell out of my chair. "That's it! We got him! He invited himself, but we will hand deliver an invitation and make it official: 'We are officially inviting you back!'"

—

Sometime in 1986, there was an announcement that a World Youth Conference was to happen in Denver, Colorado, in 1987, and Pope John Paul II was going. I saw that and I said, "That's it. How many hours does it take to fly to Fort Simpson from Denver?" We estimated it would be about four hours, so we said, "He just needs to add a few hours to his trip back to Rome."

We used our connections at the Vatican to set up a meeting. I had to do another round of organizing as the national host. Once again, it meant balancing the political aspirations of Indigenous leaders with the Catholic Church, while respecting the devout Catholics among our own people.

In February of 1987—it was a Friday, the sixth of February in 1987, I remember the day—I was in the final stages of planning the details of our meeting with the pope. I was in Ottawa and heading to Toronto to meet with Georges Erasmus (then head of the Assembly of First Nations), John Amagoalik, Smokey Bruyere and Jim Sinclair to solidify their support for me as the host once again. I was also trying to get Marilyn Kane, the president of the Native Women's Association, to be onstage with the national leaders during the visit so she could bring up the issues she was dealing with. Smokey had warned me about that. "Steve," he said, "we'll support you, but don't rock the boat. The Assembly of First Nations is never going to support that, so once you raise it, don't raise a big fuss about it."

But I was coming down with a cold and my head was congested. I didn't know whether I was well enough to fly to Toronto, but I did, and I got to downtown Toronto around noon. I went to the meeting and gave them a report on the work we'd done to secure a second papal visit, and I told them that we were going to send a delegation to the Vatican to deliver another handwritten invitation. I also pitched the idea to include the Native Women's Association, but Georges said no: "It's a political meeting, therefore only the Assembly of First Nations can talk for all Treaty and Indigenous Peoples in Canada."

So that was that. They were happy with the report and they thought I was doing well, but the Native Women's Association was out.

I was only in the meeting for about an hour, and after I left I just fell apart. I had a fever and was totally congested. I was supposed to go back to Ottawa for more meetings, but I stayed in bed at the hotel from Friday afternoon until Sunday morning.

Saturday night, I had this dream where a Spirit came to me. It came right into my room through the door. It didn't have wings or anything, but it looked like a tall woman. She never said a thing, but she put her hands on my chest, my heart, and stared straight at me with a look of compassion. I had this sense that she was a warrior, a warrior woman. And then the Spirit left. I don't know how else to describe it. It was like a Spirit came into me. I remember that dream well; I made a note of it in my notebook. I felt like I had a spiritual experience.

I woke up at four o'clock Sunday morning and my head was clear and the fever was gone. It would be over thirty years later that I would come to realize that an angel of compassion led me through a healing and cleansing ceremony at the edge of the Spirit World that night. When I awoke, my brain fog had lifted and my sinuses were clear. I felt strong, able and light on my feet. I call that my dream of the compassionate angel. I didn't know it then, but dreams would soon start to guide me in a number of ways, helping me to understand my Dene spirituality, my connection to my family and my ancestors, and myself.

Soon after that, the Vatican confirmed that we had another meeting with the pope. I thought, Okay, great, another private audience. We're gonna sit down with Pope John Paul II and discuss how it's going to happen.

This time, however, more Indigenous leaders were interested in coming along and representing their people. Jim Sinclair wanted to go again, and so did an Assembly of First Nations delegation and people like Gordon Peters from Ontario. It was getting crowded; I liked going solo, but I thought it would be okay if I did all the talking. I decided to invite Marie to Rome too.

The way the meeting worked was like this: we went from room to room in the Vatican, and every room had a different function. Finally, we ended up standing in this big room, and I thought, Okay, this is the waiting room, and then they're going to bring us into a smaller room where we're all going to sit down and talk.

But that didn't happen. Pope John Paul II came in with his own entourage and cameraman, and he went down the line that we had all formed, greeting everybody. There were probably about ten people with me and he wasn't singling me out or anything. I realized that we were just one of a thousand delegations that week for him.

After he said hello to me, I introduced him to Marie. She was wearing this beautiful white dress, and of course the pope had a white outfit on too. It was like there was a magnet between them: he started talking to her and off they went. It was almost like I had to pull that old man off and say, "Back off, that's my wife you're talking to—give it a break, John Paul, I'm talking to you!"

When he finally moved on to talk to other people, Marie stepped up to me and whispered, "You're going to lose him; you better get that commitment out of him before this is over."

So, I went and stood beside him, and I made sure I was beside him as he walked around the room. I kept saying the same thing, though I'd phrase it differently: "When are you going to come back and visit us?"

He said, "Talk to my officials." He said it quietly, out of the side of his mouth while he continued talking to everybody else. I'd get close to him again and I'd say, "So, can I tell my people that you're definitely going to come back and visit us this summer?"

And he said, "Talk to my officials."

Stephen Kakfwi, Marie Wilson and Indigenous leaders meet Pope John Paul II at the Vatican in 1987.

I went at it for a little while, following him and asking my question. When we were lining up for the official photograph, I realized I didn't have much time left. I stood beside him so I could say it again. "Can you tell me whether you're going to visit us this year?"

He spoke out of the side of his mouth again: "I told you to talk to my officials."

He kept repeating this answer, but I wouldn't have it. Finally, I said, "Are you going to come and visit us—*yes or no?*"

And he kind of blew up. "*I told you to talk to my officials!*" This was just as the pictures were being taken, so he was posing for the camera as he said it. I started laughing, and when he realized what had happened, he started laughing too. I had pushed him over the edge; the pope had lost his temper with me.

Anyway, he wouldn't commit. Later on, we had some meetings with officials and they were talking to us about the fog on the river in Fort Simpson. There's a news clip of me walking out of there, later that day, speaking in frustration to the reporter: "They want a guarantee that the weather is going to be good!"

The reporter asked, "What did you tell them?"

"Well," I said, "I thought they should have better connections to the big guy upstairs than me, but if He won't guarantee it, I'll give them a personal guarantee. I'll say, 'Look, it's going to be beautiful! Clear skies all day!'"

Once it was reported that they were worried about the weather, they tried to make it happen. And it worked out: eventually word came that they were going to come to Fort Simpson after their time in Denver. I knew that the Canadian government and the Canadian Conference of Catholic Bishops did not want the pope to say anything about the rights of Indigenous Peoples and whether we had a right to self-governance, land and resources. But we wanted him to recognize it. We knew that if we got the pope to say it and recognize it as the most basic of human rights, then we would have achieved something monumental.

So, that was what we tried to do. We arranged to have the pope sit down—in his special chair that we had built for him out of moose antlers—in a circle with Georges Erasmus, Jim Sinclair, Smokey Bruyere, Rosemarie Kuptana from the Inuit Circumpolar Conference, and the president of the Inuit Tapirisat, Rhoda Inukshuk.

What we got from the pope that day wasn't as categorical as I would have liked, but it was still something. By 1987, we didn't think there were going to be any more constitutional talks, but he called for them, and then he included everything else we had asked that he include.

I am aware that the major Aboriginal organizations—the Assembly of First Nations, the Inuit Tapirisat of Canada, the Métis National Council and the Native Council of Canada—have been engaged in high-level talks with the prime minister and premiers regarding ways of protecting and enhancing the rights of the Aboriginal peoples of Canada in the constitution of this great country. Once again, I affirm the right to a just and equitable measure of self-government, along with a land base and adequate resources necessary for developing a viable economy for present and future generations. I pray with you that a new round of conferences will be beneficial and that, with God's guidance and help, a path to a just agreement will be found to crown all the efforts being made.

It was significant that he explicitly supported what it was that we were engaged in. No other nation or international leader had ever done that for us—no prime minister or president.

I'll give you an example of the weight of those words. Shortly after he spoke, the United Nations was debating what language might be included in the UN Declaration on the Rights of Indigenous Peoples. My friend Wilton Littlechild, a prominent Indigenous leader from Alberta, was there and had spent years helping to draft that declaration, trying to help define those

Fort Simpson, 1987. Stephen Kakfwi, Pope John Paul II and Bishop Croteau stand beside each other. ©NWT Archives/Bern Will Brown fonds/N-2001-002: 10953

rights and the responsibilities of the state. He used the remarks that Pope John Paul II had made in Fort Simpson that day to support the wording in the declaration, and he put it forward as a guide for the delegates. The Vatican's representative in the UN came rushing up to Wilton and said, "You can't use those words; the pope never said that!" But Wilton could show him the official text from Fort Simpson. Wilton didn't hear back from that man. If you look at the articles in that declaration, you can see the language we urged the pope to use and the words he spoke.

After Pope John Paul II had completed his visit, I left the stage with him. There was a ramp going down to the ground behind the stage and the two of us walked slowly down it together. It was just him and me, having a chat. I said, "Thank you. We got it done. You did well today, John Paul, I have to compliment you." And we laughed again.

I still think about it now and then. I mean, to have done it once was amazing, but to make it happen a second time? You could say that when you do stuff like that, your ego can run away on you. Pretty soon you think you can walk on water. But the truth is, I am an ordinary person with an uncanny ability to see a bunch of doors in front of me and know exactly which one to step through before it closes. It was also because of our teamwork, our youth, naïveté and complete faith that we could pull it off. We thought there was nothing difficult about it: John Paul, you just have to jump on a plane in Ottawa, go to Fort Simpson, you visit us, pack up your bags and you go back to where you came from.

Simple.

CHAPTER TWENTY-THREE

DANCE WITH THE DEVIL

Over thirteen years, I worked my way from fieldworker for the Dene Nation to its president. Then, in 1987, I jumped from the Dene Nation into a leadership role with the NWT government. It was a natural progression for me, but it happened sooner than I thought it might.

As president, it was my job to work with the Dene Chiefs and Métis leaders on their vision of a comprehensive land and resources agreement. We thought we would need a new constitution for the NWT, one that would replace the existing legislative assembly, and a new form of government that was both Indigenous and public that served the Dene and all the other people living in Dene territory.

At that time, the North was in a period of significant political change. As I've mentioned, the Dene Chiefs were changing their views. Traditionally, they had resisted any involvement with the elected governments in Canada, dismissing them as governments of the colonizers. Here's an example. Back in the mid-seventies, James Wah-Shee was president of the Indian Brotherhood and he was one of the first to run for a seat on the territorial council. The Chiefs would have none of it; they ousted James from his role as president, saying, "We don't want any of our people to sit in the territorial government."

But James was ahead of his time. He used the example of Edzo, a town that didn't even exist until the territorial government chose to build it. The government built the whole town, the houses, water systems, schools, health centres—everything from the ground up. "Edzo?" he'd say. "Who wants to live there? No one. But the government built it anyway." James believed that we had to get Dene people into the territorial government so we would be the ones to decide how that money would be spent.

At that time, I did not agree. I still held the view that the territorial government was a colonial and illegitimate body; any involvement with the NWT government was a dance with the devil and I wanted nothing to do with it. It took me a few years before I changed my mind. Of course, James's perspective was practical, and that's where a lot of us ended up eventually. The socialist rhetoric had served us well during the Berger Inquiry, but we had to find some way to access the money that the territorial government had, and that meant getting our own people elected.

Portrait of Stephen Kakfwi. Published in *Native Press* newspaper, January 19, 1979.
©NWT Archives/Native Communications Society fonds/N-2018-010: 05938

So, in 1979 the Chiefs passed a motion that fundamentally changed the Dene perspective on how the NWT should be governed. The motion encouraged young Dene leaders to run for elected office at both the federal and territorial levels. The Chief's reasoning followed what James had been saying: the best way to help the people in your community was by taking effective control of the government of the NWT.

In that same year, Georges Erasmus decided that he would run in the federal election for the NDP. The Chiefs' motion allowed him to do that without resigning as the president of the Dene Nation. Georges's campaign did not go well. It caused a lot of confusion with the Chiefs, because Georges insisted that he had to follow the talking points in the NDP national platform: the cost of living and subsidies for food. I remember one evening, when people gathered in Délı̨nę in the old community hall for a meeting. I was Georges's interpreter, and everyone was saying, "What is Georges talking about? Why is he talking about the price of a loaf of bread? We have to buy it anyway. And what does 'the cost of living' mean? We want to talk about our land and our future."

But Georges stayed with the NDP platform and he lost that election. He lost a number of votes because he had alienated some of the Métis peoples, and we had underestimated how much the Dene Nation had angered non-Indigenous voters with our opposition to the pipeline. The entire business community in the Mackenzie Valley made sure Georges didn't win.

Some of the Chiefs felt badly after that election. They saw the non-Dene people in the NWT ganging up to reject the candidacy of the Dene Nation president. They didn't change their views though: they still thought the best thing for the Dene would be to have our people in elected positions so they could control where the money was spent. I was still unconvinced.

In the summer of 1987, my term as Dene Nation president was ending and there was going to be an election. I was going to run again. Some of my critics were saying that I didn't understand Treaties because I wasn't Treaty. My grandfather Gabriel had relinquished his Treaty status to qualify for his fur trader's licence and that meant my father was non-Treaty and so were all of us kids. I didn't want to respond to those critics publicly because I thought it was a crock. I've always said, "I'm Dene. You just look at me; I'm as Dene as they come." But I resented feeling like I had to defend myself, so just to put an end to it, I applied for my Treaty status and got it. I don't know if I ever went public with it at the time. I certainly didn't make a big thing of it.

I felt I had good momentum and support leading up to the election. Then, something happened—a detour I hadn't planned.

The legislative assembly held their sessions at that time in the Yellowknife Inn, and one day I went. I was interested and wanted to see how it worked. As I walked in, I saw that they were on break, so I sat in the lobby and had a coffee. Then James Wah-Shee walked in. He's a classy guy and was wearing a suit and tie. "Hi, Steve," he said. "How are you doing? It's good to see you."

We sat down with our coffees and he got a cigarette out. He looked relaxed, like the world was his. He talked for a while, and then he said, "You know, Steve, you're wasting your time at the Dene Nation. Join us. Get working on a campaign and organize your voters and your supporters in Délı̨nę, Colville Lake, Good Hope and in the Sahtu. This is where the money and the action are."

Walking back to my office later that day, I began to think that it might be time to make the shift. I had no idea then that within a few short years the Dene Nation would be decapitated. It had been created for the purpose of helping us get control of our land and our resources and to let the Dene establish a Dene government, and on that spring day in 1987, I believed that such political change was within our reach. We were succeeding. Constitutional development was advancing well and the Dene and Métis Comprehensive Land Claim Agreement was moving along. There were some successes, some failures and some disappointments, but by and large everything was moving.

That's why I was ready to consider leaving the Dene Nation to join the legislative assembly. My friend John T'Seleie held the existing MLA office, but he wasn't planning to run for another term, so that cleared the way for me to give it some serious thought.

At that time, I was in the middle of organizing the papal visit and I didn't want to cause any distractions. I kept my decision quiet, but as soon as the pope left, I campaigned like a man on fire; the territorial election was a month away. Every chance I had, I flew to Good Hope, Colville Lake, Délı̨nę, Tulita or Norman Wells. I didn't have staff, but I was organized: I made lists of people to see or call every day. I was presenting myself to everyone, even to people who had decided they didn't like me when I was at the Dene Nation, because they regarded me as one of the people who killed the pipeline. I was seen as anti-development, but I was persistent. There were a lot of conservative right-wing people and I didn't care; I was at their door or calling and asking to meet with them, again and again.

I had Good Hope sewn up; what I didn't have was Délı̨nę, Tulita and Norman Wells. It was also a little uncomfortable because George Cleary, already a well-respected community leader, was also running and I was parachuting in from Yellowknife. I remember what George said after the election: "We figured you would have momentum because of the pope's visit and your profile, but the pope's visit had a bigger impact than we thought." Before the election, though, I didn't think I could beat George. He had too much support in Norman Wells, Tulita and Délı̨nę.

When I was in Norman Wells, I stayed at the Mackenzie Valley Hotel. Jerry Loomis and his wife, Monica, were the owners. They were polite and honest enough to tell me that they were supporting George. But they saw me come in and out, day after day. Later on, they told me, "You moved a lot of people in Norman Wells just by your work ethic." I left the hotel at eight in the morning and I didn't finish until ten at night. I was working by myself and I went from person to person. I had a lot of momentum, but I didn't have a lot of time. In the end, Jerry and Monica became some of my strongest supporters.

One day I was campaigning in Délı̨nę, and Charlie Nayelle, a local spiritual leader, sent me a message: he wanted to see me. I was thirty-six and a little bit arrogant, so I said, "Well, he's going to have to wait. I'm busy; I'm trying to get people to vote for me, so if he wants to see me, I'll be done around ten or eleven o'clock tonight."

Much to my surprise, when I finished late that night, I found Charlie waiting for me in the hotel lobby. I asked him how long he'd been waiting but he didn't answer; he just smiled, shook my hand and said he wanted to talk to me. He was seen as an Elder and a spiritual leader. So, we sat down and talked, and he asked me, "Do you know the story of the prodigal son in the Bible?"

Of course. It's a parable of a father and two sons. The younger one asks his father for his share of the inheritance, but he squanders it and comes home destitute and begging forgiveness. The father accepts him back, but the older brother, who never left and was always dutiful, is disgruntled.

Charlie asked me, "Which son are you?"

"Well, I'm the wayward one, the prodigal son, of course. I misbehaved and now I'm back trying to do good work and redeem myself to my people."

"No," Charlie said. "I think you're the dutiful son who's been working the father's fields. You're like a machine: you work for the people and you do good work, but you have no heart. You must find your heart, Steve, so that when you do your work, you do it with love and compassion for your people. That is what's missing. If you find your heart, the work you do would be Sacred Work."

I wasn't sure what to say, so I just said, "Well, thank you."

I didn't tell him then, but I disagreed with him. At the time, I thought that it was a good thing if people saw me as a principled man who didn't let emotion cloud his judgment. But I never forgot that. Of course, at this time I was also beginning to realize that this was something I had learned in residential school, that it was better to be cold and not show emotion.

Years later, my mother helped me see Charlie's message more clearly. She was asking me to give some money to my younger sisters and I said no. "If they want money, they should get a job. That's what everybody has to do."

My mother got so frustrated with me; she pounded my chest and said, "Steve, you have no heart. You have no heart!"

I was surprised, but I realized that she could see something that I couldn't: even the people in my family saw me as cold, distant and aloof. I had money; I was a cabinet minister and Marie was working all the time, so we were both making good salaries. Once my mother and I had calmed down, I gave her the money and told her she could do whatever she wanted with it—give it to my sisters if she wanted. I didn't want to know about it.

The point is that I was told as a young politician that I had no heart, and it took me a long time to figure out what that meant.

———

I won the election, and as soon as I was elected as an MLA I became the minister of Aboriginal Rights and constitutional development. When the Dene and Métis were negotiating their comprehensive land claim, the NWT government was a signatory to the process. I always told the federal minister of Indian Affairs that to arrive at a successful conclusion, the government had to get rid of the extinguishment policy, which dictated that to settle any claim, Indigenous Peoples had to agree to extinguish all our rights.

The Indian Affairs ministers always promised me they would "look at it," but the Department of Justice ruled that domain. The lawyers categorically said, "No way. Canada needs absolute certainty, and the only way we can get it is by knowing that you have no rights. To make a deal you must first extinguish all your rights; you have nothing except for the rights that we choose to give back to you."

The Justice Department lawyers called it "cloud on title," because without an agreement, it would never be clear to the Crown or to industry who owned the land. They were worried that if someone bought a one-square-mile piece of property in the Mackenzie Valley, for example, the Dene or the Métis could come in later and claim it.

Although we were involved, the NWT government didn't have a direct say in Indigenous Rights. That was primarily between the federal government and Indigenous people. We had influence over wildlife, land and water management, and subsurface rights, so we were included in the talks, and because I was Dene, I was free to speak and take positions that I thought would best support the Chiefs.

Another big obstacle was bureaucracy. Back then and even to this day, bureaucrats are unwilling to acknowledge the sovereignty of the Dene and Métis peoples. They see the NWT government as the only legitimate government.

Around this time, there was a growing economic disparity between the Inuvialuit, those living in the northern part of the Mackenzie River valley and delta, and the Sahtu and Gwich'in people who lived farther south in the valley. The Sahtu and the Gwich'in had not a penny in their pockets while their northern neighbours, the Inuvialuit, had millions in their bank account. This all happened because the Inuvialuit had negotiated their own regional claim through the Committee for Original People's Entitlement, or COPE. The Inuvialuit had negotiated their own claim, extinguished their rights and settled, and in return they got back some rights and privileges, but they also got money. A lot of it. They bought an airline, now called Canadian North, as well as the Northern Transportation Company, a barging company that supplies the communities along the Beaufort Sea and in the Mackenzie Valley.

The Gwich'in and Sahtu First Nations were living next to these wealthy neighbours who were leaving them behind economically, so they thought they'd be better off with a regional claim like COPE. The Dene Nation was discouraging them, however. We were still hoping to represent the interests of all Dene and Métis in a comprehensive claim.

Finally, in 1991, that comprehensive claim was presented to the Chiefs. Georges Erasmus told everyone to reject it because it had extinguishment in it. His brother Bill Erasmus, then the Dene Nation president, had helped the secretariat that negotiated the claim, but even Bill didn't support it. That meant that no one was there to represent the interests of the people who wanted to accept it or at least wanted the chance to vote on it.

In addition, the Gwich'in and the Sahtu not only were poor but were also feeling pressure because there was talk about another pipeline and they didn't feel ready to deal with it at all. They needed money and they needed some sense of control. So, the Gwich'in people told their Chiefs, "We need something like what the Inuvialuit have. We can't keep going like this." Despite this, the Chiefs wanted to take the deal to their communities so there could be a fair vote. The Sahtu said the same thing.

Unfortunately, a majority of the Dene and Métis Chiefs voted to reject the comprehensive claim before it could be taken to the people for a vote. So, the Gwich'in and the Sahtu said they'd had enough and left the Dene Nation. It was a crucial moment. This is when Bill Erasmus famously said, "Don't worry. They'll be back. They've got no place to go."

The Gwich'in and the Sahtu never did come back, and that was the end of the Dene Nation.

It is one of my great regrets that we didn't have the determination to see that job through. I believed that the claim should have been considered by the communities. We never had a chance to explain it to them, to go house to house and say, "Here's the deal, is it good enough for you?" The Dene Nation also failed in its hope to draft a new constitution for the NWT, to create a new form of government, so to this day we still have the legislative assembly operating under the old NWT Act, making decisions for Inuvialuit, Dene and Métis peoples, and no one knows how it might have been different.

Despite all our criticism of the legislative assembly, we were now a part of it. People like Jim Antoine and I felt we had a mandate to support the directions given by the Chiefs, to make sure there was money for the projects that mattered to them. So, that's what we did when the Sahtu, Gwich'in and Tłı̨chǫ pursued their regional claims. We were there in the legislature to back them and we were successful at it.

CHAPTER TWENTY-FOUR

THE CREATION OF NUNAVUT

As a Dene leader, I was at the centre of the long and difficult path to divide the NWT. Such a move had never been attempted in Canada before; it was the only time in the country's history where the residents of a particular area negotiated a new boundary on the national map. The creation of Nunavut, a home for the Inuit, involved negotiating one of the longest boundaries in the world, and it wasn't done by academics, lawyers or politicians. It was done by hunters and trappers, Elders and Indigenous leaders. To split the NWT in two, they had to put forward a boundary that was acceptable to the majority of people along that border—a traditional line between the Inuit and the Dene.

There were some areas that were disputed in southern NWT, areas where the Dene and Métis couldn't easily agree on a boundary. Eventually, they split it down the middle, and this happened any time there was a dispute. The Inuvik, Gwich'in, Sahtu and Tłı̨chǫ and the people in Délı̨nę and Yellowknife met with the Inuit and negotiated where the boundary would be. It was a wonderful exercise to watch.

For those of us elected to the legislature of the NWT, division posed a challenge. We had MLAs from across the North and we had to decide whether we were for or against it. Although it cost me some political support among the Dene, I supported the creation of Nunavut when I was Dene Nation president and when I held elected office in Yellowknife. I was one of the few politicians or leaders in the western Arctic who did. I made that commitment when I voted for division in the plebiscite in 1982.

It made total sense. At that time, the NWT was a 1.5 million square miles—one-third of Canada—and we had about forty thousand people across two times zones. So, as soon as I heard of the vision to create two territories, I liked it. Division was bold. I thought, I like this dream. I can help make this happen.

I had great respect for John Amagoalik, the Father of Nunavut, during these negotiations. John had this singular obsession: to do anything and everything to create Nunavut. He was single-minded, caustic, abrupt and blunt in pursuit of that. I always admired John. Even when he was being his most unfriendly self, I admired his unrelenting commitment to Nunavut.

One of the first times I met him, I was newly employed by the Dene Nation. I was also the chair of the Western Constitutional Forum, which was asked to work on behalf of western NWT should division happen. John and I worked together on the constitutional side of division. This meant we had to have meetings, and John detested meetings. At one meeting, he came in and said, "Look, I don't give a shit about this meeting and I don't care about what you're going to say, but Ottawa said I have to be here. And if I have to have a meeting, I want to speak first."

We let him speak first, then it was my turn to give a statement. He's sitting across from me and he reaches down, pulls out the *Globe and Mail* and opens it up so I can't see him. He leans back and starts reading the paper while I'm giving my presentation.

There were probably ten people in the room—his people and mine—and I never paused or said anything. I kept talking to John through his newspaper. I gave my whole presentation as if he were looking at me. I never gave him the satisfaction of reacting to what he was doing.

I'm pleased to say things got a little better over the years. As a testament to that, I was the only Dene leader invited to the celebration of the creation of Nunavut in Iqaluit.

One of the most important people in our long debate over division was a woman who got little credit for her leadership. Nellie Cournoyea is a long-time Inuvialuit leader from Tuktoyaktuk. Like me, she was also in the legislature for sixteen years and, like me, for her final four years she was premier. As a premier who was also an Inuvialuit leader, she was caught by geography and history. Inuvialuit land begins where the Mackenzie River empties into the Arctic Ocean, and it stretches east along the coastline. Though the Inuvialuit come from as far west as Alaska and as far east as the Kitikmeot Region, they identify as Inuit. That means that in the division of the NWT, their natural home would be with the Inuit in Nunavut.

Nellie was premier when these decisions were being made, and she is a very practical woman. She knew that if the Inuvialuit insisted on joining Nunavut, then the remainder of the NWT would be landlocked, unable to access the Arctic Ocean or the delta of the Mackenzie River. She also knew this would be unacceptable to everyone in the west. If she pushed to have the Inuvialuit in Nunavut, she knew that would end the concept of a homeland for the Inuit. The only way the Dene might accept division was if there was access to the Arctic Ocean and if the Inuvialuit stayed in the NWT. It was a bind for her. At that moment she was the premier for both the east and the west, so she couldn't be biased toward one side or the other. In order for her to be impartial, she designated me, through a cabinet decision, as the lead and sole spokesman on division. She knew that I was one of the few Dene leaders who would speak publicly in favour of division, and that the Inuit had always recognized my leadership.

Nellie never publicly let on that it was a hard decision to support division when her own Inuvialuit people were excluded from the new territory. I never saw her sad, though I'm sure she had moments of reflection. She did say to me that she knew all along that it was going to come to this, that she was prepared to persuade the Inuvialuit to accept the boundary and vote with their heads and not with their hearts so that the Inuit could have Nunavut.

When the vote for division was held, 56.5 percent of people in the whole of the NWT voted. In the west, 48 percent—fewer than half—of the people voted, and of those people, only 25 percent voted to support division. In the east, the turnout was much higher: 72 percent of the population voted. Of this, 87 percent voted for division. So, it passed. The reason we succeeded is that Nellie used her credibility among the Inuvialuit to speak in favour of division, and I was the only western Arctic leader pushing for it, so we swung the crucial votes for the creation of Nunavut.

On April 1, 1999, the map of Canada changed.

CHAPTER TWENTY-FIVE

STONEFACE

You put me in my place
You gave me my Stoneface
You tried to take my pride
But I learned how to hide
Stoneface

You took me from my home
And everything I'd known
Left me all alone
In the great unknown
Stoneface

—Stephen Kakfwi, "Stoneface,"
from the album *New Strings on an Old Guitar*

One day, Don Morin and I were sitting in a cabinet meeting. I was a minister at the time and Don was the premier. It was a strategy discussion and we were dealing with a particularly difficult issue, but none of the ministers wanted to touch it. So, John Todd, who was then the finance minister, turned to Premier Morin and said, "Donny, why don't you ask Steve to do it?"

I was sitting right there.

Don said, "Good idea, let's give it to Steve. We can always give him the shitty jobs—he doesn't have any friends anyway!"

We all laughed, but it tells you how I was seen by my colleagues. And it was true; that was part of my image. I didn't joke around and I didn't socialize with the other ministers or patronize the premier. I did whatever job I was assigned to do.

In another cabinet meeting, the minister of education said he was getting pressure from people in the communities who didn't want any more Dene or Inuit teachers. They felt that the best teachers were from southern Canada, and the minister told them he agreed.

But I disagreed. I had been the previous minister of education, and I said, "We hire trained Northern Indigenous Peoples first, not from the south.

It is government policy."

I challenged him, and that argument was going back and forth. I got frustrated and said, "You know, I don't believe this! Why don't you take a stand, you little wimp!"

I was sitting on the other side of the cabinet table. Lucky for me it was a wide table, because the guy jumped up and took a swing at me. He just missed. His fist must have been a hundredth of an inch away from my nose. It happened so fast that I didn't even move. The other ministers jumped up, grabbed the minister and sat him down. The premier turned to me and said, "Steve, I think you have something to say to your colleague." Name-calling is apparently worse than throwing a punch and is not allowed.

Everybody was waiting for me to apologize. I just looked at the minister and said, "Excuse me. Are you upset about something I said?"

Then he really exploded. He jumped back to his feet and the other ministers had to restrain him again. They kicked me out of that cabinet meeting. The good news is that they eventually went back to the original policy of giving priority to Northern teachers.

—

I had a reputation as a reliable minister who got things done, but there was one time when a friend of mine pointed out the price of my carefully guarded stoicism. It was during a heated question period. I was getting challenged. One of the questioners was a good friend of mine, Vince Steen from Tuktoyaktuk. Vince was quiet and easygoing and just wanted answers, but for whatever reason, I'd decided that I was going to be terse with my answers.

During a break, the premier motioned to me. He said, "Steve, you should take it easier with your answers. I just talked to Vince and he said to me, 'You know what? Nobody could be born that arrogant!'"

Don laughed. So much for my stoic self. I went over to Vince and apologized.

Another thing that set me apart from others in the legislature was my relationship with the Chiefs. A lot of the MLAs didn't grow up working with the Chiefs and didn't realize the importance of them to the way the North was run. Jim Antoine and I worked almost as if we were MLAs sent to the legislature by the Chiefs. We had a mandate from the Chiefs to settle the issues of land, resources and self-government. We signed agreements with the Gwich'in and the Sahtu, and we had an agreement-in-principle with the Tłı̨chǫ. It went to cabinet, but it stalled. The other cabinet members weren't sure that they wanted to sign it. The people who were present at that meeting would later tell me that this was the only time they'd ever seen me lose my temper. After my outburst, they said, "Well, since you feel so strongly about it, all right then."

A few days later, I got a call from the Tłı̨chǫ Chief, Joe Rabesca, thanking me for pushing the agreement through. I always believed that despite being elected representatives, we had to honour the wishes of the Chiefs and the Elders.

When Don Morin resigned as premier, I put my name forward to replace him. To my great surprise, my friend Jim Antoine ran as well. Ours is a consensus-style government: there are no parties and there isn't supposed to be any formal opposition. The person who gets the greatest number of MLAs supporting them becomes premier. On that occasion, Jim got the MLA votes and he became premier for about a year and a half. When we held the next election, Jim decided he didn't want the job again, so I went for it.

I knew exactly how many MLAs were supporting me, so we discussed whether it would work to appoint cabinet ministers who didn't. I didn't feel comfortable with them. So, when we announced the names of the MLAs in my cabinet, some of the most experienced ministers were excluded. They wanted to know why and the answer (which we never made public) was that they weren't supporting me. I chose to go with people that I could trust rather than have ministers who were hostile. Those disgruntled former ministers created what they called the Oversight Committee.

They operated more like opposition, and this was in a government system that is supposed to have no parties or opposition. It was because of their criticism that I faced two motions of non-confidence during my time as premier.

You see, I didn't believe the early warnings, people telling me how stressful it is when you're the leader, how you always end up looking over your shoulder. Over the years, I worked with all the National Chiefs at the Assembly of First Nations. They were all strong, confident men and yet they all had moments when they'd talk to me about their critics, saying they were "out to get" them. I felt the same when I was premier. Every time an MLA spoke against me, I'd take it as a full-scale assault. After a while, I kind of lost my perspective. All I was thinking was, If you speak against me, you're out to get me.

As a result, leaders end up cultivating a public image as if it's armour. It's what you put on when you're going to battle. It's a defence mechanism that you slowly develop and the more it works, the more you use it. Mine was to be unflappable and stoic and to rarely smile.

Stoneface.

For all the years I was in public life, I never flinched. It was Premier Nellie Cournoyea who first called me Stoneface and I didn't object. I didn't smile either.

In fact, throughout the sixteen years that I was in the NWT legislature, there was not one official portrait taken of me where I was smiling. No, there was one. I saw it in the Ottawa office and I asked them to take it down and stayed there until they did it.

I never raised my voice in meetings, but to tell you the truth, there was nothing gracious about my manners either. I was abrupt and confrontational, which was my way of being strong and decisive, as if to say, "This is what I think and this is the way it's going to be; this is what we're going to do and here's how we're going to do it."

I was never part of the political "boys' club"—the people who spent much of their time together at receptions and in restaurants and bars. I didn't like that and never wanted to be a part of it, so I wasn't. What mattered to me were the people of the North. By the time I was elected to the legislature, I knew every community in the NWT and I knew all the Chiefs, Métis leaders and regional and local leaders as well. I knew what they needed and that was important. Other MLAs, from places like Yellowknife, had no idea of the relationship I had with all those leaders.

For instance, I was once in the members' lounge at the legislature with a new MLA from Yellowknife. I thought, Well, I'll try to be social. I'll go over and do the chit-chat.

It didn't go well.

"Hey there, I'm Steve Kakfwi. How are you? Welcome. So, how are you doing? What communities do you know? Which Chiefs do you know and how many communities have you travelled to?"

"Well, I actually haven't travelled to any communities."

"You haven't been to Behchokǫ̀?"

"No."

"Providence?"

"No, can't say I have."

"Hay River?

"No."

"Norman Wells?"

"No."

"Inuvik?"

"No."

"How about Dettah?" (This community is a twenty-minute drive from Yellowknife.)

"No."

"Oh. What about Ndilǫ?" (Right beside Yellowknife!)

"No, I've never been there either."

"What?! You haven't been to Ndilǫ and you grew up here? You haven't been outside Yellowknife?" By then I was starting to raise my voice and the other MLAs in the lounge were listening. "Are you telling me you spent your whole damn life in Yellowknife and you never went outside of it, and now you're going to vote on money and legislation for people you don't even know? What the hell is that?"

So much for my attempt to do the chit-chat.

CHAPTER TWENTY-SIX

THE THREE CHILDREN OF STONEFACE

Somewhere in the darkness
Somewhere in the night
I found the will to live
'Cause love showed me the light
Stoneface

—Stephen Kakfwi, "Stoneface,"
from the album *New Strings on an Old Guitar*

I learned a lot from my family about love. Kyla is our eldest, and though she didn't know it at the time, she taught me a lot about affection. When Marie became pregnant, I was struggling with this thought: Am I going to be able to love my child? What is it like to have your own child coming into the world, one that comes from you?

I had this fear that I would feel nothing, have no compassion at all, because people have said that I go through life guarded. All the years in residential school and the different traumas I experienced conditioned me to think, Don't feel anything. Hit me with a brick and I'll just keep acting as if nothing happened.

But when Kyla was born, I was in a different world. It was a miracle. It is a spiritual, divine feeling to hold a newborn that is your child. I couldn't even come close to grasping the feeling: I was in awe, a million miles away, and yet right there kissing a little baby that was my baby girl.

With Kyla I also learned about hugging. With Marie, it was something I had struggled with. I'd see Marie, and she'd be happy to see me so she would hug and kiss me, and then I'd be all over her immediately. She'd have to push me away. In my upbringing, affectionate kissing didn't exist. Kiss me and that's a sexual kiss; hug me and that's a sexual hug. Kyla and Marie were the ones who taught me about hugging. Kyla hugged all the time, until she was a teenager: when she came home, when she left, when she was going to bed, when she got up and when she came to say good morning. When her younger sister, Daylyn, was born, it was the same thing. Kyla and Daylyn were hugging each other, their mother and me all the time, and then Keenan came along and it was the same thing all over again. I eventually got around to thinking, I want to teach my mother… I want to hug Mum. How I was going to do it was incredibly stressful.

Marie could hug my mother easily and Kyla would hug the bejesus out of her. And though my mom was a bit uncomfortable with that at first, after a while, you could see her change: she would see Kyla or Daylyn or Keenan and she'd reach out to them herself. I wanted that kind of affection.

I remember the first time I decided I was going to hug my mother. We had all travelled to Good Hope, and when we arrived at Mum's house, Marie, Daylyn, Keenan and Kyla went straight over and hugged her. I followed and Mum was watching me, wondering what I was doing. I reached for her and she didn't reach for me; she didn't know what I was doing. I hugged her quickly, like I wanted to get it over with.

On the next visit, as the kids were hugging her, Mum was on full alert.

I was hesitating and fumbling around, but eventually I made it across the room and hugged her. After that, it was easier. Sometimes I'd forget, and I'd see that she was watching me, thinking, Where is he going to sit, what am I going to say and will he hug me? By the time she was in her nineties, we were hugging all the time. Kyla and Marie opened the door to that.

—

It was about 1990 when I started getting close to my mother, brothers and sisters. It all began with a family dinner, which Marie and I suggested.

I had previously told Marie, "We've never, not ever, had one family dinner where Mum and Dad and all the kids sat together and enjoyed a big meal. It never happened."

Marie said, "Well, what about after your dad died? Did your mother and you guys ever eat together then?"

"I don't think so," I said. "I don't remember any time."

"Well, why don't we organize one?"

So, we planned one on a summer evening, when my mother was trying out the old folks' home in Good Hope; she wasn't sure she wanted to move permanently into the home, so she was trying it out for a few months. When we told my mother about the meal, she said, "Well, go ahead."

But my God, did it ever stress her out. The idea of all of us congregating around her was just more than she could bear. She didn't like the idea that we were going to have to sit down and talk. In fact, all of us were jittery about it. It was a completely new experience.

"What are we going to say?"

"Who are we going to sit beside?"

"What will we eat?"

"How do we start?"

The day came, and a number of us were going to be there: my sisters Cathy, Rita and Yogi, my brother Everett and his soon-to-be-wife, Mabel, my nieces Bonnie and Beatrice, and Marie and me and our three children, Kyla, Daylyn and Keenan. Marie was excited, and I think Rita and Yogi thought it was great, too, but some of us were unsure about it. You'd have to go back to the Christmas of 1969: that would have been the last time we came close to having a family dinner. I know that Mum was thinking, Let's get this over with so I can relax.

I think I know why the idea of a family dinner was hard for Mum. She was away for so many of the years that her children were growing up. Once, when I was probably around five or six, my mother came back from another one of her stays at the TB hospital. We were waiting for her. We'd been talking for hours, planning her return: "Oh, when Mum comes back, I'm going to behave, I'm going to help do the dishes, I'm going to sweep the floor..." So when she walked through that door, we were all so happy to see her, jumping up and down and running up to her and hugging her and kissing her, and she was exuberant as well. It was a great moment.

But then she went away again, probably when I was about eleven years old, and when she came back that time, there was no hugging. I still remember the day. We came back from school and we stood by the door of our house and looked across the room at our mother, who was sitting at the kitchen table with Dad and some other people who were visiting. We just stood there and looked at her. I didn't say anything and neither did Jean, Everett or Cathy. For some reason, we couldn't find it in ourselves to run across the room and hug her. I think it was one of those times when you hesitate, and if you hesitate for a moment too long, you can't move. I think we were also so tired of her coming and going and we didn't know what to make of it anymore. There was some sort of fatigue or indifference starting to grow. The questions were swirling in our heads: How long is she going to be here? Why did she leave in the first place? Does she even care about us? And I think she was hurt by the fact that we didn't run to her.

But we went ahead with that family dinner in 1990. We put a big tablecloth down on the floor and all of us sat down. I think maybe I said the prayer, or maybe Everett, and then we ate. After we had finished eating, I remember Mum saying, "*Kah-Dee*?" Well, are we done now?

"No," we said. "We have some pies. We have dessert coming."

We got those out and we got through the dessert and it still wasn't fast enough for Mum.

During all that, Everett got up and said, "Well, I've got a little announcement: Mabel and I have decided to get married."

We were happy for them and that made us relax a little more, but Mum, you could tell she just wanted to get it over with.

We had many more family dinners after that and Mum eventually got to enjoy them and relax. So, she got used to the dinners and she got used to the hugs—hugs, I should say, that she never initiated, but she got increasingly comfortable with them all the same.

In 1997, Chief Gordon Yakeleya of Tulita invited me to go hunting. The Mountain Dene often invited me to hunt sheep and caribou with them in the fall, so I accepted the invitation, but I told the Chief that I wanted to bring my daughter. Nobody took girls hunting, but I wanted all my children to be comfortable with guns, hunting, travelling in boats and being out on the land. Chief Yakeleya said it should be okay, so we got Kyla all the gear she needed as well as a rifle, a Browning .243 lever-action rifle, a beautiful gun and good for caribou and sheep.

She was about thirteen at the time and she wanted to do it. I said to her, "I'll be there all the time. We'll travel south together by boat on the Mackenzie River, and then we'll go up the Keele River into the mountains. It might rain, it might get cold, it might get hot and we're going to travel with other men. The Chief is going to take care of us, but he is in charge and we have to be quiet; we can't complain and we can't ask too many questions. It's a hunting party. We're going to be moving fast, eating lightly and quickly, and setting up camp. You and I will share a tent."

"Okay, Dad."

So off we went to Tulita. There were two boats and the Chief invited us to travel with him in his boat. Before we left, the Chief talked to everybody in his group. In Dene, he said, "This guy is going to operate the boat and when he's tired this guy's going to take over. I'm going to sit in front. Steve and his daughter, they'll be hunting and travelling with us. And you, George Campbell, you're going to be the cook."

George was the most surprised and sheepish-looking guy in the boat, but he said okay. And that's how we started. Everybody was travelling light, and once we were on the move, we went fast: we'd come ashore for washroom breaks, everybody goes, done. We keep going. We're thirsty, we come ashore, make a quick fire, make tea, eat a little bit, clean up and go. When we were travelling into the mountains, the elevation was increasing and we were against the current, so we weren't just meandering around.

In early afternoon, Chief Yakeleya said it was time to have lunch, so we pulled off to the shore. George made a big fire and got a pail of water boiling, then took out a couple of big whitefish, cut them up and threw them in the pot. Fifteen minutes later and our boiled fish was ready. We ate, threw the leftovers in a container and cleaned up, and away we went.

That evening, we set up camp some way down the river. George boiled pork chops, which was pretty tasteless, but we ate it along with some bannock and crawled into our tents for the night.

The next morning, we woke up to a beautiful day. George was still the designated cook, and I was wondering, What is he going to boil this time?

He went down to the river, got his pail of water and put it on the fire. It started boiling, and Kyla and I watched as he went to the grub box, took out a big container of sliced bacon and threw all of it in the boiling water. For Kyla, that was it. She turned to me and whispered, "Dad, is he going to boil *everything*?"

"I hope not, but he might!"

We had George's boiled bacon with a dozen eggs he'd thrown in there too. Afterward, somebody started saying we should start cooking our own stuff, so it got a little better.

We spent five or six days up in the mountains, and Kyla was great. We had rain and a little bit of snow, the river was low and then it was high after the rain, and she never once complained. The hunting was great too: we got some sheep, moose and caribou. And that was her first big hunting experience.

—

I like the way my family has grounded me. Sometimes I was not aware of it and sometimes it surprised me—like the time when the MLAs were trying to vote me out of office with a non-confidence motion. It was a hectic time. There was a lot of anger on both sides, and I was even getting phone calls to my house. At some point, my son Keenan phoned the local radio station. He was about twelve years old. He said, live on air, "I think he should stay because I love him and he's my dad."

When he was older, Keenan honoured an Elder, an act brought on by a vision of mine. It was some years after Everett passed on and Rabbi, our childhood friend, had decided to go to university at the age of sixty-five. He'd been accepted as a mature student at the University of Alberta, so I offered to help Rabbi find a place to rent but he said he didn't need any help. I saw Rabbi again later that summer before his courses were due to start and asked him again if he had a place to stay in Edmonton.

"Steve, don't worry about it," he said. "It's all taken care of."

Then September came and I got a late-night call from Rabbi. "Steve, I'm in Edmonton. I'm in a motel 'cause I don't have a place to stay. I'm going to go broke pretty soon. I wonder if you could help me?"

I kind of lost it. "Rabbi. I talked to you twice about this and you wouldn't listen. You know what? This is too damn bad. I'm tired and it's late. I can't help you. Good night!"

I got up the next morning and as I was coming down the stairs I noticed that Keenan was up before me, which was unusual. I was halfway down the stairs when I heard the voice of my brother Everett, clear as a bell. He talked to me in Dene. "Ah, he's a nuisance," Everett said. "Yes, he's irritating. But help him. Help him anyway."

My son knew right away that something had happened. "Dad, are you okay?"

"Yeah, I'm okay."

"Dad," Keenan said. "What just happened?"

I said, "Your uncle just spoke to me."

So, I told Keenan about Rabbi's phone call the night before and that I had hung up on him, and then I told him what my brother had said.

Keenan said, "Dad, if your brother speaks to you from the Spirit World, then we've got to do it. I'll help you. I've got everything in storage in Edmonton that we'd need to furnish a one-bedroom apartment. Let's drive down and set that up for Rabbi. That's what your brother wants you to do."

My first thought was no. I was so damned mad at him. But Keenan persisted. "Call my old landlord," he said. "He might have a place for Rabbi."

So, reluctantly, I called the landlord. He said, "You know what? That guy already filled out an application with me for an available apartment, but how can a man be sixty-five years old and have no credit rating? It's like he doesn't exist. He has no credit card and he's never rented a place in his life. What kind of a person is that?"

I explained that it was because he had grown up and lived in Good Hope where there is nothing to rent and nobody needs credit cards.

"I can't rent it to him." The landlord was firm. "I don't even know if he has a bank account… but," he said, "I'll rent it to you!"

So, I agreed and Rabbi had a place to stay—just like that.

A few days later, Keenan and I drove to Edmonton and helped the movers with all the stuff he had in storage—right down to paper napkins and toilet paper. So, at the end of the moving day, there's Rabbi sitting at his kitchen table with this smirk on his face. He looked at me and he said, "Of course, you had to do this for me."

I said to him, "The ONLY reason that I came down is because my son wanted to help and because of Everett."

Rabbi never forgot that. He always asked after Keenan. A couple of years later, he got cancer and passed away in the winter. In the spring of 2019, when I went back to Good Hope, I wanted to visit Rabbi's grave. I went to the cemetery and looked everywhere for him but I couldn't find him. Finally, I decided to go to the area where my family is buried: my grandparents, my parents, my sister Jean and Everett. When I got to Everett's grave, there, buried right beside him, was Rabbi. I thought, You know, they started off in the cradle together and, after all those years, here they were lying side by side. It couldn't have ended better.

—

One of our favourite family stories involves our youngest daughter, Daylyn, when she was about seven years old. We'd been invited to a celebration in Colville Lake. Several couples were getting married and my sister NeeNee was one of the brides. Colville Lake is a remote community northeast of Good Hope with only about seventy people living there, so it was a big event and we wanted to be there. The NWT bishop at the time, Bishop Croteau, thought he should be there, too, so he flew in.

There's a little log church there, about twenty by forty feet, and that's where the event was held. Everything seemed set for the big celebration—but the wine was missing. Somebody had made off with it. So, we had a Catholic bishop and no wine, but we were told that someone got hold of something to replace it and the service went ahead.

It was a beautiful, clear day with no wind, and it became increasingly hot. That afternoon, the church was packed and it was like a sauna inside. Some of us were all dressed up and everybody was sweating. Little Daylyn was sitting there with Kyla and Keenan, wide-eyed and taking it all in.

I think everybody was hoping it would be a fifteen-minute ceremony, but it was an hour and the church kept getting hotter. Once the ceremony was over, the bishop got up to start Mass. This was always the worst part of church because you never know how long the sermon is going to be. So, Bishop Croteau starts, and I think he threw his original sermon away because all he said was, "God loves you. You are all his children, so pray and be good. Today we have witnessed some young women and men be married in the eyes of God."

He then reached toward the wine alternative. It was a big plastic jug of water and beside it was a package of Kool-Aid. Daylyn was fixated on the bishop. Others in the congregation were paying attention, too, and the bishop smiled, pleased with the sudden interest he had generated. "Marriage," he said, "is like putting this package of Kool-Aid into this jug of water: once it is done, you can never divide them again. It is easy and natural; all you must do is wait for them to mix."

He poured the red powder into the jug and paused dramatically; Daylyn was riveted. "But just water and the Kool-Aid are not enough. It is still not a real marriage, because something important is missing. Do you know what that might be?"

Nobody cared to answer.

"What is missing is in fact the most important part of the marriage." He stepped back dramatically, whipped back his long white garment, reached into his pocket and flourished a bag of sugar for all to see. My daughter's eyes popped even wider. "Yes. The sugar is the love in a marriage; it makes everything sweet. Without the sugar or the love, everything is flat. So, my young people, I say to you, love one another as you do today for the rest of your lives—and keep the sugar in your marriage."

The bishop beamed and concluded his sermon. He performed the Eucharist with bread and Kool-Aid, which he blessed. When Mass ended, everybody rushed out into the summer evening gasping for some cool air.

The church was still like a sauna and the bishop himself began to disrobe beside the altar, but Daylyn was undeterred. "Mom, can I go see that man up there?"

Before we could answer, she jumped over the pew onto the next bench and scurried up the aisle to see the bishop. She scrambled up there and presented her little self in front of the bishop, and the bishop looked down at her and said, "Why, hello, little girl. What is your name?"

"My name is Daylyn."

"And what can I do for you, little girl?"

She gulped and said, "Please, can I have some of that *juice*?!"

The bishop laughed as Marie and I were walking up the aisle to take her away. The bishop said of course, poured her a cup and, while laughing, said, "Maybe your mom and dad could use a little bit of this as well."

We didn't know it then, but someday we would.

CHAPTER TWENTY-SEVEN

THE DENE AND THE DIAMONDS

N ot every Dene that went into the legislature was asked by the Chiefs to go there, but some of us still felt like we had a mandate and we got that mandate in large part from the Chiefs. When the Chiefs said they wanted housing and one of us was the minister of housing, they'd come and meet with us. We knew every community in the valley and what the people needed in those communities, so we understood what the Chiefs were talking about. The other key reason to be in the legislature was to help our people benefit from the resources of the North.

Like diamonds.

In 1991, a few prospectors discovered evidence of kimberlite and carefully tracked it to its source, and there they found diamonds. It was an epic find, one that could be worth billions of dollars.

Dene leaders were increasingly looking for economic initiatives, projects that would benefit their people and bring jobs and contracts. But when diamonds were discovered in the early nineties, we realized that none of us had any idea of what diamonds were about. We could see that the Tłįchǫ land was being completely overrun: overnight there were prospectors running through the communities, staking areas that went right through their villages. There were even people jumping out of helicopters with stakes.

The Tłįchǫ were focussed and strategic. They knew they couldn't stop the rush, but they could use it as leverage in negotiations with the federal government for a regional agreement on land, resources and self-government. The first mining company, BHP Billiton, understood the uncertainty: they would have to invest billions, but there was the cloud on title to deal with. So, while the diamond rush expedited the whole Tłįchǫ process, we were still moving relatively slowly. Ministers like Mike Ballantyne, Gordon Rae, John Todd, Jim Antoine and I had many questions. How do you value diamonds? How do they get priced? Who sells them? What do diamond cutters do? What do the mining companies do? Who are the players? What are their roles? What does the government have to do with it?

We had to scramble. There were many trips to New York, Antwerp and London, where you find the people who work in the diamond business, a business that felt kind of secretive and mysterious. We quickly learned that this was a different kind of business than we were used to. I'll give you an example: I met with De Beers in London. When I got there, I checked into my nice hotel and then I went out. When I came back to the hotel, my room had been broken into. It was a professional job; I was up on the sixth floor, so somebody had crawled up to my window from the outside, cut a nice, neat circle in the windowpane, reached inside and opened the window latch. They went through all my stuff meticulously and stole some pictures of my family. We reported it to the police and the hotel moved me to another room.

The diamond dealers in Antwerp, they looked like they were wearing suits from the fifties. I'd say, "Well, can you show me some diamonds?" and they would sigh, reach into their shirt pocket, take out a piece of paper and unfold it, showing me a small handful of diamonds. And they were always saying, "Oh, the market is not good, the prices are low, it's hard to make money."

We needed to prepare for the day when we would hopefully sit down with a company and negotiate an agreement. We knew that we wanted to be involved in the construction of the mines and in the operating phase. We wanted to be players and we wanted benefits for our people. For the construction, we wanted a certain number of Northern people to get a percentage of the jobs, and of that, a certain percentage of them to be Indigenous. We wanted an evaluation facility to be built in the North so that the diamonds weren't flown from the mine site to Antwerp or New York to be examined, as was the original plan. We wanted the government to be able to judge the value of the rough diamonds that were to be shipped out, so we insisted that an evaluation facility be based in Yellowknife. Finally, we wanted a monthly allocation of a certain size and type of diamond available for cutting and polishing in the North.

The first company we had to deal with was BHP Billiton. They were one of the biggest mining companies in the world at the time and they would barely look across the table at us when we met with them. Eventually they realized that they had to deal with us to get environmental and other approvals in place if they wanted to start on time, so they decided, pretty reluctantly, I think, to try to make a deal. We got some contract and job matters resolved, but we couldn't agree on the evaluation facility and they wouldn't agree to allocate us any diamonds to be processed in the North; they said it didn't fit into their business plan.

We were at loggerheads. John Todd, our finance minister, said that if the mining companies were not willing to make some Northern accommodations that he'd happily introduce a tax on them that would be big enough to choke a horse. That statement made the news and the company took note because their shareholders saw the comment, but it still wasn't enough to get an agreement. Premier Don Morin was also getting frustrated with the slow pace of the negotiations and said that if there wasn't some progress soon, the NWT would just leave all the diamonds in the ground.

BHP Billiton thought he was bluffing and we all assured them he was not. They started to move a little bit once again, but nowhere near enough.

At one point in the process, I heard that a diamond-cutting firm based in Victoria, BC, had reached an access agreement for diamonds with BHP Billiton. I was the minister of economic development at the time, so that night I jumped on a plane to Victoria and met with the owner of the diamond-cutting firm. He was quite happy to meet with me—in fact he was flattered that a minister would fly all the way from Yellowknife to southern BC to meet him.

He said that BHP had agreed to give him a monthly allocation of diamonds, but they hadn't worked out the details yet. So, I said, "If you come to the North and set up a facility there, we'll support you and you can do the cutting and polishing there." He said he had plans to do that already.

When I got back to Yellowknife, I announced at a cabinet meeting that I had achieved an agreement to have some of the diamonds cut and polished in the North. I didn't tell them any of the details, the who or what, I just said I got it.

John Todd went ballistic, saying he didn't know what I had done but that he was convinced I had sold out the North.

But I hadn't. I had figured it out. BHP was saying, "No, we're not going to give a monthly allocation to the government of the NWT"—but they hadn't shut the door on monthly allocations to the private sector. We really didn't care who did the work, as long as it was done in the North. All we had to do was get a diamond cutter to say, "Yeah, we'll set up a facility in Yellowknife and we'll do the cutting and polishing there."

The trick was to get a certain size and quality of diamond handled in Yellowknife so that it would be economically worthwhile. The cutters said they could do it without subsidy, so BHP was happy. We also had agreements for the contracting, jobs and training, making sure there were specific provisions for Northern and Indigenous workers and contractors. Soon after that, BHP's first Northern diamond mine, the Ekati mine, was in production.

Another diamond mine was surveyed in the early nineties. That one would be called the Diavik mine. Another huge mining company, Rio Tinto, was in charge of this one. Rio Tinto had a group based in Yellowknife that was doing the negotiating for them, and it was impossibly difficult to deal with them. It went on for over a year and a half. We couldn't get anywhere

on the evaluation facility, we couldn't get anywhere on the monthly allocation of diamonds and we were having slow negotiations on the percentage
of jobs and contracts we'd have during the construction phase, as well as
what the arrangements would be during the operational stage.

The negotiations were still dragging on through the summer of 1999.
Some of our people went on holiday and Rio Tinto, based in London, England, did not seem interested in talking to us. All they offered was a Rio
Tinto executive who happened to be flying through Calgary. That man
grudgingly agreed to give us half an hour of his time at the airport, at eleven
o'clock at night. We were not impressed, but I offered to meet with him.

I got his name and had my staff research him, but instead of going
to Calgary I sent a message to the president of Rio Tinto. I said, "This is
unacceptable. If you want to operate a diamond mine in the NWT, then
you have to come to terms with the fact that we're the government here and
that right now we're not happy. The offer of a half-hour meeting at eleven
o'clock at night at an airport in another city is no way to conduct business.
I'm flying to London next week and I need a meeting."

To my surprise, a message came back. "I'd be happy to meet with you;
just say when you are arriving and we will make the arrangements."

So, I flew to London and had a meeting with Robert Wilson, Rio Tinto's president and CEO. The offices there are built like palaces with marble
everywhere. The wealth is incredible.

Robert was a gentleman and he was happy to receive me. He said,
"Okay, what can I do for you?"

"I need to finalize the agreement to have our contractors and workers
guaranteed," I explained. "We have already done it with the other diamond
mine so I don't know what the holdup is, but we're tired of your group hard-
lining with us. We've had enough of it."

"Well, that sounds reasonable to me. We'll push them to agree. If that's
what you've done with BHP Billiton, there's no reason why we can't do the
same. What else?"

"We want the evaluation facility to be in Yellowknife. We don't want
you to fly the diamonds out of your mine straight to Europe. They must
come through Yellowknife. There's a good airport where we could build an
evaluation facility."

"Okay, that sounds reasonable. What else?"

"We want a monthly allocation."

"No, I can't do that," Robert said. "We're not interested in subsidies
having anything to do with our operation."

"I'm not talking about subsidies. We want monthly access based on size and quality of diamonds that we can cut and polish in Yellowknife. We already have a cutting and polishing business with allocations going to BHP Billiton. The private sector can be involved, from Europe or the United States or Canada, but they have to work out of Yellowknife. It's already being done."

"Well, then, I don't see any reason why we can't, as long as there's no subsidies involved. What else?"

"That's it."

It took us fifteen minutes. When I told him how long we had been negotiating with his staff in Yellowknife without reaching any agreement, he asked me what I thought of them.

"I think, to be quite honest, that they're all dead from the arse up."

This made him laugh. I asked for our agreement in writing and he said he would do it—and he did. He honoured it. I guess word got out in Yellowknife among his staff about my comment, but I didn't mind.

Ultimately, the diamond industry has been great for this part of the NWT. When diamonds came along, the two gold mines in Yellowknife, Con and Giant, were starting to wind down. Yellowknife would have been economically devastated without those two gold mines, but the diamond mining activity happened at the right time and was picking up the slack; there was no hiccup at all. We were lucky that way. It was one of those things where everything fell into place. And it's been good for our people. It has made a difference.

Chapter Twenty-Eight

The Devil in Me

I want to talk about the counselling sessions that helped me through the trauma of residential school, but I should start by talking about the devil, my preoccupation with the devil.

The Federal Day School in Fort Good Hope was a public school, but there was a crucifix hanging on every wall. Every few days the priest would come to school and teach us about the catechism, God and the story of Creation. He'd talk about and Jesus and Mary and all the saints and angels—and they all had white skin. Then there was Satan or Lucifer, the bad one. He had dark, dark skin like me, and claws, horns and a forked tail, and he was surrounded by fire and screaming, dying people. The priests, brothers and sisters would always tell me, "That's where you're going to go if you're a bad kid."

And I always thought I was a bad kid because that's what they told me. Sister Hebert said it outright. "You are just like a little devil."

I thought the devil must be everywhere, the way that God was everywhere. That's one of the remnants of being raised in the grips of the Catholic Church and growing up in a religious community. Maybe I got indoctrinated more than other people. Maybe my imagination was more vivid than the other kids, but I believed it and I was horrified by it.

When I lived with Uncle Albert and Auntie Dora in 1960, my cousin Michel and I had to sleep upstairs in the attic. Michel slept at the far end of the attic and he always came back late, long after I went to bed. I slept closer to the stairway; it was brighter there and I was scared of the dark. Sometimes I didn't want to go to bed, so Uncle Albert, a fiddler and a good storyteller, would tell me stories. He told me one about the devil.

"There was this town where people were really bad," he said. "They liked to drink and dance, and the priest tried to talk to them but he wasn't getting anywhere. Finally, one day, this dark stranger came to town. He had a top hat, gloves and big boots, and the women liked the way he looked. That night, there was a dance in the community hall and all the people were dancing when that man walked in. He had power: people were watching him. After a while he chased the fiddler off the chair, grabbed the fiddle and started playing 'The Devil's Reel.' It's sharp and it's fast, and he's really playing and the strings are starting to smoke, and the people couldn't stop dancing. It's like they were hypnotized. Right in the middle of it all, the priest came bursting through the door with a big pail of holy water and said, 'Devil begone! Satan begone!'

"He threw that holy water all over the devil and it burned him: he was screaming, and then he got mad. He took off his hat and there were his horns; he tried to pull off his gloves but his big talons poked through them. His tail was swishing around out of his pants and his big toenails burst right through his shoes!"

My uncle looked right at me and called my Dene name out in this loud voice, "Dee-win! Dee-win! That was the *devil!*"

He bent over and slapped his knees with laughter. Then he said, "All right now, you go to bed."

Oh God, I didn't want to move, I didn't want to get up, but I did. I walked across the floor and had got halfway up the stairs when Uncle Albert started imitating "The Devil's Reel": "*Da-dada-da-dada-da-dada-da,* that was the devil, Dee-win! *Dum-dada-dum-dada-dum,* Dee-win, that was the *devil!*"

I froze halfway up the stairs. He laughed again and said, "Go get your blankets. Come down here. You can sleep on the couch."

It sounds like he was being mean, but we were having fun. Some of the Dene who've been to residential school are not affectionate people. My uncle, aunt and cousin had all been to residential school and they were kind to me but they were really not very affectionate.

—

In 1985, when I was working and travelling as the head of the Dene Nation, I still hadn't faced my own demons from residential school. I had not uncovered those memories. In the fall of that year, before I quit drinking, I was in Ottawa a week or two every month.

There were three or four trips when, during my free time (and you have a lot of it when you're waiting to meet people in Ottawa), I was obsessing about the devil. It was a difficult time; I was distant from my family and I was drinking, always tired and never sleeping. I was convinced that the devil did exist and that the evil was inside me.

When I was in a hotel, I'd rent a VHS player and the movie *The Exorcist.* I was obsessed with two scenes from that film: one is the image of two dogs fighting, with the wind swirling around them in a desert. That was familiar to me; I've seen dogs in the North get so angry that they'd kill one another. They become oblivious to everything except the dog they're trying to kill.

The other scene is when the priest, Father Damien, is trying to get the demon to leave Regan's body. He's tired and getting weak, and suddenly you can see in his eyes that the demon is starting to possess him, moving into his body. The priest gets angry and he loses it, and at the last second, just when he realizes what's happening, he lets go of Regan and jumps out of the window, killing himself.

The more I drank, the more I watched this stupid movie. I was convinced that I was possessed, that the devil was in me, that evil was inside me, so I kept drinking to numb the fear.

I haven't watched *The Exorcist* since. In fact, I don't watch any horror movies. I like to sleep at night and I don't need any more demons. I like to think that I'm still kicking their asses out the door one by one, until I kill them all.

But it would be another ten years before I even thought about therapy. In 1998, when I was confronting my memories of the abuse at residential school, Marie and I thought that it would be good for me to get some professional counselling.

I was under this crazy notion that I'd go to Edmonton, see a counsellor, tell my story and cry my eyes out and I'd be okay in about two weeks. That would be that. So, I was quite surprised and angry when an Elder said it would take a bit longer that. "Well, what?" I asked. "A month, two?"

"No, a little longer than that."

"Like, six months, a year—what is it?"

"Put it this way: every day that goes by and you talk about the abuses you suffered, it gets a little easier."

That's when I realized that he was talking about my whole lifetime. He's talking about years, and there was no guarantee that I'd ever be better, or normal. I don't even know what normal is.

I talked to a counsellor about the abuse I endured at Grollier Hall, but as I talked about that, it turned out I had memories of my school that year as well. I attended grade three at Sir Alexander Mackenzie School. It was both an Anglican school and a Catholic school, but the Catholic kids and the Anglican kids were kept apart from each other. They were taught in different classrooms. At night, the Anglican kids went back to Stringer Hall and us Catholic kids went back to Grollier.

Sister Leduc was my grade three teacher. She was a bit of a relief for me because—while she still dressed in a habit, which gave her that stern look—she was, for the most part, strict but never angry. She never hit anybody or strapped anybody. For me, that was compassion, especially compared with Sister Hebert, who seemed to take pleasure in hurting me.

There was a young girl in the class named Anne Porter. She never spoke, and at the smallest provocation, like if Sister Leduc asked her too many questions, she'd start crying. She was an Inuit girl and she was on the verge of tears all the time. I remember that she was the saddest little girl and I always wondered why.

There was another student, an Inuk named Wesley Joe. He was always late and he often fell asleep in class. He wasn't living with us at Grollier Hall; he lived in town, in Inuvik. Sister Leduc constantly berated and ridiculed him, and I remember he always seemed so indifferent, like she was the least of his problems, whatever his problems were. It shows you the kind of kids we were: there was Anne Porter, who Sister Leduc tried to be gentle with because she always broke into tears, and there was Wesley Joe, who couldn't do anything right.

One of the things I remember about that class is that I had to memorize the multiplication table, the whole thing. One times one, one times two, all the way up to twelve times twelve. I memorized it and I passed grade three. The strange thing about it is, going into grade four in the fall of 1960 in Good Hope, I had completely forgotten the multiplication table. Like, what is this? I think part of the result of that trauma from Grollier Hall was that my mind blanked out certain things and I guess the multiplication table was one of them.

One of my strongest memories of that class came when Easter was approaching. Sister Leduc said it was the biggest day in the Catholic calendar, and to celebrate she wanted us to draw a picture that we would mail to our parents. She asked me who I wanted to send my picture to, and I said, "I want to send it to my mother. She's in a hospital in Edmonton."

"Okay, I will do that."

I drew this picture of Jesus floating in the air in front of his tomb, with a big hole in the rock and an angel sitting on this round rock that had been rolled away. It was elaborate. I guess that's why I remember it, and I was proud of it because the sketch looked great. So, I coloured it in with some crayons. There was a lot of light, because he radiated light and it was Easter morning, but, you know, working on the same thing week after week, there are only so many details like leaves and trees you can work on. So, after a while, everything was coloured and I felt I was done. The only parts of the drawing that I didn't colour were Jesus's hands, feet and face, so his skin was white like the paper I used. But Sister Leduc said I had to put some colour there to finish it.

So, I tried a little bit of yellow and pink or something, and it went well until I started to try to put some shade in it. When you put too much crayon on paper it loses its translucence, so his skin started to get darker and darker, and after a while the crayon was caked on his face. He started to look just about as dark as I am and it didn't look right because Jesus is supposed to be white. I was in a dilemma. What do I do? I couldn't take the crayon off and it was too late to start over again, so I handed it in to Sister Leduc. She took a long look at it and said she would send it to my mother.

At the end of that school year, in the last two days of class, Sister Leduc asked some of us to stay and help her clean up, and I thought that was great: the longer I could stay away from Sister Hebert and Grollier Hall, the happier I was. So of course I stayed, and Sister Leduc was happy with that. When we were cleaning up, I came across some papers and there, in the stack, was my drawing of the dark Jesus, the drawing she said she would send to my mother. All that time, I believed my mother had received the drawing for Easter. I didn't know what to make of it, but I didn't say anything. I didn't want to know the answer. Whatever the reason, I felt badly that I made him that dark and I felt badly that my mother never got to see it.

But I passed grade three, which was a good thing, I suppose, and Sister Leduc gave out Catholic gifts. I got a rosary. It was a transparent, emerald-green plastic. To me, it felt like a gift from God, because it made me feel like I was okay. *Sister Hebert said I was a little devil and that I am dark like the devil, but Sister Leduc didn't say that and she gave me a rosary, so I must be okay.*

I carried it around in my pocket until I went back to Good Hope, and when I got back I showed it to my grandparents as if to say, "Look, I was such a good kid, the nun gave me a gift." I didn't really believe that, though. I didn't tell them about the abuse and the beatings. I don't think there was anybody in the world that I felt I could confide in. If Mum and Dad were around, I couldn't confide in them. I was convinced that I really was bad; I was a bad kid because I was fighting all the time and that meant I was somehow evil. I believed it because if Sister Hebert was a nun, she must have the ability to see it inside me. And that's why I was so unlovable: I was touched by evil.

I never told anybody about it until after I was married.

As for that green rosary, I wore it around my neck that summer like it exonerated me. One day, I was hanging out with my friends at one of our favourite swimming holes, the place we called Fiddlesticks. I dove in, and when I was dog-paddling my way back to the surface, somehow my hand got caught in the rosary and it broke. When I climbed out of the water, I realized it was gone. I kept diving to look for the darn thing, feeling around in the muck and the silt. I looked for it day after day but I never found it.

A lot of these stories came out in the counselling sessions that I had.

I had a hard time with counselling once I started talking about the abuse and suffering. I once described it as letting somebody put their arm into my mouth and reach down my throat to the pit of my stomach and start pulling. That's how it felt the first time. The first time I let go, I couldn't stop it; it was like my body was pushing out everything that it could possibly push out. I'd hung on to this ugly, poisoned, festering boil since 1960, and suddenly I couldn't get rid of it fast enough. It was like an explosion. You cry. You can't breathe.

I thought, Okay, help me get the tears out so I can get on with my life. But I really had no idea. That's when I realized why people commit suicide. Before, when I heard about adults or kids who were committing suicide because they were sexually abused, I thought, you know, Wimps, nothing but wimps. But I hadn't realized the depth of it until those counselling sessions. The pain, the waves of anguish—it was unbearable. It's like throwing up and not having time to breathe, just throwing up and throwing up and throwing up. It's endless and you feel like you're dying.

I told my counsellor about the dark room and the endless abuse at Grollier Hall, and during the session I also realized that it wasn't just Grollier Hall. I remembered a time when I was fifteen years old and three of us kids were going back to Grandin College in Fort Smith. We had to sleep overnight at the home of a teacher in Norman Wells along the way, and that teacher put out bottles of scotch, rum, rye and gin and said, "You guys have a good supper and then after supper, help yourself. Just don't go outside."

What did he think was going to happen? We ate and the three of us sat down on the carpet and we tried every bottle that was in that collection and, of course, all of us zonked out. We were fifteen years old. When I woke up, I was in bed with that man. I don't remember anything except waking up and I'm filthy and sticky and puking and hungover, and I'm naked in bed with that guy. I later confronted him about it in a letter, and I've always regretted writing it because he wrote back and said, "What are you complaining about? You enjoyed it as much as I did."

Because of this comment, all through my high school years I thought I must be gay. Why else would that have happened? But I was fifteen years old. That was clear as anything. I woke up with this man. I had been raped in my sleep.

So, for years, every time someone asked me whether I remember any time when I was sexually abused, I always said no. I would lie because I couldn't live with it. It's a difficult thing to explain, but that's where I was.

When I first disclosed it in Edmonton, the counsellor told me that it was important to know that my body was reacting naturally when I was unconscious and that it wasn't my fault. Then we talked about Grollier Hall. We talked about it and I had lots of tears. After about an hour and a half, we finished up that session and I called a taxi. They told me it would take fifteen minutes, so I went to the washroom. I was in there for forty-five minutes. I was so sick: I had diarrhea and I was throwing up, and it felt like my whole body was in a state of revulsion. When I finally got out of the washroom, the staff asked whether they should be concerned and I just said, "Something I had for lunch, I guess."

They called another cab for me, but when I got back to my hotel room it got worse. There was nothing left in my stomach, but I was still dry heaving and having diarrhea. There was snot coming out of my nose, it felt like there was stuff coming out of my ears and I couldn't stop crying. I thought I was going to die; I thought I was going to choke on my own vomit, except there wasn't any vomit. There was nothing left inside me. It was as if my body was so sick of holding on to this stuff that when I finally disclosed, it pushed *everything* out it possibly could, like it needed to be purified. It was a near-death experience.

You can't breathe—you're choking—you're crawling around on the hotel floor—you're lying in the bathtub—you soil your clothes—you lose control of your body again and again.

I got back to my room at the Westin Hotel around four o'clock and that went on for four hours. I got to a point where I almost started drinking again. I had been sober for over twelve years, yet I remember lying on the floor and thinking that if I weren't so physically weak, I could just open that mini-bar, thinking it'd be so good, you know, to medicate. If I had only two vodkas, I thought, I'd be okay.

At eight o'clock that night, I had my last set of clean clothes on and I got to the door and said out loud, "Okay, I think I'm ready to go now." To nobody in particular, just: "Okay, I think I'm ready to go out now."

I went down to the lobby and I said to the concierge, "I'm starving and I want to treat myself to something. Can you recommend a good place to eat?"

And they replied, "There is a food festival happening right now, one block from here, with food from every corner of the world; you could have African food, you could eat Chinese, Korean, French, German—everything."

It was like God timed it. He was there for me; he arranged it so that when I walked out of that hotel room, I could sample all the best dishes of the world. For years after that, I always timed my visits to Edmonton when that festival was on. It was my treat. As they say, "My happiness is my revenge." But the Elder and counsellor were right: the process of overcoming the trauma of residential school abuse is a lifelong journey.

In the spring of 2021, the Tk'emlúps te Secwépemc First Nation announced that they had uncovered the remains of 215 children buried near Kamloops Indian Residential School. I had visited that school many years before the discovery, just as the initial work of the Truth and Reconciliation Commission was starting. It was the summer of 2008. Marie was appointed as one of the commissioners and she was eager to get to work, travelling the country and meeting Survivors. On one of those trips, a tour throughout Alberta and British Columbia, I was Marie's chauffeur. She was so busy that she'd sit in the back seat so she had room to spread out all her notebooks, calendars and cellphone numbers.

At one point we ended up in Kamloops, where we were going to tour the old residential school. There was a large group of people there and, while I wasn't a major player, Truth and Reconciliation was also my issue and I wanted to help. We were all walking up this slope from the parking lot to the building and everyone was going too slow for me, so I was up ahead. Suddenly this feeling went through me; it was like a cold wind, a cold Spirit that went right through me. It made me shudder and turn around so I wasn't facing the building anymore, and a person behind me asked if I was okay. I said I was fine but I wasn't as I approached the old residential school.

Everything about that building and the air around it was wrong. It was like walking through a garden where it's warm, beautiful and full of flowers, and then suddenly you're in a room where everything is ice cold, grey and lifeless. It's hard to describe, but that's what it was.

Once we were all inside, I was trying to take part in the discussion but I just couldn't. I was nauseous and had a headache and I wasn't sure whether I was going to throw up or lose consciousness, so I went outside for a while.

When I came back in, I wanted to walk through the whole building. I ended up in the basement, and I think the basement was the hardest part of it all. There was an old man sweeping and then washing the floor, and there was something about the way he was doing it; it was almost the saddest thing I saw that day. He looked sad, but I was thinking about the thousands of children who did the same thing: wash the building, wash the floor, wash the walls, take a mop and push it around.

And it was near that building where they found hundreds of unmarked graves of children. Perhaps I had felt the presence of all those children who were lying underground; perhaps it was the Spirits of those children crying out for acknowledgement.

Chapter Twenty-Nine

Trouble at the Top

At the end of October 2001, I was in my second year as premier. That's when I got into some trouble.

It started with one of my cabinet ministers. We are all supposed to file a report with the ethics commissioner when we enter public life and I guess this minister missed a couple of things in her report. Some MLAs were outraged and called for an investigation. My principal secretary, John Bayly, was on the phone with the ethics commissioner when the minister in question walked into John's office unannounced. The minister had a habit of doing this—walking into offices without knocking. It's illegal for anybody to eavesdrop on a telephone call, and it seemed as if the minister might have been in the room for some time before John realized it.

There was quite an outcry about it and naturally there was a discussion about whether to remove me as premier because it had happened on my watch. The Oversight Committee pushed for a non-confidence motion. I was offended. I had spent my whole life in service and suddenly people were implying I didn't have principles, as if I were a new upstart. I'd been around twenty years. I decided to take the weekend to decide whether I was going to stay or not.

At the time, the Native Women's Association of the NWT was having a meeting in Yellowknife with women from all the communities. They invited me to dinner and I said sure; it sounded like a comforting thing to do.

I ended up spending the whole evening with them and part of the next day. They all came over to me in their quiet way to give me their statements. They wanted me to stay in office, and as the women provided their quiet words of encouragement, there were other calls of support coming in from the Chiefs and the Métis leaders. It was a good moment and it got me thinking, so I went back to the legislature on Monday and announced that I wanted to stay. A CBC report published October 29, 2001, titled "NWT Premier Kakfwi Wins Vote of Confidence," states:

> Premier Stephen Kakfwi fought off rebellion in his legislature Monday and announced his decision to stay on the job. "I want to serve," Kakfwi told a full assembly and a packed public gallery. "I want to finish my job."

Shortly after, MLAs voted 13–1 in favour of a motion express-
ing confidence in the government. Four abstained.

That was the first serious challenge to my leadership when I was premier.
Sadly, it led to the resignation of my principal secretary, John Bayly, and my
chief of staff, Lynda Sorenson. It has always troubled me that civil servants
are as vulnerable as they are to the whims of politicians.

Lynda's departure led to a motion of non-confidence in my leadership
a year later. My cabinet had appointed her to the rank of chief of staff, the
first time such a position had been created in the NWT. When she left, we
set her severance package at that level but my critics disagreed and they
took the issue all the way to the auditor general of Canada for a ruling. It
was a controversial decision, but the auditor general ruled in their favour. I
was facing a motion of non-confidence.

The Sunday evening before the vote of confidence, I figured that it was
all over. But later that night, I got a call from Chief Abe Wilson from Fort
McPherson. His call was unexpected, and then it went beyond expectation.

He sounded weary. "Steve, I support you. The Chiefs support you, but
I didn't want to just say it, so at eight o'clock this morning, I went to every single house in Fort McPherson and I asked the people myself. I asked
them, 'What do you want me to do? Shall I support Steve? What do you
want me to say?' Everyone says they support you, Steve. I walked around
town between 8 a.m. and 10 p.m., and there were four houses that wouldn't
say anything and one family that said they don't support you. Every single
other house supports you."

He had been out for, what, fourteen hours? He said he was going to call
his MLA once he hung up. "I just want you to know that," he said.

I never forgot that call because I didn't have a strong working relationship with Chief Abe Wilson. I was so moved by the length and extent to
which he worked to say, "It's not just me; it's my whole community that
supports Steve Kakfwi."

It's moments like that where suddenly you feel more solid, more em-
powered than ever.

The next morning, MLAs were telling me how the Oversight Committee was putting pressure on them to vote in their favour. But at the same time,
busloads of people from Behchokǫ̀ and other communities were arriving in
Yellowknife to back me. My support from the Chiefs and especially from the
Tłıchǫ was strong. Many people, Indigenous and non-Indigenous, came to sit
in the public galleries and in the end the motion of non-confidence was easily
defeated.

But while I survived the motion, it's important to remember that it was challenges like this one that cost Lynda her job. I have always believed that civil servants never get the credit or the respect that they deserve. Lynda had been a nurse earlier in her career and while she worked with me, she was quietly corresponding with constituents of mine who were disabled or had disabled children. There was one young man, Vital Manuel from Good Hope, who was confined to a wheelchair. He was very determined, though; he wanted to go to school and then work with us in Yellowknife. Lynda made sure that he got a job and he worked under her supervision for ten years. Vital passed away in 2005 but I later found some pictures of him that Lynda had taken and framed them and sent them to his parents.

Lynda also kept meticulous notes throughout my time as a leader. She carefully filed them in a way that made it possible for me to maintain a historical record of years that were important to me, and also to the Dene.

CHAPTER THIRTY

WALKING OUT ON THE PRIME MINISTER

"Territorial leaders have accused Prime Minister Jean Chrétien of leaving 'a legacy of neglect' of northern and Aboriginal Canadians by brushing off their concerns and forcing their leaders to reject the federal-provincial health accord Thursday.

"'For whatever reason, [Jean Chrétien] thought he could get away with ignoring us,' Northwest Territories Premier Stephen Kakfwi said in Ottawa. 'Here's a prime minister who brags about how much he loves the North … and he came up with a flat zero.'"

—Kim Lunman, "PM Draws Fire for Shunning Territories in Health Talks," *Globe and Mail*, February 8, 2003

In my last year as premier, I led a confrontation with Prime Minister Jean Chrétien. It was a first ministers' meeting in Ottawa and we'd all come to talk about health-care funding.

I was one of the three Northern premiers present. As usual, we were the little guys: when every provincial premier gets millions, we get $100,000 here and there. It's done on a per capita basis, but we've always argued, quite forcefully, that because of our remoteness, the vastness of our territories and our many small communities, we have much higher costs associated with medical services. We can't operate on a per capita basis.

Before the meeting, I had suggested to Yukon Premier Dennis Fentie and Nunavut Premier Paul Okalik that we should walk out of the meeting if we weren't given a response to our assertions, and we all agreed. So, we're sitting in this meeting and Chrétien is going after the premiers of Ontario and Quebec. At the time, that was Ernie Eves and Bernard Landry, respectively. Now, I knew Chrétien: he was thinking that once he beat these two into submission, everybody else would be manageable. The others—people like the premier of Manitoba, Gary Doer—were easygoing guys, not exactly pushovers, but they weren't the "stand up and fight and give as good as you get" kind of people either.

So, we're sitting there patiently and then I asked to speak. Chrétien turned to me and I raised our concern. "We have to have a resolution to this," I said. "You have to give us something because this offer is not acceptable and we need a response."

He turned back to face Ontario and Quebec and kept talking to them as if I hadn't spoken. About fifteen minutes later, I raised my hand again and he waved me off. So, I stood up with Paul and Dennis and said, "Well, we're leaving."

Chrétien looked at us and then went right back to whatever he was saying to Quebec and Ontario. The other premiers watched us walk out and some of them told me later that they wished they had walked out too.

Why? Because we got an incredible amount of media coverage. Outside the room was a throng of media, notebooks, cameras and tape recorders. It was the Parliamentary Press Gallery and they were set up for the prime minister's news conference. There were microphones and a podium in front of a line of flags, the Canadian flag and those of the provinces and territories. Everyone was expecting Chrétien to walk out first, but then here come the three Northern premiers instead.

The reporters knew something was up. They crowded around us and somebody led us to the microphones. That's where Chrétien was supposed to sit, but we sat down instead. We had a simple message for the journalists: "We are the three Northern premiers and we find the offer that's been presented to us by the prime minister unacceptable. Our people need more than a few hundred thousand dollars for their health care, and we walked out today because Prime Minister Chrétien will not even listen to us."

We talked for a while, and as we were wrapping up, the doors opened and Chrétien came walking toward us with his entourage and the other premiers. So, we got up and pranced out of the room, but the damage was done: we had completely stolen his thunder. Chrétien watched us walk away—that's one thing about Chrétien, the guy never missed a thing—and he knew it was too late. Lucky for us, we hadn't said anything too offensive.

We got good, and I mean *really good*, media coverage. The next day we flew home on an Air Canada flight, and the passengers gave us a standing ovation on the plane. They recognized us; we were all over the national news. A week later, I was in Calgary with my children, boarding a bus headed up to Edmonton. As the bus pulled out of the parking lot, the driver announced, "On board with us today is the premier of the Northwest Territories, the only premier courageous enough to stand up to Jean Chrétien." There was another standing ovation, and the kids got some soda.

Our people back home were proud of us. Here were three little guys taking on the big bully, and he thought he was only fighting with Quebec and Ontario.

The point of the story is that it worked. A few days later, he called me. "I am inviting you back to Ottawa. We'll have a nice dinner and then we will come to some sort of agreement."

So, we all flew back to Ottawa. We had dinner at the prime minister's home at 24 Sussex Drive, and the next day we had a meeting with the Clerk at the Privy Council, Alex Himelfarb. In the end, we came back with a few million dollars more than what was originally offered to us.

That's what happened. And we were all good, though Chrétien would never actually tell you if he was ticked off with you. He responded to the incident in the media by saying he was going to respond to us anyway and that it was a whole lot of fuss over nothing. In 2003, he invited all the premiers to accompany him on one of his trips to promote Canadian business. We flew over on his Team Canada jumbo jet. Marie was with me and we were relaxing in wide, comfortable seats. Chrétien was walking down the aisle, hobnobbing with everybody: "Oh, this is my friend; how are you? I'm glad to see you..."

When he saw me, he said, "Oh, you! You're the troublemaker! What are you doing here?"

"You invited me," I replied. "And this is my wife, Marie."

The plane hit some turbulence and he excused himself and went back to his seat. And that was the end of our conversation.

In later years, I got to know two of our other prime ministers well. Both Joe Clark and Paul Martin joined me in the Canadians for a New Partnership initiative after the Truth and Reconciliation Commission delivered its report. We are still good friends after all those years; they have a good understanding of Indigenous priorities in Canada. Paul came closer than most with his Kelowna Accord, but that was shot down by Prime Minister Stephen Harper.

CHAPTER THIRTY-ONE

I'D BETTER LEAVE BEFORE I DECIDE TO STAY

You stood right by my side
Right through this crazy war
You gave me love I needed
I never had before
But when you cried and reached for me
I turned so cold and didn't care
I pray that you'll forgive me
I left you standing there

Someday I may be sorry
for some things of long ago
Have I become a stranger?
Do you know me anymore?

—Stephen Kakfwi, "Someday I May Be Sorry,"
from the album *New Strings on an Old Guitar*

I was working in the yard with my son in the fall of 2003 when I made the decision to leave public life. We were putting shingles on the side of a shed. Every day I'd climb up there on the scaffold and ponder my future. My mind was telling me to stay, to run again, and my heart was telling me it was time to leave. So, I'd get up there and do the shingling and I'd come back down at the end of the day and I was still not clear about what I was going to do. Then one day it just came together. "It's a good time to leave."

I wasn't prepared to do a second term as a premier, and once I decided, it never troubled me again. I didn't tell anybody except Marie and the children, but it was a great feeling to think, I've made a decision and it's the right one.

There was absolutely no doubt about it. My last day as a premier was in December 2003. I'd served my time, and I remember starting to go to my office and taking things out of there, all my pictures and personal notes. I slowly stripped my office of any sign that I had ever been there. So, by the time

I left that office, there was absolutely nothing in there, not even a pencil, that belonged to me. It was like an empty hotel room: you came, you stayed, you packed up, you're leaving. And I remember walking out of there the very last time in December, walking out to the darkness of the winter afternoon, and I realized, You know what, I don't have any emotion about it at all. It was just like I was walking out of a warehouse where I did some work for a little while. I had no emotional attachment to either the building or the institution. I liked the idea of walking out into the cold darkness of the winter. I was a free man. After sixteen years in the legislature, I was thinking, I don't have to be accountable to anyone, and I'm going to be free again for the first time in over twenty years, since 1983 when I was elected as Dene Nation president.

Proud is a difficult word to say, but I am proud of the service I did. I respected the institution, the legislature, because it served all the people of the North, and although I was Dene and my political base was the Dene people and their Chiefs, I also had lots of support among non-Dene residents in Yellowknife and in Norman Wells, Fort Smith, Hay River and Inuvik. That made me feel great to know that I could serve the Dene and non-Indigenous people as well.

I didn't have a plan to do anything except to sit at home and sleep when I wanted, and only do things that I wanted … I didn't want to be driven by duty or obligation.

There were friends of mine who said, "So, what are you going to do? Sit at home for a while? You know, you should look for some work. You're not ready to retire."

And I said, "Well, I don't want to think about that right now. It's too soon. I just want to enjoy the euphoria of being unattached."

So, that's what I did. I spent Christmas at home with the family. It was great. And then in January, I thought, Well, what am I going to do?

"I'm going to go outside to my backyard," I decided, "and I'm going to split wood and make fire. No matter how cold it is, I'm going to do that." It was January 2004, dark and cold, and I sat out there for hours, but somehow there was comfort in that simple act.

I soon started to get phone calls from people, asking me to work … offers of contract work. So that's what I did. I have this uncanny sense that when opportunities are going to come, other doors are going to open and I'm just going to step through one or two of them and everything will take care of itself. I just need to wait for it and they'll come to me. And that's what happened: I started working for communities and I started getting calls to speak at conferences and workshops, and I was doing a lot of work with some environmental organizations.

I never got calls from the NWT government. The new premier had lots of appointments to make, but I never had one call to say, "Steve, would you be willing to serve on this board or in this role?"

It's not like I expected it. The fact of it is, I hate being on boards. I find it boring. But I was never even asked, from the place where I worked for sixteen years. So I noticed that.

Eventually I ended up having what you would call a classic mid-life crisis. I was still dealing with issues from residential school and I had chronic insomnia. I slept about four or five hours a night, and that was on a good night. By 2003, I was not in good shape. By 2004, I don't know if I was mentally well, because I couldn't sleep and I was in serious trouble. I'd wake up and I'd be still absolutely dead tired, and I couldn't get back to sleep. Your mind starts to play tricks with you. Even on sunny days, you think the days are just grey. I was suffering from depression and everything that comes along with extreme fatigue. You know, I was over fifty when I left politics, and I started to think, How long can I maintain this role of getting contracts and speaking engagements before people realize there's nothing there, that I'm running on empty?

What made it all worse was that I was having issues with Marie as well. For most of the time that I was in politics, Marie worked as a journalist. She was with CBC on air and as a manager in radio and TV. What that meant was, we couldn't—and we didn't—talk to each other about work; it was too likely to put either one of us in a conflict-of-interest position and we had to respect that. Then, when I was elected premier, Marie had to give up her career at the CBC. That was a huge adjustment for her and now I was sinking into my own depression. I didn't confide in Marie. I had decided that I was on my own. The more withdrawn I got, the more distant I became with everybody. I was trying to convince myself that "I'm only happy when I'm alone; I don't need anybody around. I don't need anybody to talk to." It wasn't true, but it was a good line in my head and I was sticking with it, but it drove me slowly to the edge of the darkness.

I remember talking to a friend of mine in Ottawa. George Braden and I were talking over dim sum, and he said, "Oh, it's time to go. You should go get some sleep."

And I said, "Well, let's finish our lunch."

"You're tired. You just fell asleep on me."

"No, I didn't."

"Steve, you fell asleep. You were talking to me. You closed your eyes and you fell asleep."

I had no idea.

Around that time, I started wearing these brightly coloured scarves. There were days when I thought, Why am I getting up? It's probably dark and gloomy outside, there isn't a colour out there in the world. So, I started wearing all these colourful scarves—red, yellow, gold, bright green and turquoise—and every day I'd put on a different one. Up until last year, that was one of my coping mechanisms.

One time, I decided to leave Yellowknife. I jumped on a plane to Edmonton and I stayed in the Met hotel on Whyte Avenue. The Met had a nice fireplace, which is why I picked it. I went to sleep about ten or eleven o'clock at night as usual. I fell asleep propped up in a chair while watching the fire. I woke up once, turned the fire off, and when I woke up again it was eight o'clock in the morning. I looked at the time and I sat up and counted the hours. I had slept over nine hours, and I could feel it through my whole body. I broke down in tears because it was the first time I felt like it was possible to be normal; it was possible to be like most normal people and sleep for six hours or eight hours. That was a normal night's sleep, and I hadn't had one for years—I couldn't even remember the last time. And here I was in Edmonton, running away from home and waking up at eight o'clock in the morning, having gone to bed at ten o'clock the night before. This was an enormous moment. I was thinking, Whatever the hell is the matter with me, I'm going to fix it all by myself. If I'm in a depression and suffering from insomnia, I'm going to fix it, I'm going to power out of it and I'm going to fix it.

And I was plagued by thinking, How do I do this? I wouldn't be in this position in the first place if I were able to love. But I've never felt I could love, whatever that means for a normal person. I've read about it; I know I studied the damn thing. I knew how you're supposed to feel, and I knew how I felt about my children… about Marie and my family. But I had always wondered if I really loved them. Like, what if my love wasn't 100 percent? Maybe it was like 3 percent. That's how I always thought because I had created this persona: distant, "stoneface," defiant, angry. The stoic, dark side of me was winning: I was in the grips of it and feeling unhinged.

When Marie and I split up, of all the friends that we had, I don't remember anybody ever calling me and saying, "Oh, Steve, like, how are you?"

At first, I was walking around thinking, Oh, that really hurts. You know, how could they? I thought they were my friends too.

After a while, of course, the defiant part of me came and kicked in and said, "I never liked them that much anyway. And it's okay because I don't want friends anyway. I mean, didn't somebody say that about me one time? That I didn't have any friends?"

I found a vacant one-bedroom apartment at Fraser Arms East, so I borrowed a sleeping bag and I moved in and that's where I stayed. I was also trying to recover from the flu at that time. One day, my daughters, Kyla and Daylyn, came to check on me and Daylyn said, "Do you have any change of clothes?"

Kyla said, "Dad, how long have you been wearing that sweater?"

And I realized then that I'd been wearing the same old grey sweater since the beginning of December when I went to Edmonton, and this was well into the middle of January. I mean, I'd always tried to be presentable—dress shirt and sports jacket—and here I was wearing this shabby old wool sweater that was starting to wear through at the elbows, and my kids were starting to tell me, "You should take better care of yourself."

I guess they must have had a family meeting and said something like, "Dad is staying in this one-bedroom apartment. There's not a thing in there except a foamy and a sleeping bag." Marie arranged to send up furniture; I got a bed, a desk and a couch. That's where I lived for about a year and a half. I hardly had any visitors. For some reason, I thought everybody else was the problem.

One of the only things that was good about living alone was that I went to all kinds of concerts and music festivals. Once I saw that Bob Dylan was going to play in Vancouver—the next day. So, I flew all the way to Vancouver to see him. Close to the theatre, this scalper came up to me and said, "Bob Dylan concert tickets here!"

"Well, how much ?"

"Hundred and fifty."

"Where's the seat?"

"Front row."

"Okay, I'll take it."

I showed up that evening and I told the woman taking the tickets that I'd come all the way from Yellowknife. She said, "Well, I hope you really enjoy it."

So, I went in and found my seat in the front row, but I couldn't see the stage because the speakers were in the way. So, I jumped back up and I went and saw the same woman. She said, "Are you okay? You already got your ticket."

"Yes, but I ended up with a seat where I can't even see the front of the stage. I spent a lot of money to come here."

She dug around and she said, her face beaming up at me, "I got something for you. How about a seat in the third row, right in the middle?" Only my strict Catholic upbringing prevented me from hugging the lady right then and there.

So, the concert began and I had a really great time. I don't normally get animated at all but this time both my feet were tapping.

I went to see Steve Earle in Lake Louise, too, and I also went to both the Calgary and the Edmonton Folk Music Festivals, by myself. It's the best way to go. By yourself. When you have somebody else with you, you're always going, "Well, do you want to stay? Do you want to go?" By yourself, you just do whatever the hell you want.

At some point or other, I started to like myself again. I got to thinking that the work I'd done was the work of somebody who had some principles, some values. I had married a beautiful, remarkable and loving woman who was also my best friend and we had raised children who were good children.

The only person I ever really believed loved me was Marie, but I didn't know how to say, "I'm sorry. I made a mistake." I actually remember thinking, You know, I wonder if I will ever heal. I wonder if I'll get beyond the trauma and the pain and suffering that I had in my childhood after years of residential school. Could I ever really love—totally, unconditionally? And what would that be like?

Then, one day my son, Keenan, decided to go on a holiday with his mother and helped drive her to Edmonton. I was in Calgary. They called me and they said, "It'd be really good if you could come by because we're on holiday and you could have dinner with us."

That's what my son wanted. "I'd just like to have dinner with the both of you."

So, I took a bus up from Calgary and we had dinner, and it went really well.

That evening, I said to Marie, "Let's go for a walk. Just a half-hour walk."

It went well. It was cautious, but it went well. So, the next day we had breakfast together and then went for another walk. It was great. I wasn't exactly clicking my heels walking down the road after that, but close to it. You know, I was thinking that it was possible to be happy and get back together—then I'd come back to life, feel good about myself. I was thinking, This feels so familiar and just like the way it was and the way it's supposed to be. This is the Marie I remember and this feels like the joy I felt the first time we were together in Edmonton in 1976.

That's how it started again. I came back to Yellowknife, and there was a George Jones concert playing. I bought five tickets. I called Marie and the children and I said, "I have all these tickets; let's all go together." So… that was the beginning of us getting back together.

Stephen and Marie. Photo by Pat Kane of Yellowknife

My friend George Braden said, "Steve, maybe you had to fall apart in order to get yourself back together, and you're just taking the good pieces you like and leaving all the others out of it. You're rebuilding yourself piece by piece. That's how I see it."

I realized that you have only one life on this earth, so that gives you some very important questions.

How do you wanna spend your life?

How hard do you want to work at being a difficult, ornery, disjointed person—or how hard are you really willing to work to get along with people?

I'm a screwed-up, traumatized introvert. I'm anti-social, bordering on having a compulsive disorder, but there's something good about me and I'm going to project as much of it as I can on the world.

And Marie. She is the prism. She can take ordinary light and bring out all the colours of the rainbow for me to see. Through her, I realized I could see the beauty of a lot of things around me that I never allowed myself to see before.

CHAPTER THIRTY-TWO

IN THE WALLS OF HIS MIND

He tries to be a father
For his wife and his children
And he hides the pain
That will drive him insane
And that voice each night
That is quietly crying
Somewhere in the walls
And the halls of his mind

—Stephen Kakfwi, "In the Walls of His Mind,"
from the album *In the Walls of His Mind*

I started to write songs again when I was separated from the family and eventually I started recording them. Within a year and a half, I'd produced two CDs. They were good therapy; they're my statements of times when I was feeling a certain way. There's one song called "Will You Love Me Tomorrow?" and it's about the realization that I never really had much faith or trust in others. There were other songs called "How Far Will I Fall?," "Afraid to Feel" and "If I Could Find the Words," so you can see what I was thinking at the time.

The first time I ever sang in public with my guitar was January 2001. It was unexpected, both for me and for the people who were there.

It started with a fiddler named Kole Crook out of Hay River. He was a charismatic, lively and spiritual young man. He travelled everywhere to get to know as many Elders as he could, so he'd go to Wrigley, to Fort Good Hope, and if he ever needed money, he just took out his fiddle and played. The guy was amazing. One time he was in Edmonton. He went to the airport and he didn't have enough money for a ticket, so he cracked open his fiddle case and started playing, right there at the airport. In a matter of an hour, he made enough to buy himself a ticket and he went home with that.

He was in Good Hope for the Christmas of 2000 playing for a dance. After it was over, Everett took him to the airport. He knew that my brother could play guitar, so while they were waiting at the airport, he asked Everett, "How come you don't perform? You play guitar. You're learning the fiddle. Why don't you play?"

And my brother said, "I'm kind of shy."

And Kole told him, "Everett, the Creator gave some of us gifts, some of us a big gift of being able to play and to sing; sometimes it's just to play guitar, sometimes to sing, sometimes to play the fiddle, but no matter how big or how small that gift is, the Creator gives it to you for a reason. It's to make people happy. So, don't think like that. Think that the Creator gave you this gift to make people happy, to dance, to laugh and cheer them up."

Everett liked that, so he agreed and said okay.

Kole climbed on that plane and about thirty minutes later, the plane crashed into the side of the mountain. No one survived.

I was in Ontario with Marie and her parents for Christmas that year, and I got the call from Everett. Everett told me about the crash and what Kole had said about getting a gift from the Creator. I came back early for the funeral.

It's strange how things work out sometimes, because just a couple of weeks earlier I'd met my daughter Kyla's new boyfriend. He was interested in her, but the two of them, they were scared of me. They regarded me as "the Grumpy," so they were wondering about the best way to introduce him to me. The young guy fretted about it, and finally Kyla said, "You know, my dad just loves Bob Dylan."

"Oh, I have a three-CD set of Bob Dylan songs. Does he have that?"

"I know he doesn't have that."

"What if I brought it to him and offered to lend it to him?"

"That might work."

So, just before Christmas, Kyla brought him over and he wasn't even inside our house before he was blurting out, "Mister-Kakfwi-nice-to-meet-you-here-is-a-collection-of-Bob-Dylan-CDs-I wonder-if-you'd-like-to…"

"Thank you!" I swiped them away and stomped off. I think the two of them were so relieved. I went through the songs later. There were about thirty-six songs in the set. Some of them I'd never heard before. One stuck in my head. It's called "Lay Down Your Weary Tune." And it was still in my head when I went to Ontario for Christmas.

When I came back for Kole's funeral, I woke up in the middle of the night with that song playing in my head again. I didn't know the words, but I was dreaming that I was singing it. So, at about three o'clock in the morning, I got the CD out and played it, and as I listened I wrote down the lyrics.

A lot of friends showed up at Kole's funeral a few days later. Afterward, his family organized a wake for him at the community hall. It was just full of people. People like George Tuccaro and John Tees and a lot of other musicians performed there. George was the MC and I told him I'd like to try the

Bob Dylan song. So, later, when I walked into the community hall, George saw me and he said, "Heeeyyy, Premier Steve Kakfwi's here. Let's get him up to do a song!"

And everybody was surprised. "What? He sings? He plays guitar?"

I went up and I took out that song sheet I had in my pocket, and I sang "Lay Down Your Weary Tune." That was my very first performance.

I was inspired by Kole's words: no matter how small a gift your musical ability might be, the Creator gives it to you to entertain. So, that's why I did it.

The song that changed everything for me, though, is the one I wrote called "In the Walls of His Mind," the song I wrote during the flight from Norman Wells to Yellowknife in 1998.

> I remember the years
> They took all the children
> And they locked them away
> Where they taught them to pray
> There were children each night
> Who were quietly crying
> They are in the walls
> And the halls of my mind

The halls and the walls are a reference to Grollier Hall itself because I came from a small log house; Grollier Hall was huge and scary, just all these hallways, doors and storage rooms—a hell of a place to send a kid from a small log house.

I started writing the song... because everybody was starting to talk about Grollier Hall. I was there. I knew what happened. But I was also a minister in government at the time, so I had to think about my career and the people who have always said, "Oh, he shouldn't be here, he shouldn't be the minister. He's not qualified." I didn't want to give those people any reason to say, "That poor guy, no wonder he can't do his job. He's so traumatized."

The songs gave me confidence that I didn't have before. It got so I wasn't too shy to play music. I got invited to music festivals and when I wasn't invited, I invited myself. Eventually, I started playing some of my own songs.

I even played at the 2002 Premiers' Conference in Halifax. J.P. Cormier, a Celtic musician from the Maritimes, was performing. Somebody told him that I sang and played guitar, so, to my surprise, at a big dinner up at the Halifax Citadel, he called out to me and said, "I'm sorry to embarrass you, Mr. Kakfwi, but there's no other way to get you up here. Please join me and sing a song."

And so, I performed a song with him. Afterward, he said, "You know, I enjoyed that so much. I need you to come back again."

I think we did two or three songs together, entertaining the other premiers.

After I'd stepped down as premier, Lois Edge invited me to perform at an Indigenous health conference in Winnipeg. She asked me to sing just one song, "In the Walls of His Mind." I was thinking, This is crazy. I have to fly all the way down to Winnipeg and it takes me fifteen minutes onstage and I'm done.

But playing that music, and that song in particular, was powerful. The audience connected to that song. People who'd been to residential school recognized what I was saying in that song. They said, "That's my song."

Afterward, I went to a healing conference in Edmonton. The organizers wanted me to sing "In the Walls of His Mind" at a morning workshop in front of seventy-eight Elders and then talk about it with them. I thought, Who wants to hear my song, or any song, at nine o'clock in the morning? Right off? First thing at a conference?

And they said, "Look, it's important. Just do it and we'll take it from there."

I wasn't too sure. I liked to sing in the evening with the lights on and my Bob Dylan sunglasses. Waking up a bunch of Elders at nine o'clock in the morning wasn't my idea of how to perform, but I did it anyway.

I remember introducing it. I said, "You know, I went to Grollier Hall, a residential school up North, when I was nine years old… Here's a song I wrote about it."

I had added a new verse that I'd written just for them.

> Do you remember the years
> When you were the children
> And they locked you away
> And taught you to pray.
> Do you still hear your voices quietly crying,
> Somewhere in the halls and walls of your mind.

They started to stand up, one at a time, until all seventy-eight of the Elders were standing. Some of them were crying, just standing there sobbing. Some just stood there with tears in their eyes. Old grandmothers were sobbing. It took me everything to finish the song. When the song was over, they called a break. There were many support workers there to help the Elders.

Afterward, one Elder told me, "I went to Aklavik. I was not even nine years old. I went there with my brother. When my brother died, they sent me back to school that day. They didn't even tell me what they did with his body. To this day, I don't know when or where he was buried. That's what you made me remember." That was Charlie Snowshoe from Fort McPherson.

I started to realize that a song can be more than entertainment. It has the power to help people heal.

Later, I was asked to sing that song at a reunion for all the kids that went to Grollier Hall between 1959 and 1985. I didn't want to go. The organizers, people like Johnny Banksland and some of the Inuvialuit leaders, called me one day and said, "We're organizing our conference; we want you to come and sing your song."

"Okay, I'll come. But just one day and then I'm leaving. I don't want to stay. I don't want to be near that place."

Grollier Hall itself had already been torn down, but the federal school building was still there and that's where they wanted to have the gathering. The organizers kept calling me. Banksland had spent his whole life in residential school, and he was saying, "Well, Steve, can you stay for one day and just sit with us?"

I agreed to. But then a week after that he called back and said, "Well, we had a meeting and we really want you to stay two days. And you've got to sing that song at least twice."

"Oh, okay. I'll stay two days."

A week after that he called again, "We really want you to stay for the five days. Just sit with us."

"I'll think about it."

And a few days later he called back and said, "Steve, look. All of us, we had another meeting. We think you have to chair this meeting. You have to do it."

I caved. "Okay, I'll do it."

So, I went there and I chaired this gathering and I saw people I hadn't see since 1960. Some of them said they were there when they were six years old, or seven, eight or nine; some of them went for a year, some of them went for five years, ten years. And they were all just looking around in the school, Sir Alexander Mackenzie School. That's when it occurred to me that the public school we were gathering in was built at the same time as Grollier Hall. It's all the same design and material.

Banksland had asked me to start the conference by saying a prayer and singing my song, then everyone was going to break out into groups. Again, I don't like to sing in the morning, but I went up there anyway. They'd never heard me sing or play before, all these former students, so they were kind of intrigued. Some of them were in their fifties and others were already in their seventies and eighties.

I started out by saying, "Look around you. Look at the walls, the varnished plywood, the tiles on the floor, the cover on the windows and the gymnasium. It's all the same as Grollier Hall."

I watched as everybody looked around. They could see the similarity too. Then I started the song. It's the only time in my life where I was singing and there was a sense of both power and panic, a huge surge of energy, pain and anguish. There were over seventy people there. The whole room burst into tears, but they were not just crying—they were wailing, as if somebody was tearing their hearts out. I was watching this and I don't know how many times I just about stopped singing. Fortunately, we had a lot of support workers, healers and counsellors in the room, so I finished the song.

You could see the support workers taking control of the room, letting the former students know that help was there, that they were there, and that got us through. After I finished the song, I just kept talking and talking and things calmed down, but I didn't sing it again for two days. When I did, people were crying again, but it was a different kind of cry. It was a cry about sad memories. But that first morning, I think I unleashed some horrific memories for all these people who attended Grollier Hall through the years. And the song had been therapy for me too: the first few times I sang the song, I couldn't finish it. I'd fall apart.

—

I've spent some time trying to understand why music matters so much to me. It started with the church, but music is also a part of my Dene roots, my family roots, and the influences just kept coming as I got older.

My father used to take us to church, and the times I remember best are in the spring and summer and fall, because the sun shining into the church in Good Hope made it an awesome place. Some of the windows were yellow, purple, green and red stained glass. And the church itself was remarkable: it had a deep-blue ceiling with painted yellow stars, just like the universe. And once they started the Gregorian music—man, you're pretty damn close to God.

I used to watch my father while he was singing. He knew all the songs in Latin and I used to watch his lips to see if he was mumbling it or he was pronouncing them, and I was always impressed because he was pronouncing the words. Latin words. It never occurred to me then that he'd learned it all in residential school, but my aunts and all the parents in the church, they were all singing these songs and it sounded beautiful.

Uncle Jonas also played the church organ for over fifty-five years. Just a few years before he died, a couple of nuns came to town and took over the church. They wanted to do everything, so they kicked out all the lay people and my uncle never played again. It kind of makes me angry thinking about it. Uncle Jonas was also taught how to play fiddle by my uncle Albert, so he'd play guitar and sing songs. He was the community fiddler for twenty or thirty years.

Every Sunday in the summertime, in the warm weather after church, Uncle Jonas would get his friends John and Ernest Cotchilly to come over and play guitar. They'd sit outside my grandfather's house on a bench and play guitar and the fiddle, have a little jam session. You could hear it some way off, and that's kind of a nice memory I have of growing up, listening to this kind of music. I enjoyed it enough to try to sit still and hang out there. People would be walking by and listening. It made them happy, and some of them stopped to listen too.

My father also sang Dene songs. I vaguely remember him singing when my mother was gone. He was in his thirties, and while my older sister and younger brother stayed with my grandparents, Everett, Jean and I stayed with my father most of the time. Sometimes after the lights would go out, we would pile into bed with him. I guess he was lonely. In the dark, he would sing this Dene love song that he made up for my mother. Everett knew the song, and he's the one that reminded me of it. He said, "You know, Steve, you used to cry listening to Dad singing in the dark."

In another one of my songs, I honour my father. There's an old CBC recording of him singing "First Sign of Spring," and we took that old recording and mixed my voice in with his. It was my way to ask my father for forgiveness—and to forgive him as well, to make peace with my father. He died in 1975 and here I was, thirty years later, still dealing with that.

I also wanted to use my music to honour the leaders and Elders I grew up with. I wanted to write about some great Chiefs that I knew, men like Alexie Arrowmaker, Chief Johnny Charlie and Elders like Lazarus Sittichinli.

Michael Grandjambe wrote a love song for his wife. She was from Bear Lake. He married her and after a few years they split up. I think he told her to go back to her parents. A few years later she ended up having a child with another guy, but Grandjambe changed his mind. He wanted her back. But what to do? He had to deal with the fact that he had sent his wife away to fend for herself, and now his wife had a child with another man.

Then she went to the hospital with TB. Many women went to the hospital at that same time, so there was this whole community of men whose wives were in the hospital. The men included my father and my uncle Cassien Edgi, Joe Masuzumi and Charlie Masuzumi. These men were raising kids by themselves.

Around that time, in 1957, the first tape recorder came to the mission in Fort Good Hope. The mission invited everybody to come and record messages to the wives who were in the hospital in Aklavik. That's when Grandjambe recorded the song to send to his wife.

It's a powerful love song. It's in Dene and the original tape is in the archives of the Prince of Wales Northern Heritage Centre in Yellowknife. I put my version of Grandjambe's love song on my CD. I wanted to honour the original version of the song, so we started it simply—just my voice and a drum—and we ended it the same. But I wanted to add my own touch, too, so we mixed in the Vancouver Symphony Orchestra as well.

I recall many times throughout my childhood when there were drum dances in Good Hope. All the older guys that drum would go there and they'd make a fire because they needed to warm the drums to keep them tight. So, they'd drum and people would dance—and when there was a dance, there was nothing but that drumming the whole night long. They'd also have fiddle dances and those dances would go all night as well.

When people came back from trapping they'd often do their stick gambling. They'd gamble for money and fur. There were usually two lines of men, two teams facing each other, and they'd try to outguess each other, figure out who was holding their stick and in which hand. They'd go at it day and night, and the drums kept it all going. As kids, we used to listen to it as long as we could, late into the night, and eventually my father or mother, if she was there, would send us home. But we'd be in bed and there was little use being there because the drums went all night and we could hear them from bed. We just listened to them. In the morning, we'd wake up and go back and they'd still be playing. They stopped, usually when the sun started to get hotter, and then in the afternoon they'd start again with their stick gambling. People were so happy to be back in town. It was the end of another trapping season.

So, that's how I first started to appreciate songs and music. Latin hymns at church, my uncles with their guitar and fiddle and, of course, the drum dance music.

—

One day, I was in Yellowknife talking on the phone with my friend Randall Prescott. Randall is a musician and producer and has a studio near Ottawa where he'd recorded a number of my songs. He said, "Do you know any Dene songs?"

"Yeah, I know a couple."

So, I called Joe Rabesca, who at the time was the Grand Chief of the Tłı̨chǫ, and I told him I needed three drums so I could record. A couple of days later, he sent a car and two guys down from Behchokǫ̀ to Yellowknife. They delivered the drums right to my house. I thought, This is a good sign.

I packed up those three drums and went to Ottawa and started recording.

First, we had to decide what to do with the songs because they have no names and some of them have words and some of them don't. I created some titles. One is called "Spirit of Yamogha" because I like Yamogha. In Dene legends, he's a defiant supernatural being and a fighter.

If you fly from Good Hope toward Norman Wells, you fly over a mountain ridge that rises about six hundred feet. At the top of that ridge, there's a prominent pinnacle sticking out of the rock face. We all know that as Yamogha's Rock. That's where he was fighting when he was cornered and, rather than admit defeat, turned himself into a rock. That was the last anybody saw of Yamogha.

But these Dene legends actually start with Yamogha's brother, Yamoria. He was sent by the Creator to get rid of the giant animals—that's what we call the dinosaurs and giant beavers and eagles, the animals that were threatening to wipe out the Dene. So, Yamoria created a balance and set down the laws of nature. There's a landmark named after Yamoria across the Mackenzie River from Tulita: three round, reddish outlines of rock represent the skins from the last three giant beavers he killed and nailed up. Legend says that he cooked them and the fat from those beavers spilled onto the shore upriver from Tulita. When you see smoke coming out of the seams along the shoreline there, it's a spiritual sign. I've only seen it once with my friend Bob Overvold. It was a powerful spiritual moment for both of us.

I had to ask questions about these legends because the church discouraged those stories. My parents were quiet about them. We never heard much about Yamoria or Yamogha when we were kids.

⁓

Everett was a big musical influence too. He was always interested in music. As a kid he wanted to play guitar, but the guitars in town were pretty beat-up. Eventually, he discovered a guitar at the Bay: a flat top made of spruce selling for fifteen bucks. To his surprise, my mother went and bought it, so he tuned it up and he started playing it. He took to it naturally. The spring before he passed away, he was visiting me in Yellowknife. I was sitting in my office, listening to a live recording of Bob Dylan singing "Song to Woody." Everett walked in, heard the song and grabbed my guitar that was hanging up on the wall. When Dylan started picking out the acoustic part, Everett started picking along with it, almost note for note. Then he sort of shrugged, put that guitar back on the wall and walked out.

I actually got to meet Dylan once. He was playing at a concert in Calgary and Marie and I decided to go. I was still premier at the time and Melody Morrison was the principal secretary to the cabinet and arranged for us to go backstage. So, we met Dylan after the concert. He's a small man and he has a unique way of moving: he came out of the curtains and, because it was too dark to see properly, he was sort of shuffling to make sure he didn't trip on the cables and the cords that were strewn everywhere. As he moved, he was peering around trying to make us out.

"Mr. Dylan," I said. "Over here."

He nodded, shuffled over and then took our hands. We introduced ourselves and I told him that I'd been playing his songs, and even changing the lyrics to suit my audiences. One of his songs is called "Only a Hobo" and I told him that I would change it to "Only a Trapper."

"Good, good," he replied. "That's what they're for."

After a little while, we both stopped talking like we'd run out of things to say, but Marie always helps when this happens. She stepped in and got the conversation going again. Dylan was interested in where we lived and I presented him with a Dene moosehide jacket. He took it and rubbed his hands over it, taking in the aroma of the smoked hide. When he slipped it on it fit him perfectly and he seemed happy to have it.

"Thank you," he said. "I'll be taking this to my farm in Minnesota where I'll need it to be warm in the winter."

Bob Dylan is the one who first got me thinking about becoming a musician back when I was at Grandin College. I'm never very good at it, but I've got to do what I dreamt of doing as a kid: I grew out my hair so it was bushy, and I shuffled nervously onto more than a few stages with a guitar and a harmonica, wearing my dark glasses and singing the songs that I wrote.

CHAPTER THIRTY-THREE

SACRED WORK

Not long after Marie and I got back together, I began to realize that there was an emptiness inside me, as if a spiritual essence had been taken away from me. I couldn't fix it through the Catholic Church, or any church. I tried to fix it by spending time with Elders, hunting and fishing, living on the land and trying to connect to all of Creation, but I just didn't know how to do it.

All I knew was that to be spiritual doesn't mean just being connected to God; it means being connected to everything around you—your wife, your children, your family and community—in a deep, profound way. It also means being connected to the ants and the mosquitoes, the birds and the fish, the moose—all of Creation. Being connected to all of Creation is what being spiritual means to me. As I started to learn that, somebody gave me Dave Courchene's phone number. They said he was a spiritual leader and a keeper of Traditional Knowledge from Manitoba. I called him and he said, "Well, I'm down in BC conducting ceremonies. Come and join us; I'd like to see you. Just sit and listen and be a part of what we're doing."

So, I went. I think it might have been the first time I said out loud that I had to get ready to die. I didn't want to die, but I didn't want to die the way I was, with this big emptiness inside of me, all this rage and pain and fear inside of me. I wanted to learn how to live, to enjoy everything that was around me. I wanted to be able to centre myself so that I was at peace wherever I was, and I knew I couldn't do it unless I became more spiritually centred and aware.

Dave said, "Well, you've come to the right place." We had a laugh about it, and he said, "I think you're already there because you know what's missing. I work with people like that all over the world, from Peru and Scandinavia, all over the United States, from Alaska and Yukon. I know Traditional Healers, people who use Traditional Medicine, the Knowledge Holders and the people who carry the Traditional Ceremonies, so maybe you should travel with me and I'll help you get there. You'd be good company."

His father, Dave Courchene Sr., had been the first head of the Manitoba Indian Brotherhood. Dave Jr. was encouraged to follow in the footsteps of his father and be a political leader, but he didn't feel like it was meant for him. One year, he had a vision that told him he was supposed to work for people, to help them regain everything that we had and that we had lost. So, he went to the Anishinaabe people, to the Ojibwe people of which he was a part, and to the Lakota in the United States and southern Manitoba, and he learned from the Elders, Healers, Medicine People and holders of these Sacred Traditions. They bestowed upon him a mandate to set up a lodge and a movement that would help people regain all the ways in which we used to be connected to the land—to the animals, water, air, birds, insects, all of Creation. That lodge became Turtle Lodge, and his vision was to "learn the land, learn about Creation, connect to it, and relearn the ceremonies that our people used and the ways of prayer." That's what he spent his whole life doing and he became a great teacher and guide for me.

I also had a long history and friendship with the former National Chief of the Assembly of First Nations, Ovide Mercredi. He was trained as a lawyer, so his mastery of the English language is great, and he is always aware of everybody that is in the room when he speaks. He always knew who he was talking to. During the constitutional discussions at the Charlottetown Accord, he was at his best. My admiration for Ovide was established at that time and we've become close friends over the years.

I invited Dave and Ovide to join me in an organization called the Indigenous Leadership Initiative (ILI), a gathering of Indigenous leaders from across Canada who are working to protect and preserve traditional land, and to give Indigenous people an increasing say in that work. Most of the funding comes from big American foundations like the Pew Charitable Trusts, the Hewlett Foundation, Ducks Unlimited and the Gordon and Betty Moore Foundation.

We all started talking about establishing a national guardians program, with which we could give money to communities where their people were ready to start guarding, monitoring and taking care of their own Traditional Territories.

Dave, Ovide and I thought that there was too much partying among the Indigenous leaders and others involved. We thought that leading our communities, deciding what to do with land and resources, was Sacred Work, and that you couldn't be doing this in the daytime and then switch to beer and martinis at night. We said, "It's not going to be a nine-to-five job. It's got to be based on our understanding that we are spiritual people, that we are more connected to the land, the wildlife, than anybody else. This is our land, our culture and our history. So, when we train these people to be guardians, to protect the land, we must have ceremony. You can't just start doing this and then say, 'Okay, it's five o'clock now, I'm done. I think I'll have a glass of wine.' If you're going to work with and on the land, you must be

Three friends, Stephen Kakfwi, Ovide Mercredi and Dave Courchene. Photo by a kind stranger

without drugs. It's Sacred Work." We were firm about this, and when the time came to have our contracts renewed with the ILI they vaguely told us, "We'll be in touch." I knew they were done with us. None of our contracts were renewed.

For a while, I worked with environmental organizations like the World Wildlife Fund (WWF). I'd have a contract or be on a retainer. I was kind of their VIP, the high-profile public Indigenous person. If I agreed with what they were trying to do, I'd accept their invitation to Ottawa to see a minister, but if I didn't agree, I didn't go. My attitude always was that they could hire me, but they could never tell me what to say. I decide what I say, what I do and how things are done.

It all worked fine so long as that was how things were done, but I often had to take a stand. For example, after two years of working for the WWF, I had to leave. At a meeting one day, I think it was in London, England, they said, "We have a mandate and we want you to work with us. We are going to save the polar bears and we're going to do it with the Inuit—but if we have to, we'll be doing it without the Inuit."

I said, "So, how do you think you're going to do that without the Inuit?"

"Well, we expect the Inuit are going to oppose the conservation measures we propose because they harvest the bears for their fur and meat."

"Look," I replied. "The Inuit are my friends and I would never tell them how to manage the wildlife on their land and territory—and neither can you. I'm not going to support that."

The other issue that we disagreed on was the caribou calving grounds. The Inuit around Rankin Inlet and Baker Lake live close to caribou calving grounds, and again, the WWF came to me and said, "We are going to mount a campaign to save the caribou and protect the caribou calving grounds. Once again, if we can't do it with the Inuit, we're going to do it without them."

And again, the same argument from me: I cannot support that and I won't.

After those two incidents, I walked away. International organizations looking out for the interests of wildlife, the ones that mount huge animal welfare and anti-fur campaigns, always make one fundamental mistake. They see it all as empty land: no Inuit, no Dene, no Inuvialuit, no Métis. We are never a part of the equation.

Greenpeace took that hard line in the early eighties: they put the welfare of animals above the welfare of our people and we never forgave them. They were entitled to lobby against the fur trade, but they never accepted that there were people, our people, who were being hurt as well. I told them that we were the front-line people who protect the land and resources, but the Greenpeace leaders couldn't see that, so we never wanted to see those people up North again. In the nineties, they came to Fort Good Hope and apologized, but I never recovered from their earlier slight because I felt like they had turned the world against us. Our people had been independent economically, with so many of us still hunting and trapping, but the animal rights groups tried to destroy us.

Around this time, we were trying to create a protected area in the Ramparts Wetlands, just south of Good Hope, and we were close to reaching an agreement. There's a river that runs through this area called Ramparts River (in Dene the name translates to Big Spruce River), and that whole area is a major migratory nesting area for ducks. There are thousands of little lakes there. The Elders know that if anything should ever happen to the Mackenzie River—if it became polluted or started to dry up—and it could no longer provide for us, we could use the Ramparts Wetlands for moose and ducks.

In the end, when the ratification of the protected area was supposed to happen, the new Chief and Council were against it, and so were the leaders of the Land Corporation. I was in this awkward, lonely position of publicly fighting the elected leaders of Good Hope and telling people to ratify that agreement. I worked at it the same way I did for the Berger Inquiry, going house to house, speaking to one person at a time.

I left Good Hope the day before the vote confident that the people would choose to protect the Ramparts Wetlands. My cousin Wayne Kakfwi and I went up the river hunting to Norman Wells and there we shot a moose. I said to him at that time that I'd done everything I could, and that we would win the vote.

The ratification vote happened and we got a yes to protect the area in the Ramparts Wetlands. It was pushed through by the Elders, people like Frank and John T'Seleie; they helped carry the vote, but it took months before leaders accepted it. People who were at one of the public meetings called me afterward and said, "You know what they're saying about you at the meeting? That you're nothing but an outsider, and we don't like outsiders coming and telling us how to vote or having them negotiate agreements for us."

I couldn't believe it. It was a full year before I went back to Good Hope. Today, though, the young leaders have changed their minds and the people see that it was a good project. They are grateful for it and the hard work of implementing the agreement.

CHAPTER THIRTY-FOUR

THREE BROTHERS

He says he'll be just fine
Every time he's crossed that line
What more will he do?
What more will he take you through?
Just pray for him each day
To know why he is that way
And don't take it to the heart
The way he is with you

—Stephen Kakfwi, "Don't Take It to the Heart," dedicated to
Tommy Kakfwi, from the album *New Strings on an Old Guitar*

When I left Fort Good Hope as a young man, I left two brothers behind: Tommy and Everett. We didn't see much of each other after that. We led our own lives and we had our troubles with drinking, but we got clean eventually. I got sober in 1986, Everett a few years later and Tommy in 2013.

In 2010, Everett was diagnosed with colon cancer. The doctors told him they couldn't cure him, so for the last year he was alive, I spent a lot of time with him. We went to see Elders, Healers and Medicine People, and two of the Elders that we saw told him, "Only the Creator can heal you or tell you how long you can live. What we could do is teach you how to enjoy every moment, every minute, every hour of what you have, which is today. The Creator gave you today. How are you using it? If you're feeling sorry for yourself, if you're mad, if you're whining and complaining, it's hard for us to ask the Creator for more days for you. You've got to show that you're using what you're getting."

Everett said to the Healers, "I'd like to learn how to do that and I want my brother to learn it with me."

So, we went on this journey together: learning how to be positive, to accept death as part of life, to try to be good to everybody around us and to live every moment that we've got.

In June 2011, the Truth and Reconciliation Commission was holding an event in Inuvik where they would hear from residential school Survivors from Grollier and Stringer Halls. Marie was one of the three commissioners, so I was going to be with her. By that time, Everett was feeble, down to about 110 pounds, and still losing a lot of weight. He was living in Good Hope and he really wanted to travel to Inuvik, but he had no place to stay: all the hotel rooms were booked, people were billeted out and accommodations were at a premium. Since Marie and I had a hotel suite, a one-bedroom with a couch in the living room, I told him he could sleep on the couch. So, off he went to Inuvik, as frail as he was.

I picked him up from the airport and brought him into town. He was hungry, so we had dinner at the hotel restaurant. He was excited about the event and we were talking about when we were kids at Grollier Hall, but he started falling asleep.

"Everett, you're falling asleep."

"I know. I can't help it."

We had a good laugh about it, and I said, "Well, why don't you go upstairs and go to bed?"

"I can't do that. If I go to bed now, I'm not going to get up until tomorrow. I want to go there, look at the schoolyard and see if I can remember anybody."

As tired as he was, we paid our bill and went across the street and into the schoolyard. We sat down at a picnic table and we stayed there for about two hours: we sat there while countless people came by to say hello. Some of them knew him, some of them knew me, and even though he was exhausted, Everett was enjoying himself. By the end of the day, he was so tired that I practically had to pack him back to the hotel. He stayed on the couch and we had a bedroom in the back, and that's how Everett spent four days with us. He was up before me every morning; if I got up at five, he was already up and waiting for his coffee. So, I'd make coffee and then sit down with him and talk.

Our cousin Peter Mountain was also in town because his sister Mary was in the hospital. She was dying. We got hold of Peter and he said his accommodations weren't very good, so Everett said, "Well, why don't you come stay with us? You can sleep on the floor."

"Okay," Peter replied. "That's better than where I'm staying."

Then we had two of them staying with us, and it was an awesome little holiday for my brother; he was so fond of Peter and he always loved Marie. Every morning, I would wake up and the two of them would be there, saying, "Well, we're waiting for our coffee."

I thought that might have been Everett's last adventure, but about a month later there was a big meeting in Colville Lake, where Everett had grown up as a teenager. He'd left residential school when he was fifteen and for years after that he went hunting and trapping with people from there. Even though he was frail, he wanted to go there one more time. Gene Oudzi, one of his childhood friends, lived there and he was going to let Everett and me stay in his extra log house by the shore. I thought, Great, the two of us will have this beautiful log house together, down by the lakeshore. But this time, Everett flew in with his wife, Mabel, and they kicked me out. "This is a honeymoon and you're not invited."

Not long before Everett passed on, he phoned my sister Cathy. They were always in touch. He told her, "I'm getting weak and I'm going to need help before I die. I don't want anybody else to touch me, so I want you to come and take care of me."

Mabel couldn't do it by herself, so Cathy said yes and she was there for the last few weeks of his life. Then one day Everett called me and said quietly, "You should come soon, Steve, because I don't think I have too much time left."

Marie and I were on the next plane to Good Hope. That was how he got ready to pass on: very quietly. Soon after we got there, he asked Marie to sing to him and she did. Then, after four days of him not eating, we all thought he was close to the end. But one night he said to me, "Tomorrow morning, I want you to make me some good coffee; I like your coffee. Later in the day, I want to have a big meal, some meat, mashed potatoes and vegetables, and I want to have some dessert, and then I want to have another coffee, and then I want to watch TV."

Everybody thought, What the heck's going on here? He was being so defiant. Suppertime came around and we brought him a plate and propped him up. He ate, but when he'd had enough, he waved a hand at nobody in particular, as if to say, *Take it away.*

Then it was dessert. He had a cake with a little bit of ice cream and whipped cream, and when he'd had enough of it, he waved again. *Take it away.*

Then it was coffee. I made the coffee, a good dark roast, and he drank that, and then it was time for TV. So, we lifted him out of bed, brought him into the living room and propped him up on a couch, and he watched TV. Finally, he started to fall asleep.

"Well," Cathy said, "you had enough TV? Maybe you should go to sleep now."

"Yeah, who cares about TV anyway."

To us, this whole episode was his way of defiantly saying, "I'm not ready to go. I'll decide when I go."

About three days later, he passed away.

~

Although Everett passed away in September 2011, it wasn't the last time he spoke to me.

The following February, Marie and I were in Vancouver. It was a Sunday morning. We were staying at Hotel Vancouver; Marie had worked late the night before but I was up, as usual, at five o'clock, and I was pacing, waiting for her to get up so we could do something. At nine o'clock, I'd just about had enough.

"Can you do something for me?" she asked. "Can you get me one of those special coffees?" She was so cozy in the big bed and wanted to get a little more sleep.

I grabbed a couple of Thermos cups and stomped out of the hotel room, down the hall and outside, and made my way over to Robson Street. It was a cold morning—kind of drizzling, sometimes raining, always windy—and I was in a bad mood. I was missing my brother and I was feeling the emptiness of the city. I got to Robson Street and headed west; I could see a Second Cup coffee shop across the street. I was just getting to the corner when there was a blast of wind and I felt something pass right through me. I stopped dead in my tracks and I heard my brother's voice. "Steve, you're the one that's alive… how come you're not happy?"

I turned and looked down Robson Street to the east; the clouds parted and the morning sun came through and shot right down the street, hitting me. I started crying and I was all by myself. Part of me was embarrassed. Across the street, outside the coffee shop, I saw two old street people huddled together. They looked like they were about seventy years old; they were cold and wet and sharing one cup of coffee. I walked across the street and got coffee and treats for Marie and me. I came back out and asked the two Elders sitting on the pavement, "How come you're only drinking one cup?"

"That's all we got," they said. And they were so happy, ignoring me and passing that hot coffee back and forth. I gave them some money and I thought, What the hell is the matter with me? My brother is right. I should be happy and here I am ruining my whole day.

I took those coffees back to Marie and I was in a much better mood.

~

My other brother Tommy is a couple of years younger than me. He was very sick with TB when he was around six years old and he just about died. They say that he was skin and bones when they put him onto a plane and flew him to the hospital in Aklavik.

I wasn't there when they took him away. Everett, Cathy and I went to Grollier Hall a few days later, and I didn't see Tommy for another five months. While we were at residential school, we were told that we were going on a little plane. They didn't say where we were going, but they took the three of us out of school, put us on a plane and flew us to Aklavik. We landed at the shore, climbed up to the top of the bank and then walked to the hospital.

It was foggy, grey and miserable when we got to the hospital. All Saints Hospital in Aklavik was an old wood-frame building, everything creaked and it looked like it was ready to fall down. We walked slowly into the hospital and there they stood, in a line, all in their housecoats and hospital gowns: my grandfather, my father, my sister Jean and little Tommy. They were just standing there, deathlike; they weren't coming to hug us or anything. It was eerie. Everett and Cathy were so happy to see everybody, so they ran up to them, but I couldn't handle it. I hadn't seen them for five months. I was only nine and I had thought they were all dead. I started sobbing. I couldn't look at them and I couldn't catch my breath.

Cathy and Everett went with everyone, so I followed. I ended up talking to my grandfather first, and then my dad and Jean, and then little Tommy. They told me that our mother had also been staying there but she got too sick, so they took her to a hospital in Edmonton. My grandmother was there but she had TB in her spine so she was bedridden. At one point, my grandfather said to me, "Your little brother Tommy was so sick, they thought he was going to die. In the afternoons, when they put us down for our rest period, sometimes I could hear him crying. Tommy was upstairs and I was downstairs, so I asked for him to be put in the same room as me. I told them that if he's going to die then I want to be with him, that he shouldn't be alone in the room."

Many years later, Tommy told me what really happened. "Every time I was supposed to sleep in the afternoon, one of the hospital staff would come into my room and, because I was alone, sexually abuse me. I remember crying, but I guess I was weak; either I couldn't cry loudly or I could and nobody paid attention. Suddenly, they moved everybody around and next thing my grandfather was with me, so the abuse stopped."

After our visit on that day, Everett, Cathy and I were put back on the float plane and sent back to Grollier Hall. I think about that day now. Six members of my family hospitalized with TB, three of us in residential school and at least two of us were being sexually abused.

When Tommy got better, three or four years later, he also went to Grollier Hall. In the summers, Tommy would try to hang around with Everett and me; we were his older brothers and he idolized us. When we were talking about the things we did, he would try to jump in and tell us something and we'd brush it off. "Oh, yeah… whatever."

After a while, Tommy stopped trying to hang out with us. It wasn't until we were in our fifties that I found out about all the sexual abuse that he'd gone through at Grollier Hall. We could have known that earlier but we didn't take him seriously. So, Tommy never got close to me or Everett.

Tommy had many careers: he worked on the oil rigs, in the seismic camps, for Good Hope Recreation and for the Housing Corporation. In 2013, he finally quit drinking and that's when we became close.

Everett had a hand in this. You see, Tommy lived a turbulent life with lots of drinking. He'd often be in Yellowknife and living on the street. I'd try to help him, usually just because my mother or Everett requested it, but I'd always find him back on the streets. I got fed up with him.

Just before Everett passed away, he said to me, "Steve, I'm not going to be around soon. Don't give up on Tommy. If I could quit drinking, then he could quit drinking."

Everett had been a notorious drinker in Good Hope, so I made him that commitment and I stuck with Tommy. I still didn't have a lot of patience with him. The last time I saw Tommy drinking, he was standing in front of the Canadian Imperial Bank in Yellowknife. It was a beautiful day in the summer and I was driving by with my car window rolled down, and he's leaning over the rail and calling out to me, "Hey, bro! BRO!"

He was smiling from ear to ear. I said hello as I drove past, but I wasn't planning on stopping. Then Everett, clear as anything, spoke to me from the Spirit World. He asked quietly, "Steve, how's my brother doing?"

Hearing Everett by this point was the most normal thing in the world. I thought, Well, I don't know how Tommy's doing. So, I parked the car and walked over to the bank. Tommy was just, "AYY, BRO!"

I asked him how he was doing, and he said, "I'm doing GREAT!"

I asked, "Where are you staying?"

"Staying with FRIENDS!"

"Tommy, where are you staying?"

"Last night I stayed at the Salvation Army. I don't know about tonight." Finally, he said, "I'm not doing that good."

"Well, let's go have a coffee." I took him to Javaroma and over coffee he opened up to me. I told him about what Everett had said before he passed away: "Don't give up on Tommy."

Tommy had gone to a lot of treatment programs before, but after this, he finally got sober. Years later, I asked him how he did it.

He answered right away. "I saw the light go out of my best friend's eyes and I saw the light dim in my cousin's eyes. The three of us were on the streets of Yellowknife and now they're both gone. I realized then that somebody cares for me, somebody loves me, and that's all it was. It was like I could hear a voice a million miles away, and that's the craziest thing. You, Everett, our sisters and Mum, you guys made me feel like you cared for me no matter how much I messed up. That's how I did it."

When Tommy finished the treatment, he went back to his house in Good Hope and the house was in complete disarray. He had no clock, radio or TV, everything was broken or missing—and the front door was the best indication of how crazy things had been for Tommy. It had three doorknobs: one was a little higher by a foot and closer to the middle of the door, the third one was even further past that, and only one of them worked. How and why they ended up there, and who put them there, has been a complete mystery since then.

He had the whole house cleaned up and in working order within a few weeks, but the three doorknobs stayed for a few months. One day, the old Chief, Charlie Barnaby, came for a visit. He was very happy to hear Tommy was back in town and sober.

When he arrived, he wasn't sure which doorknob to use and was worried that the state of the door was an indication that the house was in bad shape, but it looked great and Tommy and old Charlie had a good visit. Charlie got up to leave and headed toward the front door. The entrance was fairly dark. There was a pause and a fumbling sound, then he yelled out, "Tommy, what doorknob am I going to use here? There are too many doorknobs; I can't get out!"

They laughed and they laughed, and Tommy helped the old Chief open the door. Tommy has a new door now, and it has only one doorknob.

Tommy was elected Chief of Good Hope in 2021, and we talk every two or three days. When I'm in Good Hope I stay with him, and we just laugh. We're constantly laughing. We are both happy to have finally found each other after forty years.

CHAPTER THIRTY-FIVE

SAYING GOODBYE TO GEORGINA

Are you afraid to feel, afraid to feel?
Will you ever know what it's like to heal?

Do you know what you're hiding?
Will you ever be able to know what you should keep?
Then she held out the promise, of all that I needed
And she showed me the key to what I had hidden so deep

—Stephen Kakfwi, "Afraid to Feel," from the album *Last Chance Hotel*

I never felt that my mother and I were close. I know she loved me but she didn't act like she did and she never said she loved me.

Back in the early eighties, I was the one who had to tell her that her eldest grandchild, Melvin, had taken his own life with a rifle. It happened during one of those rare times when my mother was out of Fort Good Hope, relaxing in Yellowknife and visiting some friends. She was in the Gold Range; the band was playing and she was sitting with one of her oldest friends, enjoying a beer and the music, and I had to go in there and take her home. You know, it was so hard because she was smiling and relaxing, and she didn't know why I brought her home. She thought I didn't want her to stay out late. But then I told her that her fourteen-year-old grandson, my nephew Melvin, had taken his own life. She was in shock. It was the first holiday she'd ever taken. When the news sank in, she went into a period of deep grief. She went back to Good Hope the next day. Even today, that suicide haunts us. We all feel like we could have done something. It happened soon after Marie and I moved from Good Hope to Yellowknife. Back then, there was still a lot of drinking in our family; Everett, Cathy and I were still drinking heavily. These were the years we started to get closer as a family.

In the fall of 2012, my mother suddenly lost feeling in the lower half of her body and had to be medevaced out of Good Hope. It was like she was paralyzed from the waist down. They sent her to Inuvik and in October of that year I went to visit her. It turned out she was quite happy. She was in what they call extended care. For a woman of that age from Good Hope, it was about as close to a holiday as she ever had: no worries about gathering wood or water or finding and preparing food.

That year she didn't even care to go home for Christmas, but sometime in March or April, when the sun started to come back and the days warmed a little, she started to say, mostly to my sisters, "Well, I'm just about ready to go home now."

My nieces, Bonnie and Beatrice, who are closest to her, told her in strong terms, "You can't go home. You're paralyzed. You need two people to take care of you, to move you around, to make sure you don't get bed sores. One person can't take care of you, so the only way you can go home is if you learn to walk again."

In the spring of 2013, Marie and I went to Scotland. We went to the remote island of Iona off the west coast. It's not easy to get there: you have to take a ferry to the Isle of Mull and then follow a long road to the next ferry that takes you to Iona. There's a Celtic Christian monastery there that goes back to the year 563 that's built out of rocks. People told me about the tradition: you write down whatever it is you're praying for and you put your prayer in this basket, and then you say your prayers and you hope it comes true.

I was a skeptical Catholic but I didn't want to be disrespectful, so one evening I decided I would do it. I wrote the note, but I made two copies so I could have one to keep, because I figured, what if it came true? Who would believe me and how will I know that I did this and it wasn't just a dream?

I knew that my mother wanted to go back to Good Hope at least one more time; if she could, I figured she would choose to die there, so I talked to the Creator. "You know, my mother is in her nineties, and she's had a good but very hard life. She's gone through a lot of pain and suffering and she wants to go home, but she can't because she's paralyzed. I am asking and praying that my mother can walk again so she could come home for the last time." That was the prayer.

The next thing we know, my niece is calling us and saying, "Did you hear about Granny? The nurses are saying she's got feeling in one of her feet and she can move her toes!"

Well, we thought, that's promising.

The next month, my niece called again. "You wouldn't believe this, but Granny's got feeling in her other foot—she's moving the other foot!"

Everybody got to talking. "You know what? She's up to something. I think she has decided she's going to start walking again so she can go home."

And sure enough, that's what she did. First, she could move her foot, then she could lift her feet on both sides, and then she started doing exercises so she could lift herself up by her arms from the wheelchair. By the fall of 2014, she had started using a walker with the help of a nurse, and by about November, she was strong enough to use the walker by herself.

I told the nurses at the hospital that if she became strong enough, I wanted to take her home for Christmas. They said, "Yeah, if she continues at this rate, she'll be strong enough for that."

I don't know if the prayer had anything to do with this. Maybe one day she just decided, *I'm going to walk so I can go home for Christmas.* Whatever the reason, she became strong enough and we put her on a plane in December.

I went to spend the Christmas of 2014 with her in Good Hope and Marie, the kids and the grandkids stayed in Yellowknife. It was the first time I spent Christmas alone with my mother. Everett was in Yellowknife, so Mum and I stayed at his house.

I told her about the prayer that I had written for her in Scotland and she just said, "Well, it must have been a good prayer."

It was a strange time. We sat alone in the house, and it was a very spartan house. Every day people would stop by, some of her friends, as well as some younger people. It was a steady stream of people who came to pay their respects and welcome her home. We had visitors every day, but even so my mother and I didn't have much to say to each other. We sat together for long periods, saying nothing.

I spent a week with her and then Tommy and our sisters took care of her for the rest of the holiday. When New Year's came, she said, "I'm done, I don't want to be here anymore. I'll go back to the hospital in Inuvik where they take good care of me. This is my last visit; I'm not coming back." So, we brought her back to the hospital.

A year later, in January, she phoned me. "I don't want to live anymore," she said. "I'm ready to die, but I want you to arrange for everybody to come see me."

"Okay, sure. I'll do it."

I started arranging different times for everybody to go and I put myself right in the middle. I didn't want to go early and I didn't want to go too late. When it was my turn to visit, I flew up to Inuvik and stayed there five days. I figured it shouldn't be three days—that would be too short—and it couldn't be seven days because that would be too long… so I settled on five. I was a little bit sensitive about it all. I wasn't sure how to handle it, and sure enough, it all came up on the last day.

My departing flight was taking off at about two o'clock in the afternoon, so I went to see my mother at about eleven. Cathy was there. We sat in her hospital room, not saying anything. It was getting close to noon, so it was time for me to go. I hadn't said a word to my mother and she hadn't said anything to me. Finally, Cathy said, "Mum, you should say goodbye to Stephen, because you guys aren't going to see each other again. He's leaving, he's going back to Yellowknife today. You know that."

And my mother looked at her and said, "Well, if he has to go, then he should get going."

"Mum," Cathy said. "What a thing to say!"

My mother was looking right at Cathy. She didn't look at me at all. I was standing there thinking, Well, the heck with you too.

But then I thought, You know what, no. I'm not going to let her do that to me.

So, I said, "Okay, Mum." I was about eight feet away from her. "I'm going to say goodbye."

I got on my knees and hobbled across the floor on my knees to her in her wheelchair, just being funny, with my arms out. She turned, reached for me and said, "Thank you for everything. Thank you for everything, Stephen."

"Well, I love you, Mum, and thank you for everything. Thank you for putting me on this earth and being there for me."

And that was it. You know, it could have been a disaster. I could have just walked out, and it would still be bothering me to this day. But we turned it around and it has made all the difference.

I have thought about it a lot. You see, she spent almost ten years in residential school—from the time when she was five years old until she was fifteen. She became indifferent about a lot of things and I never knew that. My mother was eighty years old before she even told us that she had spent all those years in residential school. She wasn't affectionate and neither was I, unsurprisingly: I was my mother's son and I took on some of her traits. Thankfully, Marie, Kyla, Daylyn and Keenan were into the hugging business, and Mum and I picked it up.

In February 2016, my mother announced that she was going to the Spirit World. My father had come to her in visions, asking her to join him. We saw her reaching out and calling him by name. In her other visions, her deceased parents, Vital and Louise Barnaby, and her brothers and sisters also came to take her home.

Just a few days before she passed away, she asked Cathy, "Can you bring me some snow?"

Now, anybody who lives in the North might say, "It's March. You must be sick of the snow and of winter. Why would you want someone to bring you some snow?"

But she said, "Bring me some snow, and not snow from the top, but from underneath. I want the crystal-ice snow. "

Cathy went outside and brought her back a little container of snow, and Mum was marvelling at it. Cathy said she looked like somebody who had never seen snow before.

That's how my sister put it. She said, "Mum was holding it in her hands and she was looking at it, you know, and it was melting a little bit. And then she said, 'It's so white and so pure.'"

And my sister said, "You know what? Mum never talks like that. I've never heard Mum say something was 'pure' in her life. That's not a word she used. She was already in a different space."

People who talk about their near-death experiences, they say that everything, people included, starts to have its own energy, its own light; wherever Mum was, looking at the crystallized snow, she was admiring and loving its energy.

"I don't know why she said that," Cathy said. "But I'll never forget it."

We buried our mother, Georgina Kakfwi, on March 18, 2016, in the Catholic church cemetery in Good Hope, the same church where she had been baptized ninety-five years earlier.

Whenever I hear birds singing, it brings back memories of when we were together as a family in the bush camp. I can still hear her laughter and feel her Spirit. My mother is one with the earth.

CHAPTER THIRTY-SIX

BORN IN THE BOWL OF A PIPE

You drum, you sing your song

There is light in the deep of the dark

An Elder, she spoke these words

"Our happiness is our revenge"

My friends, we faced the demons

We healed our wounds inside

And now we know the darkness

We can truly love the light

—Stephen Kakfwi, "Love the Light"

Some of our Elders had special gifts; my grandmother Domitille certainly did. Years ago, people would go to her and say, "My uncle has gone up country; he is coming in from Colville Lake this month by dog team. Do you know when they're going to arrive?"

She'd sleep on it and the next day she had an answer for them. She was accurate enough that people went to her on a regular basis. Back then, there was no telephone or bush radio, but she would figure it out. What she did was travel in her dreams. She'd fly over the land and spot where the people were camping, and then figure out the distance to town.

When I was a kid, I remember people coming to visit her. She would send them away and they'd come back the next day, and she would say, "I don't know who's there, but I see three dog teams coming in tomorrow night from Colville Lake, or from up Rampart River." She did that until the early sixties, when people started getting bush radios. As far as I know, traditional people that had gifts didn't ask for money or payment. Instead, you'd give them whatever you felt like—a piece of fur or some meat, or you'd cut wood for them. They don't consider it their gift; it's the Creator's gift they carry.

My grandfather passed away when I was a young man, just twenty-four years old. My grandmother said he was asking for me, wondering where I was, but I was in Edmonton.

I did see him again, though; I saw him in 1986 just before I quit drinking. January 28 of that year I was in Ottawa at the Four Seasons Hotel, and I was on a two-week bender. I woke up that morning and crawled out from a jumble of blankets. I didn't know what I did the night before, but I recalled arriving in a taxi from Montreal in the middle of the night without even a winter coat. It seemed like I hadn't eaten or slept for a week. I turned on the TV just in time to see the space shuttle *Challenger* launch into a beautiful clear sky and then explode. It was horrific—and then I thought, That's me. That's exactly what's going to happen to me if I keep doing this.

I was in such bad shape later that night that I started hallucinating. I still hadn't eaten and I couldn't sleep so I was either still drunk or going through withdrawal. My grandfather came to me in a dream that night and he said, "My grandson, do you want to live?"

I thought I was on my death bed, but my grandfather reminded me that I had the power to decide where I went from here. That's when I decided I had to quit drinking, and I did.

I spoke with his Spirit throughout my political career whenever I got in trouble. I never prayed to anybody; I didn't call for Jesus or the Virgin Mary or the saints. Instead, I talked to my grandfather. I'd always start out by saying, "Grandfather, you asked me to do this work. Where are you? I need help."

Usually things would turn for the better for me after this, but one time in the late nineties, I was a little too ambitious. I wanted to shake up the cabinet, consolidate a bunch of portfolios. I believed I was right but I wasn't getting much support. So, I called out to my grandfather. "I need some help. This is what I want to do and I can't seem to do it myself. Can you help me?"

That night I had a dream of my grandfather scolding me. He said, "Grandson, why do you keep asking for things you don't need? Everything you need is around you; you just have to look. Look and you'll see. You can do everything by yourself now."

It was such a powerful message, although I didn't get it at first. He scolded me, so at first I felt as if he didn't want to help me and it didn't feel good. It was only later that I realized what he was saying. He was telling me, "You're a mature man now. You're capable of everything and you don't need my help. Don't ask me anymore; be aware of what you have. Stay focussed. Everything you need is around you." After that, I never asked him for help again and that was the last time he talked to me.

My grandparents were devout Catholics. They never questioned their faith, but they never denied their own Dene spirituality either. They just didn't talk about it; better for the church not to know. I was also raised Catholic, but when I went to residential school I lost my devotion to the church. I grew up with a big empty hole in the middle of me and I tried to fill it, sometimes not with the best of things.

It's true for many Dene that the whole spiritual essence of who we were was taken away from us, and it became impossible to recover because we developed these shields. We became too guarded, too distant from the spiritual aspect of what we were. We did things as machines, with a limited ability to love somebody and be compassionate. For instance, when you go out on the land as a traditional Dene, you must first connect to the land and the Spirit; you can't just jump on your snowmobile and go get a moose and come back. There is a real connection ceremony. I didn't get it at first; if I wanted to go for ducks, I went. If I wanted to get moose, I'd go out and get a moose. It was a functional kind of thing. Of course, I loved being out there, but the spiritual part of what we were supposed to do was missing. It always had to start with ceremony, an acknowledgement of the Creator and the land.

Some of my dreams deal with this loss of identity and tradition. There is one dream that changed my life; it was so powerful that the moment I woke up I wrote down the details. It was February 10, 2013, at 2:11 in the morning—three years before my mother passed away. I was staying in a Best Western motel in High Level, Alberta. I dreamt that I was walking along and approaching what looked like hundreds of people surrounding a fire glowing a reddish-yellow light at the top of a little hill. Somebody was in the middle of this fire, and someone said to me, "It's your mother. We're visiting your mother." I didn't go up to where they were gathered because I didn't want to say, "Hey, I'm her son. Get out of the way so I can see my mother." I wanted to walk around and see if I could get close to her without pushing my way through. I didn't want to offend anybody.

I started to circle this group of people standing around the fire, and as I was going around, I arrived at a different place. The wind picked up and shifted coarse sand and pebbles near the base of a rock, revealing underneath something that looked like an old campsite. There were charcoal, ashes, a pipe stem about fourteen inches long and a pipe bowl that was charred and reddish brown. Everything was burnt; it looked like an ancient fireplace. The pipe stem was charred but intact, and I could see carved into the side of it these seven crosses. In my dream, I thought it was important to count them. I decided to go toward the centre of the hill, but before I did that, I felt a tremendous rush go through my body.

I'd never felt anything like that before. It was a primal force of awakening. It's an energy that starts at your lower back, at the centre of your body, and shoots right through to the top of your head. When I woke up, I thought I had had a heart attack. I jumped about two feet off the bed. I could still feel it going through my body: I could feel it moving through my neck and into my head, then through and out the top of my head.

I thought the dream meant my mother must have died, so once I calmed down, I phoned the hospital in Inuvik, even though it was about three o'clock in the morning. I told them who I was and what I had experienced, and they told me Mum was fine. "We check on her every hour and she's sleeping well, and you should too."

Mum was highly respected as a traditional, hard-working, no-nonsense kind of woman, but I couldn't figure out why people would gather around her and pray with such reverence. I scribbled down the outline of the pipe story on a little piece of Best Western stationery. I still have that on my bulletin board at home.

And that's just the start of this story. A few years later, I met an Ojibwe Elder named Fred Kelly at the airport in Ottawa. I had upgraded my seat and I noticed when we boarded that he had a bad middle seat in the back of this WestJet plane. I felt badly so I arranged an upgrade of his seat with the flight attendant. I didn't tell him it was me, but he ended up sitting across from me.

He was happy to move and we ended up talking. He wanted to know who I was and I got to know a little bit about him. A little while after I got home, I got a short voice-mail message from him. "It's Fred Kelly. I want to talk to you. Call me any time you want."

I called him, and he said he wanted to take me out for dinner the next time I was in Winnipeg, and that what he wanted to say to me was important. So, I did that: I called him up the next time I was in Winnipeg. Over dinner, he said, "I need you to tell me about your dreams. I think you have something, but I can't tell what it is until you tell me about some of your dreams."

I told him about my accident with the truck when I was three and a half years old and he was taken with that. I told him about the times when my brother and my grandfather had spoken to me from the Spirit World, and then I told him about the dream of the fire on the hill, the pipe and my mother. He fixated on that. He said, "That dream is not about your mother; it's about the earth, everything that is sacred and holy to the Dene people. It's about the spirituality that all of us want so badly in our lives. What the Creator gave us in the first place, that's the mother in your dream. I'm not saying your mother doesn't deserve to be surrounded by friends and relatives, but I think the dream is about you. Your people are looking for the spiritual connection you all need and it's missing."

He went on. "I think you were born with a pipe. I know some of you Dene don't believe in pipes. We use them as our own way to pray. As you know, there are many ways to pray, but I think you were born with a pipe and you're trying to go back to where you came from, and I think the place is the bowl of a pipe. Maybe your people used the pipe a long time ago, we don't know that, but you're dreaming about finding a pipe and your people are searching for the Sacred Ceremonies that you used to have before the church and the colonizers came. That's what the dream's about. You had a vision, the holiest of sacred visions. It's the essence of why you're Dene. You can't get closer to the Creator than that."

We talked for about three hours. He is such an interesting man. Fred was a political leader for years, but he's also a Healer and practises medicine and, like many people, he's picked up a lot of ceremonies over the years. I see him regularly now. I was at an Assembly of First Nations conference in Niagara Falls one year and suddenly I thought, I've got to see that old man. I was hungry, so I thought I'd go eat something first and then call him afterward and see if he was in town for the assembly.

I walked out of the hotel and headed to a nearby restaurant with a patio and there, at a table right by the patio fence, was Fred Kelly. He spoke first. "Oh, I've been waiting for you. Come and join me."

"Who's sitting with you?"

"Nobody. I saved this seat for you."

It felt as if I wanted to see him and—*bang*—fifteen minutes later, there he is waiting for me. He laughed about it. He never said, "Well, you know, I can do these kinds of things." He just laughed quietly. His laugh envelops you; it feels nice. I'm not sure he's widely known for this kind of spirituality, but for me he's special.

Another time I saw him was in the spring of 2019. I was at the Lord Elgin Hotel in Ottawa, and I woke up one morning around six with this strong urge to see him. I went down for breakfast and I ran into a fellow who was mentored by Fred. This guy once had throat cancer and he was considered terminal. He lost a lot of weight, but Fred took him in and saved him using ceremony and Traditional Medicine from the land. He's still alive. His cancer has gone and never came back. He's now always there for Fred whenever Fred needs an assistant.

So, this guy thinks Fred walks on water—and for good reason—and I ran into him having breakfast at the hotel. Why he chose to have breakfast there that morning I don't know, but I sat down with him and we started talking. I said, "I had a dream and I woke up and thought that I had to see Fred. Do you know where he is?"

"Yeah, I'm picking him up at the airport after breakfast. Come with me."

Off we went, and I had a nice long ride from the airport back to town with Fred. Again, I told him about what happened.

"Yeah, I know," he said. "I wanted to see you too."

A few months after I had that first meal with him, Fred gave me a pipe.

He said, "You were born with a pipe, so I'm going to give you one. It comes from the Lakota people down in the United States. Learn to use it and carry it around with you till you get comfortable and it becomes a part of you."

And that's what I've been doing. I take it out occasionally and look at it. It's like a gun: if you handle it enough, it gets comfortable. When you smoke a pipe, and everybody smokes differently, you pray. So, I've been doing that too.

The praying has also helped me with my fixation on the devil. As a mature man, I once asked two priests whether the devil exists, and they beat around the bush and never answered the question. A while later, just after I'd stopped working, I went home to Fort Good Hope and talked to an Elder, Gabe Kochon. I was in town because I wanted to see my family, visit the church graveyard and talk to my ancestors.

Gabe spent most of his life on the land. He was a devout Catholic but also a storyteller and traditional Dene Elder. When I asked him about the devil, he said, "You know, Stephen, it's no big deal. I don't know why you're obsessing about him. He is just a guy with scorched feet. He's a guy in a myth, a story."

It was almost as if I'd been imagining that the devil was always waiting outside my front door ever since I met Sister Hebert at residential school. I'd been scared all my life, and suddenly this Elder says, "Let's open the door; let's deal with it." He opened the door for me and there was nothing there. He made it disappear.

He never said, "Steve, you're stupid and screwed up. What have you been doing all these years, carrying around that damned notion?"

All he said was, "We first heard these stories from the priests. We heard about the birth of Jesus and the angels, and that was a beautiful story. We liked that one; we liked that he was born poor with animals around him. The Christmas story is beautiful. But then the priests started talking about other things, about angels going evil and God getting mad, and they told us that God made a place of eternal fire and that's where he threw this evil angel. When they said that, some of our old people laughed and said, 'Well, so much for that guy; he must have really burnt his feet when he landed there.'"

They called him *ay kahy ttss-oh-leh*, the one with scorched feet, as if his feet had crinkled up like a piece of hide that's held over a fire too long. Gabe went on to say, "Our Elders thought it was another story, like the stories we tell. We know that some are true and some are not. The devil? It's a story."

Without lecturing me or passing judgment, he told me not to worry about it. That's when it dawned on me how much time I'd wasted in my life. At that moment I understood the power of the church to indoctrinate. That power is enormous. I mean, if you were in Good Hope a few years ago, everywhere you'd turn there was the cross: the priests used to wear cassocks with a big metal cross right through their belt; there were crosses in every classroom because the nuns were sent to the public schools to teach; when you'd walk into the church, crosses. The church was relentless. It was everywhere.

So... am I still as angry as I was when I was nine, fifteen, twenty, thirty? I've got to say that no, I'm not. And that's partly why I went to the family gravesites in Good Hope. I brought Tommy with me to the cemetery because I wanted a witness, something that became common for me later in life.

And so I said to Tommy, "You know what, I'm done working for our people. I've done this work since I was twenty-four and I'm sixty-eight now and I don't want to do it anymore. So, I have to go and talk to Everett and our parents and grandparents and tell them. I want to give them a report of what I've done and why I don't want to do it anymore. I also want to tell them that I'm no longer Catholic and that I've changed over the years, that I don't smoke or drink anymore and I don't do drugs. And I need you to come with me, Tommy, because I need a witness; in a year or two, I might not believe that I did this."

We drove there one evening in Tommy's truck and we parked down by the church. The graves are on either side of it. We walked slowly, wandering past the graves, some with crosses, others with little fences around them. It was the middle of August: it was warm and sunny with some clouds and a light breeze. It was beautiful. The grass had been cut recently; somebody cares for it. I had planned to walk to each one of my family members' graves. My grandparents are buried in one place and the graves of Mum, Dad and Everett are nearby.

I had written out a page of things I wanted to say. I was well prepared; I had most of it memorized, so I wasn't walking around holding that sheet of paper, but I had it in my pocket just in case. Before I went in, I went through it again to make sure I hadn't forgotten anything.

I spoke to my grandparents first, because it was my grandfather who sent me on what I thought was a mission. I told him, "I was thirteen when you first told me that I would be the one that would make your name known across this country, and I think your name is pretty well known. Though you never told me what it was I was supposed to do, I assumed it was about working for people and working with the Chiefs, and I've done that and I'm finished. I want to let you know that I'm done."

I said it out loud with Tommy listening as a witness. I said, "I tried to be a good person. I got married; I have kids and grandkids I raise the best I can. I used to drink and I quit, as you know because you were there. I quit smoking because my kids asked me to and I quit doing drugs, so I've tried to live a good life. I don't have anything to do with the church anymore, because I think the church has done great harm to me and great harm to everybody. The Catholic faith itself was okay, but the Catholic Church as an institution, I feel that was wrong; it was evil and it has lost its way, and it was only interested in controlling people, owning land, having a lot of money and taking care of itself. I don't see how it has done anything good for us. I. wanted to tell you myself because you were devoted, but the bishops, priests and popes, they're not good people and I'm not Catholic anymore. I still pray, and I have different ways of praying. I'll sit in the United Church sometimes; occasionally I end up in a Catholic church, but that's because I like sitting with my people there. I have also learned a new way to pray from the Indigenous Peoples in the south. I even pray with a pipe sometimes. I'm not asking permission; I'm just letting you know. I'm happy with my decision. I feel at peace with the Creator."

So that was it as I remember.

Then I talked to my father. I said that for a long time I didn't give him any credit and that I was really, really angry with him, but I was sorry for the harm and hurt that I caused him. It was only recently that I had realized how hard he worked and how much he loved us, and how difficult it must have been for him to raise us by himself with our mother gone so often. I thanked him for coming to me in the dream.

To my father, my mother and Everett, I said, "You asked me to stay close to Tommy and I did. He's here, he's sober and we're close, and I will do my part to make sure our families get together for dinners and take care of each other. Everybody is okay. Most of us have jobs and we're taking care of our children, and I thought you'd both be happy to know that we're not falling apart. We remained a good family after you left."

To my mother, I said that I was sorry that she didn't get to know her own parents or siblings well, and that they had all passed away around the same time. I told her that I had discovered the names of her great-grandfather's children, the Laporte children, in a mass grave in Fort Providence, and that their names are on the monument.

I went to the grave of my sister Jean, who passed away in 1971 as a young woman. I thanked her for helping raise me during the years when our mother was gone, and I told her that her children grew up to be beautiful people and they had children themselves, and everyone was doing well.

I stopped at the gravesite of my nephew Melvin and my niece Yvonne to say that we all missed them but that I hoped they were happy to be with family in the Spirit World.

I saved my last words for Everett. I said, "I am surprised and happy to see that Rabbi is sleeping beside you. In the dream where you asked me to take care of Rabbi I just about blew it, but Keenan was the one to make sure that I took care of it properly. It turned out well, and you asked me not to give up on Tommy so thanks to you we're here together."

This was important to me. I'd left Good Hope fifty years earlier because I felt like an outsider. Then I spent my whole life wandering the country and working, and even in my later years I was still regarded as an outsider. But I wanted to finish my work as an outsider, still feeling like I wasn't part of the community, or part of anything, really, and I was okay with that. That's me.

I still speak to my grandfather, Dad, Mum and Everett in the Spirit World. I do it every few days. Sometimes I say to Everett, "I know I'm being grumpy and feeling sorry for myself and yeah, I know, Everett, I'm the one that's alive, so how come I'm not enjoying it…" I don't get on my knees and pray and get all solemn about it. I keep it light and talk to them like I talk to living people.

When I write about having afterlife visits from my family, people might think I'm crazy, but I'm just telling it as it is. This is my reality, and it has been both a blessing and a curse because I know my own troubled spirit has prevented me from relaxing and being centred. I spent a lot of years without sleep, haunted by all kinds of things, but I'm getting better now. I'm feeling blessed; I'm feeling like I've got it. If I went to the Spirit World tomorrow, I'd be okay with that. I'm ready to go. I'd feel sad to leave my family, friends, wife, grandchildren and children, but I'd be about as ready as anybody. I guess sometimes I feel like I've already been there. I wasn't ready then, but it's all about getting ready. That's what life is all about.

The family. Back row: Amos and Laurance. Middle row: Sadeya, Kyla, Marie, Stephen, Daylyn and Maslyn. Front row: Tydzeh, Ry'den and Keenan. Photo by Tessa Macintosh

Acknowledgements

I have many people to thank for their help with this book.

Elizabeth Hay helped steer me to Westwood Creative Artists, where Chris Casuccio saw the power in the stories. The people at Caitlin Press, Vici Johnstone, Sarah Corsie and Holly Vestad, turned my manuscript into the book you are holding in your hands.

Thanks to my grandson Tydzeh for his help with the map and Bill Braden of Yellowknife for his assistance with the map and photos.

Thanks to Robin Weber at the NWT Archives for access to the photos and to Rene Fumoleau and Tessa Macintosh for their camera work over the years.

I must also thank the three psychologists who helped me unravel the reality of certain events in my life, and all the Elders who taught me why stories are so important.

I will also give a grudging thanks to a mysterious ailment that confined me for long periods to my chair, but gave me the time to pen the thousands of little notes and lines that became the stories.

Finally I would like to acknowledge Dick Gordon, whose encouragement and support made this book possible. It was his work with all the transcripts and the stories and the drafts, that helped me tie all the floating pieces together.

About the Author

Stephen Kakfwi, Northern Dene, is a lifelong leader in Indigenous Rights, environmental stewardship and reconciliation. He served as premier of the Northwest Territories, and as National Chief of the Dene Nation, representing Chiefs of Treaties 8 and 11. He led community consultations for the Berger Inquiry into a north-south gas pipeline proposal across the Dene homeland. He led and hosted the visit of Pope John Paul II to Northern Canada. A husband, father and grandfather, he shares his heroes, homeland and residential school experiences in his songs and stories.

Photo Marie Wilson